Hooking Up

Hooking Up

TOM

PRAISE FOR Tom Wolfe's *Hooking Up*

"In this millennially minded assemblage . . . the grand impresario of new journalism revisits some of his favorite targets. . . . Pleasures are to be had here—notably Wolfe's recent, previously audio-only novella, *Ambush at Fort Bragg.*"

—*The Washington Post Book World*

"As the pieces included in *Hooking Up* clearly demonstrate, he never lost his faultless reporter's nose for a great story. Or a fur-flying, guns-a-blazin' dogfight."

—Matthew DeBord, Salon.com

"His discourse on the Jesuit priest and theologian Pierre Teilhard de Chardin is a surprising pleasure. Its irony and zest alone make one hope that Wolfe stays at his keyboard for many more years to come."

—Karen R. Long, *The Plain Dealer* (Cleveland)

"Wolfe proves he's still the merry prankster of journalism. . . . When Wolfe leaves the pulpit for the pavement, his X-ray eyes still crinkle with wonder at every hilarious sideshow of the great American carnival. No one tells it better."

—Kyle Smith, *People* Magazine

"Turn to the three essays grouped under the title 'The Human Beast,' and you will be in Wolfe heaven. The first of these . . . is an exuberant history of the birth of Silicon Valley. . . . 'Digibabble, Fairy Dust, and the Human Anthill' moves from the semiconductor industry to the Internet and then, by a kind of intuitive leap, to neuroscience and sociobiology. 'Sorry, but Your Soul Just Died' delves into brain imaging and the genetic determination of character. Jesuit priest Pierre Teilhard de Chardin, closet Catholic Marshall McLuhan, and scientist Edmund O. Wilson ("Darwin II himself") are the pivotal figures in these two essays."

—Michael Upchurch, *The Seattle Times*

"Wolfe's insight, his bravura style, his fun tales, and his seamless writing skills are all on display. . . . It's immensely rewarding."

—G. William Gray, *The Tampa Tribune-Times*

Also by Tom Wolfe

The Kandy-Kolored Tangerine-Flake Streamline Baby (1965)

The Pump House Gang (1968)

The Electric Kool-Aid Acid Test (1968)

Radical Chic & Mau-Mauing the Flak Catchers (1970)

The Painted Word (1975)

Mauve Gloves & Madmen, Clutter & Vine (1976)

The Right Stuff (1979)

In Our Time (1980)

From Bauhaus to Our House (1981)

The Bonfire of the Vanities (1987)

A Man in Full (1998)

WOLFE

Picador USA
Farrar, Straus and Giroux
New York

www.picadorusa.com

Picador® is a U.S. registered trademark and is used by Farrar, Straus and Giroux under license from Pan Books Limited.

For information on Picador USA Reading Group Guides, as well as ordering, please contact the Trade Marketing department at St. Martin's Press.
Phone: 1-800-221-7945 extension 763
Fax: 212-677-7456
E-mail: trademarketing@stmartins.com

Several of these pieces originally appeared, in slightly different form, in *The American Spectator, Esquire, Forbes ASAP, Harper's, New York, The New York Times Magazine,* and *The Tatler.* "Ambush at Fort Bragg" first appeared in *Rolling Stone.*

Library of Congress Cataloging-in-Publication Data

Wolfe, Tom.
Hooking up / Tom Wolfe.
p. cm.
ISBN 0-312-42023-4
I. Title.

PS3573.0526 H66 2000
813'.54—dc21 00-058748

First published in the United States by Farrar, Straus and Giroux

First Picador USA Edition: October 2001

10 9 8 7 6 5 4 3 2 1

Contents

HOOKING UP

Hooking Up:
What Life Was Like at the Turn of the Second Millennium: An American's World*

By the year 2000, the term "working class" had fallen into disuse in the United States, and "proletariat" was so obsolete it was known only to a few bitter old Marxist academics with wire hair sprouting out of their ears. The average electrician, air-conditioning mechanic, or burglar-alarm repairman lived a life that would have made the Sun King blink. He spent his vacations in Puerto Vallarta, Barbados, or St. Kitts. Before dinner he would be out on the terrace of some resort hotel with his third wife, wearing his Ricky Martin cane-cutter shirt open down to the sternum, the better to allow his gold chains to twinkle in his chest hairs. The two of them would have just ordered a round of Quibel sparkling water, from the state of West Virginia, because by 2000 the once-favored European sparkling waters Perrier and San Pellegrino seemed so tacky.

*With a tip of the hat to Robert Lacey and Danny Danziger and their delightful book *The Year 1000: What Life Was Like at the Turn of the First Millennium: An Englishman's World* (London: Little, Brown and Company, 1999).

European labels no longer held even the slightest snob appeal except among people known as "intellectuals," whom we will visit in a moment. Our typical mechanic or tradesman took it for granted that things European were second-rate. Aside from three German luxury automobiles—the Mercedes-Benz, the BMW, and the Audi—he regarded European-manufactured goods as mediocre to shoddy. On his trips abroad, our electrician, like any American businessman, would go to superhuman lengths to avoid being treated in European hospitals, which struck him as little better than those in the Third World. He considered European hygiene so primitive that to receive an injection in a European clinic voluntarily was sheer madness.

Indirectly, subconsciously, his views perhaps had to do with the fact that his own country, the United States, was now the mightiest power on earth, as omnipotent as Macedon under Alexander the Great, Rome under Julius Caesar, Mongolia under Genghis Khan, Turkey under Mohammed II, or Britain under Queen Victoria. His country was so powerful, it had begun to invade or rain missiles upon small nations in Europe, Africa, Asia, and the Caribbean for no other reason than that their leaders were lording it over their subjects at home.

Our air-conditioning mechanic had probably never heard of Saint-Simon, but he was fulfilling Saint-Simon's and the other nineteenth-century utopian socialists' dreams of a day when the ordinary workingman would have the political and personal freedom, the free time and the wherewithal to express himself in any way he saw fit and to unleash his full potential. Not only that, any ethnic or racial group—*any*, even recent refugees from a Latin country—could take over the government of any American city, if they had the votes and a modicum of organization. Americans could boast of a freedom as well as a power unparalleled in the history of the world.

Our typical burglar-alarm repairman didn't display one erg of chauvinistic swagger, however. He had been numbed by the aforementioned "intellectuals," who had spent the preceding eighty years being indignant over what a "puritanical," "repressive," "bigoted," "capitalistic," and "fascist" nation America was beneath its democratic façade. It made his head hurt. Besides, he was too busy coping with what was known as the "sexual revolution." If anything, "sexual revolution" was rather a prim term for the lurid carnival actually taking place in the mightiest country on earth in the year 2000. Every magazine stand was a riot of bare flesh, rouged areolae, moistened crevices, and stiffened giblets: boys with girls, girls with girls, boys with boys, bare-breasted female bodybuilders, so-called boys with breasts, riding backseat behind steroid-gorged bodybuilding bikers, naked except for *cache-sexes* and Panzer helmets, on huge chromed Honda or Harley-Davidson motorcycles.

But the magazines were nothing compared with what was offered on an invention of the 1990s, the Internet. By 2000, an estimated 50 percent of all hits, or "log-ons," were at Web sites purveying what was known as "adult material." The word "pornography" had disappeared down the memory hole along with "proletariat." Instances of marriages breaking up because of Web-sex addiction were rising in number. The husband, some fifty-two-year-old MRI technician or systems analyst, would sit in front of the computer for twenty-four or more hours at a stretch. Nothing that the wife could offer him in the way of sexual delights or food could compare with the one-handing he was doing day and night as he sat before the PC and logged on to such images as a girl with bare breasts and a black leather corset standing with one foot on the small of a naked boy's back, brandishing a whip.

In 1999, the year before, this particular sexual kink—sadomasochism—had achieved not merely respectability but high chic, and the word "perversion" had become as obsolete as "pornography" and "proletariat." Fashion pages presented the black leather and rubber paraphernalia as style's cutting edge. An actress named Rene Russo blithely recounted in the Living section of one of America's biggest newspapers how she had consulted a former dominatrix named Eva Norvind, who maintained a dungeon replete with whips and chains and assorted baffling leather masks, chokers, and cuffs, in order to prepare for a part as an aggressive, self-obsessed agent provocateur in *The Thomas Crown Affair*, Miss Russo's latest movie.

"Sexy" was beginning to replace "chic" as the adjective indicating what was smart and up-to-the-minute. In the year 2000, it was standard practice for the successful chief executive officer of a corporation to shuck his wife of two to three decades' standing for the simple reason that her subcutaneous packing was deteriorating, her shoulders and upper back were thickening like a shot-putter's—in short, she was no longer sexy. Once he set up the old wife in a needlepoint shop where she could sell yarn to her friends, he was free to take on a new wife, a "trophy wife," preferably a woman in her twenties, and preferably blond, as in an expression from that time, a "lemon tart." What was the downside? Was the new couple considered radioactive socially? Did people talk *sotto voce*, behind the hand, when the tainted pair came by? Not for a moment. All that happened was that everybody got on the cell phone or the Internet and rang up or E-mailed one another to find out the spelling of the new wife's first name, because it was always some name like Serena and nobody was sure how to spell it. Once that was written down in the little red Scully & Scully address book that was so popular among people of means, the lemon tart and her big CEO catch were invited to all the parties, as though nothing had happened.

Meanwhile, sexual stimuli bombarded the young so incessantly and intensely they were inflamed with a randy itch long before reaching puberty. At puberty the dams, if any were left, burst. In the nineteenth century, entire shelves used to be filled with novels whose stories turned on the need for women, such as Anna Karenina or Madame Bovary, to remain chaste or to maintain a façade of chastity. In the year 2000, a Tolstoy or a Flaubert wouldn't have stood a chance in the United States. From age thirteen, American girls were under pressure to maintain a façade of sexual experience and sophistication. Among girls, "virgin" was a term of contempt. The old term "dating"—referring to a practice in which a boy asked a girl out for the evening and took her to the movies or dinner—was now deader than "proletariat" or "pornography" or "perversion." In junior high school, high school, and college, girls headed out in packs in the evening, and boys headed out in packs, hoping to meet each other fortuitously. If they met and some girl liked the looks of some boy, she would give him the nod, or he would give her the nod, and the two of them would retire to a halfway-private room and "hook up."

"Hooking up" was a term known in the year 2000 to almost every American child over the age of nine, but to only a relatively small percentage of their parents, who, even if they heard it, thought it was being used in the old sense of "meeting" someone. Among the children, hooking up was always a sexual experience, but the nature and extent of what they did could vary widely. Back in the twentieth century, American girls had used baseball terminology. "First base" referred to embracing and kissing; "second base" referred to groping and fondling and deep, or "French," kissing, commonly known as "heavy petting"; "third base" referred to fellatio, usually known in polite conversation by the ambiguous term "oral sex"; and "home plate" meant conception-mode intercourse, known familiarly as "going all the way." In the year 2000, in the era of hooking up, "first base" meant deep kissing ("tonsil hockey"), groping, and fondling; "second base" meant oral sex; "third base" meant going all the way; and "home plate" meant learning each other's names.

Getting to home plate was relatively rare, however. The typical Filofax entry in the year 2000 by a girl who had hooked up the night before would be: "Boy with black Wu-Tang T-shirt and cargo pants: O, A, 6." Or "Stupid cock diesel"—slang for a boy who was muscular from lifting weights—"who kept saying, 'This is a cool deal': TTC, 3." The letters referred to the sexual acts performed (e.g., TTC for "that thing with the cup"), and the Arabic number indicated the degree of satisfaction on a scale of 1 to 10.

In the year 2000, girls used "score" as an active verb indicating sexual conquest, as in: "The whole thing was like very sketchy, but I scored that diesel who said he was gonna go home and caff up [drink coffee in order to stay awake and study] for the psych test." In the twentieth century, only boys had used "score" in that fashion, as in: "I finally scored with Susan last night." That girls were using such a locution points up one of the ironies of the relations between the sexes in the year 2000.

The continuing vogue of feminism had made sexual life easier, even insouciant, for men. Women had been persuaded that they should be just as active as men when it came to sexual advances. Men were only too happy to accede to the new order, since it absolved them of all sense of responsibility, let alone chivalry. Men began to adopt formerly feminine attitudes when the subject of marriage came up, pleading weakness and indecisiveness, as in: "I don't know; I'm just not ready yet" or "Of course I love you, but like, you know, I start weirding out when I try to focus on it."

With the onset of puberty, males were able to get sexual enjoyment so easily, so casually, that junior high schools as far apart geographically and socially as the slums of the South Bronx and Washington's posh suburbs of Arlington and Talbot County, Virginia, began reporting a new discipline problem. Thirteen- and fourteen-year-old girls were getting down on their knees and fellating boys in corridors and stairwells during the two-minute break between classes. One thirteen-year-old in New York, asked by a teacher how she could do such a thing, replied: "It's nasty, but I need to satisfy my man." Nasty was an aesthetic rather than a moral or hygienic judgment. In the year 2000, boys and girls did not consider fellatio to be a truely sexual act, any more than tonsil hockey. It was just "fooling around." The President of the United States at the time used to have a twenty-two-year-old girl, an unpaid volunteer in the presidential palace, the White House, come around to his office for fellatio. He later testified under oath that he had never "had sex" with her. Older Americans tended to be shocked, but junior-high-school, high-school, and college students understood completely what he was saying and wondered what on earth all the fuss was about. The two of them had merely been on second base, hooking up.

Teenage girls spoke about their sex lives to total strangers without the least embarrassment or guile. One New York City newspaper sent out a man-on-the-street interviewer with the question: "How did you lose your virginity?" Girls as well as boys responded without hesitation, posed for photographs, and divulged their name, age, and the neighborhood where they lived.

Stains and stigmas of every kind were disappearing where sex was concerned. Early in the twentieth century the term "cohabitation" had referred to the forbidden practice of a man and woman living together before marriage. In the year 2000, nobody under forty had ever heard of the word, since cohabitation was now the standard form of American courtship. For parents over forty, one of the thornier matters of etiquette concerned domestic bed assignments. When your son or daughter came home for the weekend with the live-in consort, did you put the two of them in the same bedroom, which would indicate implicit approval of the discomforting fait accompli? Or did you put them in different bedrooms and lie awake, rigid with insomnia, fearful of hearing muffled footfalls in the hallway in the middle of the night?

Putting them in different rooms was a decidedly old-fashioned thing to do; and in the year 2000, thanks to the feverish emphasis on sex and sexiness, nobody wanted to appear old, let alone old-fashioned. From the city of Baltimore came reports of grandmothers having their eyebrows, tongues, and lips pierced with gold rings in order to appear younger, since body-piercing was a popular fashion among boys and girls in their teens and early twenties. Expectant mothers were having their belly buttons pierced with gold rings so that the shapelessness of pregnancy would not make them feel old. An old man who had been a prominent United States senator and a presidential candidate, emerged from what he confessed to have been a state of incapacity to go on television to urge other old men to take a drug called Viagra to free them from what he said was one of the scourges of modern times, the disease that dared not speak its name: impotence. He dared not speak it, either. He called it "E.D.," for erectile dysfunction. Insurance companies were under pressure to classify impotence in old men as a disease and to pay for treatment.

In the late nineteenth and early twentieth centuries, old people in America had prayed, "Please, God, don't let me look poor." In the year 2000, they prayed, "Please, God, don't let me look old." Sexiness was equated with youth, and youth ruled. The most widespread age-related disease was not senility but juvenility. The social ideal was to look twenty-three and dress thirteen. All over the country, old men and women were dressing casually at every opportunity, wearing jeans, luridly striped sneakers, shorts, T-shirts, polo shirts, jackets, and sweaters, heedless of how such clothes revealed every sad twist, bow, hump, and webbed-up vein clump of their superannuated bodies. For that matter, in the year 2000, people throughout American society were inverting norms of dress that had persisted for centuries, if not millennia. Was the majesty of America's global omnipotence reflected in the raiments of the rich and prominent? Quite the opposite. In the year 2000, most American billionaires—and the press no longer took notice of men worth a mere $500 million or $750 million—lived in San Jose and Santa Clara Counties, California, an area known nationally, with mythic awe, as the Silicon Valley, the red-hot center of the computer and Internet industries. In 1999, the Internet industry alone had produced fourteen new billionaires. The Valley's mythology was full of the sagas of young men who had gone into business for themselves, created their own companies straight out of college, or, better still, had dropped out of college to launch their "start-ups," as these new digital-age enterprises were known. Such were the new "Masters of the Universe," a term coined in the eighties to describe the (mere) megamillionaires spawned by Wall Street during a boom in the bond business. By comparison with the Valley's boy billionaires, the Wall Streeters, even though they were enjoying a boom in the stock market in the year 2000, seemed slow and dreary. Typically, they graduated from college, worked for three years as number-crunching donkeys in some large investment-banking firm, went off to business school for two years to be certified as Masters of Business Administration, then returned to some investment-banking firm and hoped to start making some real money by the age of thirty. The stodginess of such a career was symbolized by the stodginess of their dress. Even the youngest of them dressed like old men: the dark blah suit, the light blah shirt, the hopelessly "interesting" Hermès tie . . . Many of them even wore silk braces.

The new Masters of the Universe turned all that upside down. At Il Fornaio restaurant in Palo Alto, California, where they gathered to tell war stories and hand out business cards at breakfast, the billionaire founders of the new wonder corporations walked in the door looking like well-pressed, well-barbered beachcombers, but beachcombers all the same. They wore khakis, boating moccasins (without socks), and ordinary cotton shirts with the cuffs rolled up and the front unbuttoned to the navel, and that was it. You could tell at a glance that a Silicon Valley billionaire carried no cell phone, Palm Pilot, HP-19B calculator, or RIM pager—he had people who did that for him. Having breakfast with him at Il Fornaio would be a vice president whose net worth was $100 or $200 million. He would be dressed just like the founder, except that he would also be wearing a sport jacket. Why? So that he could carry . . . the cell phone, the Palm Pilot, the HP-19B calculator, and the RIM pager, which received E-mail and felt big as a brick. But why not an attaché case? Because that was what old-fashioned businessmen Back East carried. Nobody would be caught dead at Il Fornaio carrying an attaché case. The Back East attaché case was known scornfully as "the leather lunch pail."

When somebody walked into Il Fornaio wearing a suit and tie, he was likely to be mistaken for a maître d'. In the year 2000, as in prior ages, service personnel, such as doormen, chauffeurs, waiters, and maître d's, were expected to wear the anachronistic finery of bygone eras. In Silicon Valley, wearing a tie was a mark of shame that indicated you were everything a Master of the Universe was not. Gradually, it would dawn on you. The poor devil in the suit and tie held one of those lowly but necessary executive positions, in public or investor relations, in which one couldn't avoid dealing with Pliocene old parties from . . . Back East.

Meanwhile, back East, the sons of the old rich were deeply involved in inverted fashions themselves. One of the more remarkable sights in New York City in the year 2000 was that of some teenage scion of an investment-banking family emerging from one of the forty-two Good Buildings, as they were known. These forty-two buildings on Manhattan's East Side contained the biggest, grandest, stateliest apartments ever constructed in the United States, most of them on Park and Fifth

Avenues. A doorman dressed like an Austrian Army colonel from the year 1870 holds open the door, and out comes a wan white boy wearing a baseball cap sideways; an outsized T-shirt, whose short sleeves fall below his elbows and whose tail hangs down over his hips; baggy cargo pants with flapped pockets running down the legs and a crotch hanging below his knees, and yards of material pooling about his ankles, all but obscuring the Lugz sneakers. This fashion was deliberately copied from the "homeys"—black youths on the streets of six New York slums, Harlem, the South Bronx, Bedford-Stuyvesant, Fort Greene, South Ozone Park, and East New York. After passing the doorman, who tipped his visored officer's hat and said "Good day," the boy walked twenty feet to a waiting sedan, where a driver with a visored officer's hat held open a rear door.

What was one to conclude from such a scene? The costumes said it all. In the year 2000, the sons of the rich, the very ones in line to inherit the bounties of the all-powerful United States, were consumed by a fear of being envied. A German sociologist of the period, Helmut Schoeck, said that "fear of being envied" was the definition of guilt. But if so, guilt about what? So many riches, so much power, such a dazzling array of advantages? American superiority in all matters of science, economics, industry, politics, business, medicine, engineering, social life, social justice, and, of course, the military was total and indisputable. Even Europeans suffering the pangs of wounded chauvinism looked on with awe at the brilliant example the United States had set for the world as the third millennium began. And yet there was a cloud on the millennial horizon.

America had shown the world the way in every area save one. In matters intellectual and artistic, she remained an obedient colony of Europe. American architecture had never recovered from the deadening influence of the German Bauhaus movement of the twenties. American painting and sculpture had never recovered from the deadening influence of various theory-driven French movements, beginning with Cubism early in the twentieth century. In music, the early-twentieth-century innovations of George Gershwin, Aaron Copland,

Duke Ellington, and Ferde Grofé had been swept away by the abstract, mathematical formulas of the Austrian composer Arnold Schoenberg. Schoenberg's influence had faded in the 1990s, but the damage had been done. The American theater had never recovered from the Absurdism of Samuel Beckett, Bertolt Brecht, and Luigi Pirandello.

But, above all, there was the curious case of American philosophy—which no longer existed. It was as if Emerson, Charles Peirce, William James, and John Dewey had never lived. The reigning doctrine was deconstruction, whose hierophants were two Frenchmen, Michel Foucault and Jacques Derrida. They began with a hyperdilation of a pronouncement of Nietzsche's to the effect that there can be no absolute truth, merely many "truths," which are the tools of various groups, classes, or forces. From this, the deconstructionists proceeded to the doctrine that language is the most insidious tool of all. The philosopher's duty was to deconstruct the language, expose its hidden agendas, and help save the victims of the American "Establishment": women, the poor, nonwhites, homosexuals, and hardwood trees.

Oddly, when deconstructionists required appendectomies or bypass surgery or even a root-canal job, they never deconstructed medical or dental "truth," but went along with whatever their board-certified, profit-oriented surgeons proclaimed was the last word.

Confused and bored, our electrician, our air-conditioning mechanic, and our burglar-alarm repairman sat down in the evening and watched his favorite TV show (*The Simpsons*), played his favorite computer game (*Tony Hawk's Pro Skater*) with the children, logged on to the Internet, stayed up until 2 a.m. planning a trip to this fabulous-sounding resort just outside Bangkok, then "crashed" (went to bed exhausted), and fell asleep faster than it takes to tell it, secure in the knowledge that the sun would once more shine blessedly upon him in the morning. It was the year 2000.

THE HUMAN BEAST

Two Young Men Who Went West

In 1948 there were seven thousand people in Grinnell, Iowa, including more than one who didn't dare take a drink in his own house without pulling the shades down first. It was against the law to sell liquor in Grinnell, but it was perfectly legal to drink it at home. So it wasn't that. It wasn't even that someone might look in through the window and disapprove. God knew Grinnell had more than its share of White Ribbon teetotalers, but by 1948 alcohol was hardly the mark of Cain it had once been. No, those timid souls with their fingers through the shade loops inside the white frame houses on Main Street and Park Street were thinking of something else altogether.

They happened to live on land originally owned by the Congregational minister who had founded the town in 1854, Josiah Grinnell. Josiah Grinnell had sold off lots with covenants, in perpetuity, stating that anyone who allowed alcohol to be drunk on his property forfeited ownership. *In perpetuity!* In perpetuity was forever, and 1948 was not even a hundred years later. In 1948 there were people walking around

Grinnell who had known Josiah Grinnell personally. They were getting old—Grinnell had died in 1891—but they were still walking around. So . . . why take a chance!

The plain truth was, Grinnell had Middle West written all over it. It was squarely in the middle of Iowa's midland corn belt, where people on the farms said "crawdad" instead of crayfish and "barn lot" instead of barnyard. Grinnell had been one of many Protestant religious communities established in the mid-nineteenth century after Iowa became a state and settlers from the East headed for the farmlands. The streets were lined with white clapboard houses and elm trees, like a New England village. And today, in 1948, the hard-scrubbed Octagon Soap smell of nineteenth-century Protestantism still permeated the houses and Main Street as well. That was no small part of what people in the East thought of when they heard the term "Middle West." For thirty years writers such as Sherwood Anderson, Sinclair Lewis, and Carl Van Vechten had been prompting the most delicious sniggers with their portraits of the churchy, narrow-minded Middle West. The Iowa painter Grant Wood was thinking of farms like the ones around Grinnell when he did his famous painting *American Gothic*. Easterners recognized the grim, juiceless couple in Wood's picture right away. There were John Calvin's and John Knox's rectitude reigning in the sticks.

In the fall of 1948 Harry Truman picked out Grinnell as one of the stops on his whistle-stop campaign tour, one of the hamlets where he could reach out to the little people, the average Americans of the heartland, the people untouched by the sophisticated opinion-makers of New York and Washington. Speaking from the rear platform of his railroad car, Truman said he would never forget Grinnell, because it was Grinnell College, the little Congregational academy over on Park Street, that had given him his first honorary degree. The President's fond recollection didn't cut much ice, as it turned out. The town had voted Republican in every presidential election since the first time Abraham Lincoln ran, in 1860, and wasn't about to change for Harry Truman.

On the face of it, there you had Grinnell, Iowa, in 1948: a piece of mid-nineteenth-century American history frozen solid in the middle of the twentieth. It was one of the last towns in America that people back East would have figured to become the starting point of a bolt into the future that would create the very substructure, the electronic grid, of life in the year 2000 and beyond.

On the other hand, it wouldn't have surprised Josiah Grinnell in the slightest.

It was in the summer of 1948 that Grant Gale, a forty-five-year-old physics professor at Grinnell College, ran across an item in the newspaper concerning a former classmate of his at the University of Wisconsin named John Bardeen. Bardeen's father had been dean of medicine at Wisconsin, and Gale's wife Harriet's father had been dean of the engineering school, and so Bardeen and Harriet had grown up as fellow faculty brats, as the phrase went. Both Gale and Bardeen had majored in electrical engineering. Eventually Bardeen had taught physics at the University of Minnesota and had then left the academic world to work for Bell Laboratories, the telephone company's main research center, in Murray Hill, New Jersey. And now, according to the item, Bardeen and another engineer at Bell, Walter Brattain, had invented a novel little device they called a transistor.

It was only an item, however; the invention of the transistor in 1948 did not create headlines. The transistor apparently performed the same function as the vacuum tube, which was an essential component of telephone relay systems and radios. Like the vacuum tube, the transistor could isolate a specific electrical signal, such as a radio wave, and amplify it. But the transistor did not require glass tubing, a vacuum, a plate, or a cathode. It was nothing more than two minute gold wires leading to a piece of processed germanium less than a sixteenth of an inch long, shaped like a tiny brick. Germanium, an element found in coal, was an insulator, not a conductor. But if the germanium was contaminated with impurities, it became a "semiconductor." A vacuum tube was also a semiconductor; the vacuum itself, like the germanium, was an insulator. But as every owner of a portable radio knew, vacuum tubes drew a lot of current, required a warm-up interval before they would work, and then got very hot. A transistor eliminated all these problems and, on top of that, was about fifty times smaller than a vacuum tube.

So far, however, it was impossible to mass-produce transistors, partly because the gold wires had to be made by hand and attached by hand two thousandths of an inch apart. But that was the telephone company's problem. Grant Gale wasn't interested in any present or future applications of the transistor in terms of products. He hoped the transistor might offer a way to study the flow of electrons through a solid (the germanium), a subject physicists had speculated about for decades. He thought it would be terrific to get some transistors for his physics department at Grinnell. So he wrote to Bardeen at Bell Laboratories. Just to make sure his request didn't get lost in the shuffle, he also wrote to the president of Bell Laboratories, Oliver Buckley. Buckley was from Sloane, Iowa, and happened to be a Grinnell graduate. So by the fall of 1948 Gale had obtained two of the first transistors ever made, and he presented the first academic instruction in solid-state electronics available anywhere in the world, for the benefit of the eighteen students majoring in physics at Grinnell College.

One of Grant Gale's senior physics majors was a local boy named Robert Noyce, whom Gale had known for years. Bob and his brothers, Donald, Gaylord, and Ralph, lived just down Park Street and used to rake leaves, mow the lawn, baby-sit, and do other chores for the Gales. Lately Grant Gale had done more than his share of agonizing over Bob Noyce. Like his brothers, Bob was a bright student, but he had just been thrown out of school for a semester, and it had taken every bit of credit Gale had in the local favor bank, not only with other faculty members but also with the sheriff, to keep the boy from being expelled for good and stigmatized with a felony conviction.

Bob Noyce's father, Ralph Sr., was a Congregational minister. Not only that, both his grandfathers were Congregational ministers. But that hadn't helped at all. In an odd way, after the thing happened, the boy's clerical lineage had boomeranged on him. People were going around saying, "Well, what do you expect from a preacher's son?" It was as if people in Grinnell agreed with Sherwood Anderson that underneath the righteousness the Midwestern Protestant preachers urged upon them, and which they themselves professed to uphold, lived demons of weakness, perversion, and hypocrisy that would break loose sooner or later.

No one denied that the Noyce boys were polite and proper in all outward appearances. They were members of the Boy Scouts. They went to Sunday school and the main Sunday service at the First Congregational Church and were active in the church youth groups. They were pumped full of Congregationalism until it was spilling over. Their father, although a minister, was not the minister of the First Congregational Church. He was the associate superintendent of the Iowa Conference of Congregational Churches, whose headquarters were at the college. The original purpose of the college had been to provide a good academic Congregational education, and many of the graduates became teachers. The Conference was a coordinating council rather than a governing body, since a prime tenet of the Congregational Church, embedded in its name, was that each congregation was autonomous. Congregationalists rejected the very idea of a church hierarchy. A Congregational minister was not supposed to be a father or even a shepherd but, rather, a teacher. Each member of the congregation was supposed to internalize the moral precepts of the church and be his own priest dealing directly with God. So the job of secretary of the Iowa Conference of Congregational Churches was anything but a position of power. It didn't pay much, either.

The Noyces didn't own their own home. They lived in a two-story white clapboard house that was owned by the church at Park Street and Tenth Avenue, at the college. Not owning your own home didn't carry the social onus in Grinnell that it did in the East. There was no upper crust in Grinnell. There were no top people who kept the social score in such matters. Congregationalists rejected the idea of a social hierarchy as fiercely as they did the idea of a religious hierarchy. The Congregationalists, like the Presbyterians, Methodists, Baptists, and United Brethren, were Dissenting Protestants. They were direct offshoots of the Separatists, who had split off from the Church of England in the sixteenth and seventeenth centuries and settled New England. At bottom, their doctrine of the autonomous congregation was derived from their hatred of the British system of class and status, with its endless gradations, topped off by the Court and the aristocracy. Even as late as 1948 the typical small town of the Middle West, like Grinnell, had nothing approaching a country club set. There were subtle differences in status in Grinnell, as in any other place, and it was better to be rich than poor, but there were only two obvious social ranks: those who were devout, educated, and hardworking, and those who weren't. Genteel poverty did not doom one socially in Grinnell. Ostentation did. The Noyce boys worked at odd jobs to earn their pocket money. That was socially correct as well as useful. To have devoted the same time to taking tennis lessons or riding lessons would have been a gaffe in Grinnell.

Donald, the oldest of the four boys, had done brilliantly at the college and had just received his Ph.D. in chemistry at Columbia University and was about to join the faculty of the University of California at Berkeley. Gaylord, the second oldest, was teaching school in Turkey. Bob, who was a year younger than Gaylord, had done so well in science at Grinnell High School that Grant Gale had invited him to take the freshman physics course at the college during his high-school senior year. He became one of Gale's star students and most tireless laboratory workers from that time on. Despite his apparent passion for the scientific grind, Bob Noyce turned out to be that much-vaunted creature, the well-rounded student. He was a trim, muscular boy, five feet eight, with thick dark brown hair, a strong jawline, and a long, broad nose that gave him a rugged appearance. He was the star diver on the college swimming team and won the Midwest Conference championship in 1947. He sang in choral groups, played the oboe, and was an actor with the college dramatic society. He also acted in a radio drama workshop at the college, along with his friend Peter Hackes and some others who were interested in broadcasting, and was the leading man in a soap opera that was broadcast over station WOI in Ames, Iowa.

Perhaps Bob Noyce was a bit too well rounded for local tastes. There were people who still remembered the business with the box kite back in 1941, when he was thirteen. It had been harmless, but it could have been a disaster. Bob had come across some plans for the building of a box kite, a kite that could carry a person aloft, in the magazine *Popular Science*. So he and Gaylord made a frame of cross-braced pine and covered it with a bolt of muslin. They tried to get the thing up by running across a field and towing it with a rope, but that didn't work terribly well. Then they hauled it up on the roof of a barn, and Bob sat in the seat and Gaylord ran across the roof, pulling the kite, and Bob was lucky he didn't break his neck when he and the rig hit the ground. So then they tied it to the rear bumper of a neighbor's car. With the neighbor at the wheel, Bob rode the kite and managed to get about twelve feet off the ground and glide for thirty seconds or so and come down without wrecking himself or any citizen's house or livestock.

Livestock . . . yes. Livestock was a major capital asset in Grinnell, and livestock was at the heart of what happened in 1948. In May a group of Bob Noyce's friends in one of the dormitory houses at Grinnell decided to have a luau, and he was in on the planning. The Second World War had popularized the exotic ways of the South Pacific, so that in 1948 the luau was an up-to-the-minute social innovation. The centerpiece of a luau was a whole roasted suckling pig with an apple or a pineapple in its mouth. Bob Noyce, being strong and quick, was one of the two boys assigned to procure the pig. That night they sneaked onto a farm just outside Grinnell and wrestled a twenty-five-pound suckling out of a pigpen and arrived back at the luau to great applause. Within a few hours the pig was crackling hot and had an apple in its mouth and looked good enough for seconds and thirds, which everybody helped himself to, and there was more applause. The next morning came the moral hangover. The two boys decided to go see the farmer, confess, and pay for the pig. They didn't quite understand how a college luau, starring his pig, would score on the laugh meter with a farmer in midland Iowa. In the state of Iowa, where the vast majority of people depended upon agriculture for a livelihood and upon Protestant morality for their standards, not even stealing a watermelon worth thirty-five cents was likely to be written off as a boyish prank. Stealing a pig was larceny. The farmer got the sheriff and insisted on bringing criminal charges.

There was only so much that Ralph Noyce, the preacher with the preacher's son, could do. Grant Gale, on the other hand, was the calm, well-respected third party. He had two difficult tasks: to keep Bob out of jail and out of court and to keep the college administration from expelling him. There was never any hope at all of a mere slap on the wrist. The compromise Grant Gale helped work out—a one-semester suspension—was the best deal Bob could have hoped for realistically.

The Night of the Luau Pig was quite a little scandal on the Grinnell Richter scale. So Gale was all the more impressed by the way Bob Noyce took it. The local death-ray glowers never broke his confidence. All the Noyce boys had a profound and, to tell the truth, baffling confidence. Bob had a certain way of listening and staring. He would lower his head slightly and look up with a gaze that seemed to be about one hundred amperes. While he looked at you he never blinked and never swallowed. He absorbed everything you said and then answered very levelly in a soft baritone voice and often with a smile that showed off his terrific set of teeth. The stare, the voice, the smile—it was all a bit like the movie persona of the most famous of all Grinnell College's alumni, Gary Cooper. With his strong face, his athlete's build, and the Gary Cooper manner, Bob Noyce projected what psychologists call the halo effect. People with the halo effect seem to know exactly what they're doing and, moreover, make you want to admire them for it. They make you see the halos over their heads.

Years later people would naturally wonder where Bob Noyce got his confidence. Many came to the conclusion it was as much from his mother, Harriet Norton Noyce, as from his father. She was a latter-day version of the sort of strong-willed, intelligent, New England–style woman who had made such a difference during Iowa's pioneer days a hundred years before. His mother and father, with the help of Rowland Cross, who taught mathematics at Grinnell, arranged for Bob to take a job in the actuarial department of Equitable Life in New York City for the summer. He stayed on at the job during the fall semester, then came back to Grinnell at Christmas and rejoined the senior class in January as the second semester began. Gale was impressed by the aplomb with which the prodigal returned. In his first three years Bob had accumulated so many extra credits, it would take him only this final semester to graduate. He resumed college life, including the extracurricular activities, without skipping a beat. But more than that, Gale was gratified by the way Bob became involved with the new experimental device that was absorbing so much of Gale's own time: the transistor.

Bob was not the only physics major interested in the transistor, but he was the one who seemed most curious about where this novel mechanism might lead. He went off to the Massachusetts Institute of Technology, in Cambridge, in the fall to begin his graduate work. When he brought up the subject of the transistor at MIT, even to faculty members, people just looked at him. Even those who had heard of it regarded it merely as a novelty fabricated by the telephone company. There was no course work involving transistors or the theory of solid-state electronics. His dissertation was a "Photoelectric Study of Surface States on Insulators," which was at best merely background for solid-state electronics. In this area MIT was far behind Grinnell College. For a good four years Grant Gale remained one of the few people Bob Noyce could compare notes with in this new field.

Well, it had been a close one! What if Grant Gale hadn't gone to school with John Bardeen, and what if Oliver Buckley hadn't been a Grinnell alumnus? And what if Gale hadn't bothered to get in touch with the two of them after he read the little squib about the transistor in the newspaper? What if he hadn't gone to bat for Bob Noyce after the Night of the Luau Pig and the boy had been thrown out of college and that had been that? After all, if Bob hadn't been able to finish at Grinnell, he probably never would have been introduced to the transistor. He certainly wouldn't have come across it at MIT in 1948. Given what Bob Noyce did over the next twenty years, one couldn't help but wonder about the fortuitous chain of events.

Fortuitous . . . well! How Josiah Grinnell, up on the plains of Heaven, must have laughed over that!

Grant Gale was the first important physicist in Bob Noyce's career. The second was William Shockley. After their ambitions had collided one last time, and they had parted company, Noyce had concluded that he and Shockley were two very different people. But in many ways they were alike.

For a start, they both had an amateur's hambone love of being onstage. At MIT Noyce had sung in choral groups. Early in the summer of 1953, after he had received his Ph.D., he went over to Tufts College to sing and act in a program of musicals presented by the college. The costume director was a girl named Elizabeth Bottomley, from Barrington, Rhode Island, who had just graduated from Tufts, majoring in English. They both enjoyed dramatics. Singing, acting, and skiing had become the pastimes Noyce enjoyed most. He had become almost as expert at skiing as he had been at diving. Noyce and Betty, as he called her, were married that fall.

In 1953 the MIT faculty was just beginning to understand the implications of the transistor. But electronics firms were already eager to have graduate electrical engineers who could do research and development in the new field. Noyce was offered jobs by Bell Laboratories, IBM, RCA, and Philco. He went to work for Philco, in Philadelphia, because Philco was starting from near zero in semiconductor research and chances for rapid advancement seemed good. But Noyce was well aware that the most important work was still being done at Bell Laboratories, thanks in no small part to William Shockley.

Shockley had devised the first theoretical framework for research into solid-state semiconductors as far back as 1939 and was in charge of the Bell Labs team that included John Bardeen and Walter Brattain. Shockley had also originated the "junction transistor," which turned the transistor from an exotic laboratory instrument into a workable item. By 1955 Shockley had left Bell and returned to Palo Alto, California, where he had grown up near Stanford University, to form his own company, Shockley Semiconductor Laboratory, with start-up money provided by Arnold Beckman of Beckman Instruments. Shockley opened up shop in a glorified shed on South San Antonio Road in Mountain View, which was just south of Palo Alto. The building was made of concrete blocks with the rafters showing. Aside from clerical and maintenance personnel, practically all the employees were electrical engineers with doctorates. In a field this experimental there was nobody else worth hiring. Shockley began talking about "my Ph.D. production line."

Meanwhile, Noyce was not finding Philco the golden opportunity he thought it would be. Philco wanted good enough transistors to stay in the game with GE and RCA, but it was not interested in putting money into the sort of avant-garde research Noyce had in mind. In 1956 he resigned from Philco and moved from Pennsylvania to California to join Shockley. The way he went about it was a classic example of the Noyce brand of confidence. By now he and his wife, Betty, had two children: Bill, who was two, and Penny, who was six months old. After a couple of telephone conversations with Shockley, Noyce put himself and Betty on a night flight from Philadelphia to San Francisco. They arrived in Palo Alto at 6 a.m. By noon Noyce had signed a contract to buy a house. That afternoon he went to Mountain View to see Shockley and ask for a job, projected the halo, and got it.

The first months on Shockley's Ph.D. production line were exhilarating. It wasn't really a production line at all. Everything at this stage was research. Every day a dozen young Ph.D.s came to the shed at eight in the morning and began heating germanium and silicon, another common element, in kilns to temperatures ranging from 1,472 to 2,552 degrees Fahrenheit. They wore white lab coats, goggles, and work gloves. When they opened the kiln doors, weird streaks of orange and white light went across their faces, and they put in the germanium or the silicon, along with specks of aluminum, phosphorus, boron, and arsenic. Contaminating the germanium or silicon with the aluminum, phosphorus, boron, and arsenic was called doping. Then they lowered a small mechanical column into the goo so that crystals formed on the bottom of the column, and they pulled the crystal out and tried to get a grip on it with tweezers, and put it under microscopes and cut it with diamond cutters, among other things, into minute slices, wafers, chips—there were no names in electronics for these tiny forms. The kilns cooked and bubbled away, the doors opened, the pale apricot light streaked over the goggles, the tweezers and diamond cutters flashed, the white coats flapped, the Ph.D.s squinted through their microscopes, and Shockley moved between the tables conducting the arcane symphony.

In pensive moments Shockley looked very much the scholar, with his roundish face, his roundish eyeglasses, and his receding hairline—but Shockley was not a man locked in the pensive mode. He was an enthusiast, a raconteur, and a showman. At the outset his very personality was enough to keep everyone swept up in the great adventure. When he lectured, as he often did at colleges and before professional groups, he would walk up to the lectern and thank the master of ceremonies and say that the only more flattering introduction he had ever received was one he gave himself one night when the emcee didn't show up, whereupon—*bango!*—a bouquet of red roses would pop up in his hand. Or he would walk up to the lectern and say that tonight he was getting into a hot subject, whereupon he would open a book and—*whumpf!*—a puff of smoke would rise up out of the pages.

Shockley was famous for his homely but shrewd examples. One day a student confessed to being puzzled by the concept of amplification, which was one of the prime functions of the transistor. Shockley told him, "If you take a bale of hay and tie it to the tail of a mule and then strike a match and set the bale of hay on fire, and if you then compare the energy expended shortly thereafter by the mule with the energy expended by yourself in the striking of the match, you will understand the concept of amplification."

On November 1, 1956, Shockley arrived at the shed on South San Antonio Road beaming. Early that morning he had received a telephone call informing him that he had won the Nobel Prize in Physics for the invention of the transistor; or, rather, that he was co-winner, along with John Bardeen and Walter Brattain. Shockley closed up shop and took everybody to a restaurant called Dinah's Shack over on El Camino Real, the road to San Francisco that had become Palo Alto's commercial strip. He treated his Ph.D. production line and all the other employees to a champagne breakfast. It seemed that Shockley's father was a mining engineer who spent years out on remote Durango terrains, in Nevada, Manchuria—all over the world. Shockley's mother was like Noyce's. She was an intelligent woman with a commanding will. The Shockleys were Unitarians, the Unitarian Church being an offshoot of the Congregational. Shockley Sr. was twenty years older than Shockley's mother and died when Shockley was seventeen. Shockley's mother was determined that her son would someday "set the world on fire," as she once put it. And now he had done it. Shockley lifted a glass of champagne in Dinah's Shack, and it was as if it were a toast back across a lot of hard-wrought Durango grit Octagon Soap sagebrush Dissenting Protestant years to his father's memory and his mother's determination.

That had been a great day at Shockley Semiconductor Laboratory. There weren't many more. Shockley was magnetic, he was a genius, and he was a great research director—the best, in fact. His forte was breaking a problem down to first principles. With a few words and a few lines on a piece of paper he aimed any experiment in the right direction. When it came to comprehending the young engineers on his Ph.D. production line, however, he was not so terrific.

It never seemed to occur to Shockley that his twelve highly educated elves just might happen to view themselves the same way he had always viewed himself: which is to say, as young geniuses capable of the sort of inventions Nobel Prizes were given for. One day Noyce came to Shockley with some new results he had found in the laboratory. Shockley picked up the telephone and called some former colleagues at Bell Labs to see if they sounded right. Shockley never even realized that Noyce had gone away from his desk seething. Then there was the business of the new management techniques. Now that he was an entrepreneur, Shockley came up with some new ways to run a company. Each one seemed to irritate the elves more than the one before. For a start, Shockley published their salaries. He posted them on a bulletin board. That way there would be no secrets. Then he started having the employees rate one another on a regular basis. These were so-called peer ratings, a device sometimes used in the military and seldom appreciated even there. Everybody regarded peer ratings as nothing more than popularity contests. But the real turning point was the lie detector. Shockley was convinced that someone in the shed was sabotaging the project. The work was running into inexplicable delays, but the money was running out on schedule. So he insisted that each employee roll up his sleeve and bare his chest and let the electrodes be attached and submit to a polygraph examination. No saboteur was ever found.

There were also some technical differences of opinion. Shockley was interested in developing a so-called four-layer diode. Noyce and two of his fellow elves, Gordon Moore and Jean Hoerni, favored transistors. But at bottom it was dissatisfaction with the boss and the lure of entrepreneurship that led to what happened next.

In the summer of 1957 Moore, Hoerni, and five other engineers—but not Noyce—got together and arrived at what became one of the primary business concepts of the young semiconductor industry. In this business, it dawned on them, capital assets in the traditional sense of plant, equipment, and raw materials counted for next to nothing. The only plant you needed was a shed big enough for the worktables. The only equipment you needed was some kilns, goggles, microscopes, tweezers, and diamond cutters. The materials, silicon and germanium, came from dirt and coal. Brainpower was the entire franchise. If the seven of them thought they could do the job better than Shockley, there was nothing to keep them from starting their own company. On that day was born the concept that would make the semiconductor business as wild as show business: defection capital.

The seven defectors went to the Wall Street firm of Hayden Stone in search of start-up money. It was at this point that they realized they had to have someone to serve as administrator. So they turned to Noyce, who was still with Shockley. None of them, including Noyce, had any administrative experience, but they all thought of Noyce as soon as the question came up. They didn't know exactly what they were looking for . . . but Noyce was the one with the halo. He agreed to join them. He would continue to wear a white lab coat and goggles and do research. But he would also be the coordinator. Of the eight of them, he would be the one man who kept track, on a regular basis, of all sides of the operation. He was twenty-nine years old.

Arthur Rock of Hayden Stone approached twenty-two firms before he finally hooked the defectors up with the Fairchild Camera and Instrument Corporation of New York. Fairchild was owned by Sherman Fairchild, a bachelor bon vivant who lived in a futuristic town house on East Sixty-fifth Street in Manhattan. The house was in two sections connected by ramps. The ramps were fifty feet long in some cases, enclosed in glass so that you could go up and down the ramps in all weather and gaze upon the marble courtyard below. The place looked like something from out of the Crystal Palace of Ming in *Flash Gordon*. The ramps were for his Aunt May, who lived with him and was confined to a wheelchair and had even more Fairchild money than he did. The chief executive officer of Fairchild was John Carter, who had just come from the Corning Glass Company. He had been the youngest vice-president in the history of that old-line, family-owned firm. He was thirty-six. Fairchild Camera and Instrument gave the defectors the money to start up the new company, Fairchild Semiconductor, with the understanding that Fairchild Camera and Instrument would have the right to buy Fairchild Semiconductor for $3 million at any time within the next eight years.

Shockley took the defections very hard. He seemed as much hurt as angered, and he was certainly angry enough. A friend of Shockley's said to Noyce's wife, Betty, "You must have known about this for quite some time. How on earth could you not tell me?" That was a baffling remark, unless one regarded Shockley as the father of the transistor and the defectors as the children he had taken beneath his mantle of greatness.

If so, one had a point. Years later, if anyone had drawn up a family tree for the semiconductor industry, practically every important branch would have led straight from Shockley's shed on South San Antonio Road. On the other hand, Noyce had been introduced to the transistor not by Shockley but by John Bardeen, via Grant Gale, and not in California but back in his own hometown, Grinnell, Iowa.

For that matter, Josiah Grinnell had been a defector in his day, too, and there was no record that he had ever lost a night's sleep over it.

Noyce, Gordon Moore, Jean Hoerni, and the other five defectors set up Fairchild Semiconductor in a two-story warehouse building some speculator had built out of tilt-up concrete slabs on Charleston Avenue in Mountain View, about twelve blocks from Shockley's operation. Mountain View was in the northern end of the Santa Clara Valley. In the business world the valley was known mainly for its apricot, pear, and plum orchards. From the work bays of the light-industry sheds that the speculators were beginning to build in the valley you could look out and see the raggedy little apricot trees they had never bothered to bulldoze after they bought the land from the farmers. A few well-known electronics firms were already in the valley: General Electric and IBM, as well as a company that had started up locally, Hewlett-Packard. Stanford University was encouraging engineering concerns to locate near Palo Alto and use the university's research facilities. The man who ran the program was a friend of Shockley's, Frederick E. Terman, whose father had originated the first scientific measurement of human intelligence, the Stanford-Binet IQ test.

IBM had a facility in the valley that was devoted specifically to research rather than production. Both IBM and Hewlett-Packard were trying to develop a highly esoteric and colossally expensive new device, the electronic computer. Shockley had been the first entrepreneur to come to the area to make semiconductors. After the defections his operation never got off the ground. Here in the Santa Clara Valley, that left the field to Noyce and the others at Fairchild.

Fairchild's start-up couldn't have come at a better time. By 1957 there was sufficient demand from manufacturers who merely wanted transistors instead of vacuum tubes, for use in radios and other machines, to justify the new operation. But it was also in 1957 that the Soviet Union launched Sputnik I. In the electronics industry the ensuing space race had the effect of coupling two new inventions—the transistor and the computer—and magnifying the importance of both.

The first American electronic computer, known as ENIAC, had been developed by the Army during the Second World War, chiefly as a means of computing artillery and bomb trajectories. The machine was a monster. It was one hundred feet long and ten feet high and required eighteen thousand vacuum tubes. The tubes generated so much heat, the temperature in the room sometimes reached 120 degrees. What the government needed was small computers that could be installed in rockets to provide automatic onboard guidance. Substituting transistors for vacuum tubes was an obvious way to cut down on the size. After Sputnik I the glamorous words in the semiconductor business were "computers" and "miniaturization."

Other than Shockley Semiconductor, Fairchild was the only semiconductor company in the Santa Clara Valley, but Texas Instruments had entered the field in Dallas, as had Motorola in Phoenix and Transitron and Raytheon in the Boston area, where a new electronics industry was starting up as MIT finally began to comprehend the new technology. These firms were all racing to refine the production of transistors to the point where they might command the market. So far refinement had not been anybody's long suit. No tourist dropping by Fairchild, Texas Instruments, Motorola, or Transitron would have had the faintest notion he was looking in on the leading edge of the most advanced of all industries, electronics. The work bays, where the transistors were produced, looked like slightly sunnier versions of the garment sweatshops of San Francisco's Chinatown. Here were rows of women hunched over worktables, squinting through microscopes, doing the most tedious and frustrating sort of manual labor, cutting layers of silicon apart with diamond cutters, picking little rectangles of them up with tweezers, trying to attach wires to them, dropping them, rummaging around on the floor to find them again, swearing, muttering, climbing back up to their chairs, rubbing their eyes, squinting back through the microscopes, and driving themselves crazy some more. Depending on how well the silicon or germanium had been cooked and doped, anywhere from 50 to 90 percent of the transistors would turn out to be defective even after all that, and sometimes the good ones would be the ones that fell on the floor and got ruined.

Even for a machine as simple as a radio the individual transistors had to be wired together, by hand, until you ended up with a little panel that looked like a road map of West Virginia. As for a computer—the wires inside a computer were sheer spaghetti.

Noyce had figured out a solution. But fabricating it was another matter. There was something primitive about cutting individual transistors out of sheets of silicon and then wiring them back together in various series. Why not put them all on a single piece of silicon without wires? The problem was that you would also have to carve, etch, coat, and otherwise fabricate the silicon to perform all the accompanying electrical functions as well, the functions ordinarily performed by insulators, rectifiers, resistors, and capacitors. You would have to create an entire electrical system, an entire circuit, on a little wafer or chip.

Noyce realized that he was not the only engineer thinking along these lines, but he had never even heard of Jack Kilby. Kilby was a thirty-six-year-old engineer working for Texas Instruments in Dallas. In January 1959 Noyce made his first detailed notes about a complete solid-state circuit. A month later Texas Instruments announced that Jack Kilby had invented one. Kilby's integrated circuit, as the invention was called, was made of germanium. Six months later Noyce created a similar integrated circuit made of silicon and using a novel insulating process developed by Jean Hoerni. Noyce's silicon device turned out to be more efficient and more practical to produce than Kilby's and set the standard for the industry. So Noyce became known as the co-inventor of the integrated circuit. Nevertheless, Kilby had unquestionably been first. There was an ironic echo of Shockley here. Strictly speaking, Bardeen and Brattain, not Shockley, had invented the transistor, but Shockley wasn't bashful about being known as the co-inventor. And now, eleven years later, Noyce wasn't turning bashful, either.

Noyce knew exactly what he possessed in this integrated circuit, or microchip, as the press would call it. Noyce knew that he had discovered the road to El Dorado.

El Dorado was the vast, still-virgin terrain of electricity. Electricity was already so familiar a part of everyday life, only a few research engineers understood just how young and unexplored the terrain actually was. It had been only eighty years since Edison invented the lightbulb in 1879. It had been less than fifty years since Lee De Forest, an inventor from Council Bluffs, Iowa, had invented the vacuum tube. The vacuum tube was based on the lightbulb, but the vacuum tube opened up fields the lightbulb did not even suggest: long-distance radio and telephone communication. Over the past ten years, since Bardeen and Brattain had invented it in 1948, the transistor had become the modern replacement for the vacuum tube. And now came Kilby's and Noyce's integrated circuit. The integrated circuit was based on the transistor, but the integrated circuit opened up fields the transistor did not even suggest. The integrated circuit made it possible to create miniature computers, to put all the functions of the mighty ENIAC on a panel the size of a playing card. Thereby the integrated circuit opened up every field of engineering imaginable, from voyages to the moon to robots, and many fields that had never been imagined, such as electronic guidance counseling. It opened up so many fields that no one could even come up with a single name to include them all. "The second industrial revolution," "the age of the computer," "the microchip universe," "the electronic grid"—none of them, not even the handy neologism "high tech," could encompass all the implications.

The importance of the integrated circuit was certainly not lost on John Carter and Fairchild Camera back in New York. In 1959 they exercised their option to buy Fairchild Semiconductor for $3 million. The next day Noyce, Moore, Hoerni, and the other five former Shockley elves woke up rich, or richer than they had ever dreamed of being. Each received $250,000 worth of Fairchild stock.

Josiah Grinnell grew livid on the subject of alcohol. But he had nothing against money. He would have approved.

Noyce didn't know what to make of his new wealth. He was thirty-one years old. For the past four years, ever since he had gone to work for Shockley, the semiconductor business had not seemed like a business at all but an esoteric game in which young electrical engineers competed for *attaboys* and the occasional round of applause after delivering a paper before the IEEE, the Institute of Electrical and Electronics Engineers. It was a game supercharged by the fact that it was being played in the real world, to use a term that annoyed scientists in the universities. Someone—Arnold Beckman, Sherman Fairchild, whoever—was betting real money, and other bands of young elves, at Texas Instruments, RCA, Bell, were out there competing with you by the real world's rules, which required that you be practical as well as brilliant. Noyce started working for Fairchild Semiconductor in 1957 for twelve thousand dollars a year. When it came to money, he had assumed that he, like his father, would always be on somebody's payroll. Now, in 1959, when he talked to his father, he told him, "The money doesn't seem real. It's just a way of keeping score."

Noyce took his family to visit his parents fairly often. He and Betty now had three children, Bill, Penny, and Polly, who was a year old. When they visited the folks, they went off to church on Sunday with the folks, as if it were all very much a part of their lives. In fact, Noyce had started drifting away from Congregationalism and the whole matter of churchgoing after he entered MIT. It was not a question of rejecting it. He never rejected anything about his upbringing in Grinnell. It was just that he was heading off somewhere else, down a different road.

In that respect Noyce was like a great many bright young men and women from Dissenting Protestant families in the Middle West after the Second World War. They had been raised as Baptists, Methodists, Congregationalists, Presbyterians, United Brethren, whatever. They had been led through the church door and prodded toward religion, but it had never come alive for them. Sundays made their skulls feel like dried-out husks. So they slowly walked away from the church and silently, without so much as a growl of rebellion, congratulated themselves on their independence of mind and headed into another way of life. Only decades later, in most cases, would they discover how, absentmindedly, inexplicably, they had brought the old ways along for the journey nonetheless. It was as if . . . through some extraordinary mistake . . . they had been sewn into the linings of their coats!

Now that he had some money, Bob Noyce bought a bigger house. His and Betty's fourth child, Margaret, was born in 1960, and they wanted each child to have a bedroom. But the thought of moving into any of the "best" neighborhoods in the Palo Alto area never even crossed his mind. The best neighborhoods were to be found in Atherton, in Burlingame, which was known as very social, or in the swell old sections of Palo Alto, near Stanford University. Instead, Noyce bought a California version of a French country house in Los Altos, a white stucco house with a steeply pitched roof. It was scenic up there in the hills, and cooler in the summer than it was down in the flatlands near the bay. The house had plenty of room, and he and Betty would be living a great deal better than most couples their age, but Los Altos had no social cachet and the house was not going to make *House & Garden* come banging on the door. No one could accuse them of being ostentatious.

John Carter appointed Noyce general manager of the entire division, Fairchild Semiconductor, which was suddenly one of the hottest new outfits in the business world. NASA chose Noyce's integrated circuits for the first computers that astronauts would use on board their spacecraft (in the Gemini program). After that, orders poured in. In ten years Fairchild sales rose from a few thousand dollars a year to $130 million, and the number of employees rose from the original band of elves to twelve thousand. As the general manager, Noyce now had to deal with a matter Shockley had dealt with clumsily and prematurely, namely, new management techniques for this new industry.

One day John Carter came to Mountain View for a close look at Noyce's semiconductor operation. Carter's office in Syosset, Long Island, arranged for a limousine and chauffeur to be at his disposal while he was in California. So Carter arrived at the tilt-up concrete building in Mountain View in the back of a black Cadillac limousine with a driver in the front wearing the complete chauffeur's uniform—the black suit, the white shirt, the black necktie, and the black visored cap. That in itself was enough to turn heads at Fairchild Semiconductor. Nobody had ever seen a limousine and a chauffeur out there before. But that wasn't what fixed the day in everybody's memory. It was the fact that the driver stayed out there for almost eight hours, *doing nothing*. He stayed out there in his uniform, with his visored hat on, in the front seat of the limousine, all day, doing nothing but waiting for a man who was somewhere inside. John Carter was inside having a terrific chief executive officer's time for himself. He took a tour of the plant, he held conferences, he looked at figures, he nodded with satisfaction, he beamed his urbane Fifty-seventh Street Biggie CEO charm. And the driver sat out there all day engaged in the task of supporting a visored cap with his head. People started leaving their workbenches and going to the front windows just to take a look at this phenomenon. It seemed that bizarre. Here was a serf who *did nothing all day* but wait outside a door in order to be at the service of the haunches of his master instantly, whenever those haunches and the paunch and the jowls might decide to reappear. It wasn't merely that this little peek at the New York–style corporate high life was unusual out here in the brown hills of the Santa Clara Valley. It was that it seemed *terribly wrong*.

A certain instinct Noyce had about this new industry and the people who worked in it began to take on the outlines of a concept. Corporations in the East adopted a feudal approach to organization, without even being aware of it. There were kings and lords, and there were vassals, soldiers, yeomen, and serfs, with layers of protocol and perquisites, such as the car and driver, to symbolize superiority and establish the boundary lines. Back East the CEOs had offices with carved paneling, fake fireplaces, escritoires, bergères, leather-bound books, and dressing rooms, like a suite in a baronial manor house. Fairchild Semiconductor needed a strict operating structure, particularly in this period of rapid growth, but it did not need a social structure. In fact, nothing could be worse. Noyce realized how much he detested the Eastern corporate system of class and status with its endless gradations, topped off by the CEOs and vice-presidents who conducted their daily lives as if they were a corporate court and aristocracy. He rejected the idea of a social hierarchy at Fairchild.

Not only would there be no limousines and chauffeurs, there would not even be any reserved parking places. Work began at 8 a.m. for one and all, and it would be first come, first served, in the parking lot, for Noyce, Gordon Moore, Jean Hoerni, and everybody else. "If you come late," Noyce liked to say, "you just have to park in the back forty." And there would be no baronial office suites. The glorified warehouse on Charleston Road was divided into work bays and a couple of rows of cramped office cubicles. The cubicles were never improved. The decor remained Glorified Warehouse, and the doors were always open. Half the time Noyce, the chief administrator, was out in the laboratory anyway, wearing his white lab coat. Noyce came to work in a coat and tie, but soon the jacket and the tie were off, and that was fine for any other man in the place, too. There were no rules of dress at all, except for some unwritten ones. Dress should be modest, modest in the social as well as the moral sense. At Fairchild there were no hard-worsted double-breasted pinstripe suits and shepherd's-check neckties. Sharp, elegant, fashionable, or alluring dress was a social blunder. Shabbiness was not a sin. Ostentation was.

During the start-up phase at Fairchild Semiconductor there had been no sense of bosses and employees. There had been only a common sense of struggle out on a frontier. Everyone had internalized the goals of the venture. They didn't need exhortations from superiors. Besides, everyone had been so young! Noyce, the administrator or chief coordinator, or whatever he should be called, had been just about the oldest person on the premises, and he had been barely thirty. And now, in the early 1960s, thanks to his athletic build and his dark brown hair with the Campus Kid hairline, he still looked very young. As Fairchild expanded, Noyce didn't even bother trying to find "experienced management personnel." Out here in California, in the semiconductor industry, they didn't exist. Instead, he recruited engineers right out of the colleges and graduate schools and gave them major responsibilities right off the bat. There was no "staff," no "top management" other than the eight partners themselves. Major decisions were not bucked up a chain of command. Noyce held weekly meetings of people from all parts of the operation, and whatever had to be worked out was worked out right there in the room. Noyce wanted them all to keep internalizing the company's goals and to provide their own motivations, just as they had during the start-up phase. If they did that, they would have the capacity to make their own decisions.

The young engineers who came to work for Fairchild could scarcely believe how much responsibility was suddenly thrust upon them. Some twenty-four-year-old just out of graduate school would find himself in charge of a major project with no one looking over his shoulder. A problem would come up, and he couldn't stand it, and he would go to Noyce and hyperventilate and ask him what to do. And Noyce would lower his head, turn on his 100-ampere eyes, listen, and say, "Look, here are your guidelines. You've got to consider A, you've got to consider B, and you've got to consider C." Then he would turn on the Gary Cooper smile: "But if you think I'm going to make your decision for you, you're mistaken. Hey . . . it's *your* ass."

Back East, in the conventional corporation, any functionary wishing to make an unusually large purchase had to have the approval of a superior or two or three superiors or even a committee, a procedure that ate up days, weeks, in paperwork. Noyce turned that around. At Fairchild any engineer, even a weenie just out of Caltech, could make any purchase he wanted, no matter how enormous, unless someone else objected strongly enough to try to stop it. Noyce called this the Short Circuit Paper Route. There was only one piece of paper involved, the piece of paper the engineer handed somebody in the purchasing department.

The spirit of the start-up phase! My God! Who could forget the exhilaration of the past few years! To be young and free out here on the silicon frontier! Noyce was determined to maintain that spirit during the expansion phase. And for the time being at least, here in the early 1960s, the notion of a permanent start-up operation didn't seem too far-fetched. Fairchild was unable to coast on the tremendous advantage Noyce's invention of the integrated circuit had provided. Competitors were setting up shop in the Santa Clara Valley like gold rushers. And where did they come from? Why, from Fairchild itself! And how could that be? Nothing to it . . . Defection capital!

Defectors (or redefectors) from Fairchild started up more than fifty companies, all making or supplying microchips. Raytheon Semiconductor, Signetics, General Microelectronics, Intersil, Advanced Micro Devices, Qualidyne—off they spun, each with a sillier pseudo-tech engineerologism for a name than the one before. Defectors! What a merry game that was. Jean Hoerni and three of the other original eight defectors from Shockley defected from Fairchild to form what would soon become known as Teledyne Semiconductors, and that was only round one. After all, why not make all the money for yourself! The urge to use defection capital was so irresistible that the word "defection," with its note of betrayal, withered away. Defectors were merely the Fairchildren, as Adam Smith dubbed them. Occasionally defectors from other companies, such as the men from Texas Instruments and Westinghouse who started Siliconix, moved into the Santa Clara Valley to join the free-for-all. But it was the Fairchildren who turned the Santa Clara Valley into the Silicon Valley. Acre by acre the fruit trees were uprooted, and two-story Silicon Modern office buildings and factories went up. The state of California built a new freeway past the area, Route 280. Children heard the phrase "Silicon Valley" so often, they grew up thinking it was the name on the map.

Everywhere the Fairchild émigrés went, they took the Noyce approach with them. It wasn't enough to start up a company; you had to start up a community, a community in which there were no social distinctions, and it was first come, first served, in the parking lot, and everyone was supposed to internalize the common goals. The atmosphere of the new companies was so democratic, it startled businessmen from the East. Some fifty-five-year-old biggie with his jowls swelling up smoothly from out of his F. R. Tripler modified-spread white collar and silk jacquard-print necktie would call up from GE or RCA and say, "This is Harold B. Thatchwaite," and the twenty-three-year-old secretary on the other end of the line, out in the Silicon Valley, would say in one of those sunny blond pale blue-eyed California voices, "Just a minute, Hal, Jack will be right with you." And once he got to California and met this Jack for the first time, there he would be, the CEO himself, all of thirty-three years old, wearing no jacket, no necktie, just a checked shirt, khaki pants, and a pair of moccasins with welted seams the size of jumper cables. Naturally the first sounds out of this Jack's mouth would be "Hi, Hal."

It was the 1960s, and people in the East were hearing a lot about California surfers, California bikers, hot-rodders, car customizers, California hippies, and political protesters, and the picture they got was of young people in jeans and T-shirts who were casual, spontaneous, impulsive, emotional, sensual, undisciplined, and obnoxiously proud of it. So these semiconductor outfits in the Silicon Valley with their CEOs dressed like camp counselors struck them as the business versions of the same thing.

They couldn't have been more wrong. The new breed of the Silicon Valley lived for work. They were disciplined to the point of back spasms. They worked long hours and kept working on weekends. They became absorbed in their companies the way men once had in the palmy days of the automobile industry. In the Silicon Valley a young engineer would go to work at eight in the morning, work right through lunch, leave the plant at six-thirty or seven, drive home, play with the baby for half an hour, have dinner with his wife, get in bed with her, give her a quick toss, then get up and leave her there in the dark and work at his desk for two or three hours on "a coupla things I had to bring home with me."

Or else he would leave the plant and decide, Well, maybe he would drop in at the Wagon Wheel for a drink before he went home. Every year there was some place, the Wagon Wheel, Chez Yvonne, Rickey's, the Roundhouse, where members of this esoteric fraternity, the young men and women of the semiconductor industry, would head after work to have a drink and gossip and brag and trade war stories about phase jitters, phantom circuits, bubble memories, pulse trains, bounceless contacts, burst modes, leapfrog tests, p-n junctions, sleeping-sickness modes, slow-death episodes, RAMs, NAKs, MOSes, PCMs, PROMs, PROM blowers, PROM burners, PROM blasters, and teramagnitudes, meaning multiples of a million millions. So then he wouldn't get home until nine, and the baby was asleep, and dinner was cold, and the wife was frosted off, and he would stand there and cup his hands as if making an imaginary snowball and try to explain to her . . . while his mind trailed off to other matters, LSIs, VLSIs, alpha flux, de-rezzing, forward biases, parasitic signals, and that terasexy little cookie from Signetics he had met at the Wagon Wheel, who understood such things.

It was not a great way of life for marriages. By the late 1960s the toll of divorces seemed to those in the business to be as great as that of NASA's boomtowns, Cocoa Beach, Florida, and Clear Lake, Texas, where other young engineers were giving themselves over to a new technology as if it were a religious mission. The second time around they tended to "intramarry." They married women who worked for Silicon Valley companies and who could comprehend and even learn to live with their twenty-four-hour obsessions. In the Silicon Valley an engineer was under pressure to reinvent the integrated circuit every six months. In 1959 Noyce's invention had made it possible to put an entire electrical circuit on a chip of silicon the size of a fingernail. By

1964 you had to know how to put ten circuits on a chip that size just to enter the game, and the stakes kept rising. Six years later the figure was one thousand circuits on a single chip; six years after that it would be thirty-two thousand—and everyone was talking about how the real breakthrough would be sixty-four thousand. Noyce himself led the race; by 1968 he had a dozen new integrated-circuit and transistor patents. And what amazing things such miniaturization made possible! In December 1968 NASA sent the first manned flight to the moon, Apollo 8. Three astronauts, Frank Borman, James Lovell, and William Anders, flew into earth orbit, then fired a rocket at precisely the right moment in order to break free of the earth's gravitational field and fly through the minute "window" in space that would put them on course to the moon rather than into orbit around the sun, from which there could be no return. They flew to the moon, went into orbit around it, saw the dark side, which no one had ever seen, not even with a telescope, then fired a rocket at precisely the right moment in order to break free of the moon's gravitational pull and go into the proper trajectory for their return to earth. None of it would have been possible without onboard computers. People were beginning to talk about all that the space program was doing for the computer sciences. Noyce knew it was the other way around. Only the existence of a miniature computer two feet long, one foot wide, and six inches thick—exactly three thousand times smaller than the old ENIAC and far faster and more reliable—made the flight of Apollo 8 possible. And there would have been no miniature computer without the integrated circuits invented by Noyce and Kilby and refined by Noyce and the young semiconductor zealots of the Silicon Valley, the new breed who were building the road to El Dorado.

Noyce used to go into a slow burn that year, 1968, when the newspapers, the magazines, and the television networks got on the subject of *the youth. The youth* was a favorite topic in 1968. Riots broke out on the campuses as the antiwar movement reached its peak following North Vietnam's Tet offensive. Black youths rioted in the cities. The Yippies, supposedly a coalition of hippies and campus activists, managed to sabotage the Democratic National Convention by setting off some highly televised street riots. The press seemed to enjoy presenting these youths as the avant-garde who were sweeping aside the politics and morals of the past and shaping America's future. The French writer Jean-François Revel toured American campuses and called the radical youth *homo novus*, "the New Man," as if they were the latest, most advanced product of human evolution itself, after the manner of the superchildren in Arthur C. Clarke's *Childhood's End*.

Homo novus? As Noyce saw it, these so-called radical youth movements were shot through with a yearning for a preindustrial Arcadia. They wanted, or thought they wanted, to return to the earth and live on organic vegetables and play folk songs from the sixteenth and seventeenth centuries. They were antitechnology. They looked upon science as an instrument monopolized by the military-industrial complex. They used this phrase, "the military-industrial complex," all the time. If industry or the military underwrote scientific research in the universities—and they underwrote a great deal of it—then that research was evil. The universities were to be pure and above exploitation, except, of course, by ideologues of the Left. The *homo novus* had set up a chain of logic that went as follows: since science equals the military-industrial complex, and the military-industrial complex equals capitalism, and capitalism equals fascism, therefore science equals fascism. And therefore these much-vaunted radical youths, these shapers of the future, attacked the forward positions of American technology, including the space program and the very idea of the computer. And therefore these creators of the future were what? They were Luddites. They wanted to destroy the new machines. They were the reactionaries of the new age. They were an avant-garde to the rear. They wanted to call off the future. They were stillborn, ossified, prematurely senile.

If you wanted to talk about the creators of the future—well, here they were! Here in the Silicon Valley! Just before Apollo 8 circled the moon, Bob Noyce turned forty-one. By age forty-one he had become such a good skier, people were urging him to enter competitions. When his daughter Penny was almost fourteen, he asked her what she wanted for her birthday, and she said she wanted to drop from an airplane by parachute. Noyce managed to convince her to settle for glider lessons instead. Then, because it made him restless to just stand around an airfield and watch her soar up above, he took flying lessons, bought an airplane, and began flying the family up through the mountain passes to Aspen, Colorado, for skiing weekends. He had the same lean, powerful build as he had had twenty years before, when he was on the swimming team at Grinnell College. He had the same thick dark brown hair and the same hairline. It looked as if every hair in his head were nailed in. He looked as if he could walk out the door any time he wanted to and win another Midwest Conference diving championship. And he was one of the *oldest* CEOs in the semiconductor business! He was the Edison of the bunch! He was the *father* of the Silicon Valley!

The rest of the hotshots were younger. It was a business dominated by people in their twenties and thirties. In the Silicon Valley there was a phenomenon known as burnout. After five or ten years of obsessive racing for the semiconductor high stakes, five or ten years of lab work, work lunches, workaholic drinks at the Wagon Wheel, and work-battering of the wife and children, an engineer would reach his middle thirties and wake up one day—and he was finished. The game was over. It was called burnout, suggesting mental and physical exhaustion brought about by overwork. But Noyce was convinced it was something else entirely. It was . . . *age*, or age and status. In the semiconductor business, research engineering was like pitching in baseball; it was 60 percent of the game. Semiconductor research was one of those highly mathematical sciences, such as microbiology, in which, for reasons one could only guess at, the great flashes, the critical moments of inspiration, came mainly to those who were young, often to men in their twenties. The thirty-five-year-old burnouts weren't suffering from exhaustion, as Noyce saw it. They were being overwhelmed, outperformed, by the younger talent coming up behind them. It wasn't the central nervous system that was collapsing, it was the ego.

Now here you saw youth in the vanguard, on the leading edge! Here you saw the youths who were, in fact, shaping the future! Here you saw, if you insisted on the term, the *homo novus*!

But why insist? For they were also of the same stripe as Josiah Grinnell, who had founded Grinnell, Iowa, at the age of thirty-three.

It was in 1968 that Noyce pulled off the redefection of all redefections. Fairchild Semiconductor had generated tremendous profits for the parent company back East. It now appeared to Noyce that John Carter and Sherman Fairchild had been diverting too much of that money into new start-up ventures outside the semiconductor field. As a matter of fact, Noyce disliked many things "back East." He disliked the periodic trips to New York, for which he dressed in gray suits, white shirts, and neckties and reported to the royal corporate court and wasted days trying to bring them up-to-date on what was happening in California. Fairchild was rather enlightened, for an Eastern corporation, but the truth was, there was no one back East who understood how to run a corporation in the United States in the second half of the twentieth century. Back East they had never progressed beyond the year 1940. Consequently, they were still hobbled by all the primitive stupidities of bureaucratism and labor-management battles. They didn't have the foggiest comprehension of the Silicon Valley idea of a corporate community. The brightest young businessmen in the East were trained—most notably at Harvard Business School—to be little Machiavellian princes. Greed and strategy were all that mattered. They were trained for failure.

Noyce and Gordon Moore, two of the three original eight Shockley elves still at Fairchild, decided to form their own company. They went to Arthur Rock, who had helped provide the start-up money for Fairchild Semiconductor when he was at Hayden Stone. Now Rock had his own venture capital operation. Noyce took great pleasure in going through none of the steps in corporate formation that the business schools talked about. He and Moore didn't even write up a proposal.

They merely told Rock what they wanted to do and put up $500,000 of their own money, $250,000 each. That seemed to impress Rock more than anything they could possibly have written down, and he rounded up $2.5 million of the start-up money. A few months later another $300,000 came, this time from Grinnell College. Noyce had been on the college's board of trustees since 1962, and a board member had asked him to give the college a chance to invest, should the day come when he started his own company. So Grinnell College became one of the gamblers betting on Noyce and Intel—the pseudo-tech engineerologism Noyce and Moore dreamed up as the corporate name. Josiah Grinnell would have loved it.

The defection of Noyce and Moore from Fairchild was an earthquake even within an industry jaded by the very subject of defections. In the Silicon Valley everybody had looked upon Fairchild as Noyce's company. He was the magnet that held the place together. With Noyce gone, it was obvious that the entire workforce would be up for grabs. As one wag put it, "People were practically driving trucks over to Fairchild Semiconductor and loading up with employees." Fairchild responded by pulling off one of the grossest raids in corporate history. One day the troops who were left at Fairchild looked across their partitions and saw a platoon of young men with terrific suntans moving into the executive office cubicles. They would always remember what terrific suntans they had. They were C. Lester Hogan, chief executive officer of the Motorola semiconductor division in Phoenix, and his top echelon of engineers and administrators. Or, rather, C. Lester Hogan of Motorola until yesterday. Fairchild had hired the whole bunch away from Motorola and installed them in place of Noyce & Co. like a matched set. There was plenty of sunshine in the Santa Clara Valley, but nobody here had suntans like this bunch from Phoenix. Fairchild had lured the leader of the young sun-gods out of the Arizona desert in the most direct way imaginable. He had offered him an absolute fortune in money and stock. Hogan received so much, the crowd at the Wagon Wheel said, that henceforth wealth in the Silicon Valley would be measured in units called hogans.

Noyce and Moore, meanwhile, started Intel up in a tilt-up concrete building that Jean Hoerni and his group had built but no longer used, in Santa Clara, which was near Mountain View. Once again there was an echo of Shockley. They opened up shop with a dozen bright young electrical engineers, plus a few clerical and maintenance people, and bet everything on research and product development. Noyce and Moore, like Shockley, put on the white coats and worked at the laboratory tables. They would not be competing with Fairchild or anyone else in the already established semiconductor markets. They had decided to move into the most backward area of computer technology, which was data storage, or "memory." A computer's memory was stored in ceramic ringlets known as cores. Each ringlet contained one "bit" of information, a "yes" or a "no," in the logic of the binary system of mathematics that computers employ. Within two years Noyce and Moore had developed the 1103 memory chip, a chip of silicon and polysilicon the size of two letters in a line of type. Each chip contained four thousand transistors, did the work of a thousand ceramic ringlets, and did it faster. The production line still consisted of rows of women sitting at tables as in the old shed-and-rafter days, but the work bays now looked like something out of an intergalactic adventure movie. The women engraved the circuits on the silicon photographically, wearing antiseptic Mars Voyage suits, headgear, and gloves because a single speck of dust could ruin one of the miniature circuits. The circuits were so small that "miniature" no longer sounded small enough. The new word was "microminiature." Everything now took place in an air-conditioned ice cube of vinyl tiles, stainless steel, fluorescent lighting, and backlit plastic.

The 1103 memory chip opened up such a lucrative field that other companies, including Fairchild, fought desperately just to occupy the number-two position, filling the orders Intel couldn't take care of. At the end of Intel's first year in business, which had been devoted almost exclusively to research, sales totaled less than three thousand dollars and the workforce numbered forty-two. In 1972, thanks largely to the 1103 chip, sales were $23.4 million and the workforce numbered

1,002. In the next year sales almost tripled, to $66 million, and the workforce increased two and a half times, to 2,528.

So Noyce had the chance to run a new company from start-up to full production precisely the way he thought Shockley should have run his in Palo Alto back in the late 1950s. From the beginning Noyce gave all the engineers and most of the office workers stock options. He had learned at Fairchild that in a business so dependent upon research, stock options were a more powerful incentive than profit sharing. People sharing profits naturally wanted to concentrate on products that were already profitable rather than plunge into avant-garde research that would not pay off in the short run even if it was successful. But people with stock options lived for research breakthroughs. The news would send a semiconductor company's stock up immediately, regardless of profits.

Noyce's idea was that every employee should feel that he could go as far and as fast in this industry as his talent would take him. He didn't want any employee to look at the structure of Intel and see a complex set of hurdles. It went without saying that there would be no social hierarchy at Intel, no executive suites, no pinstripe set, no reserved parking places or other symbols of the hierarchy. But Noyce wanted to go further. He had never liked the business of the office cubicles at Fairchild. As miserable as they were, the mere possession of one symbolized superior rank. At Intel executives would not be walled off in offices. Everybody would be in one big room. There would be nothing but low partitions to separate Noyce or anyone else from the lowliest stock boys trundling in the accordion printout paper. The whole place became like a shed. When they first moved into the building, Noyce worked at an old, scratched, secondhand metal desk. As the company expanded, Noyce kept the same desk, and new stenographers, just hired, were given desks that were not only newer but bigger and better than his. Everybody noticed the old beat-up desk, since there was nothing to keep anybody from looking at every inch of Noyce's office space. Noyce enjoyed this subversion of the Eastern corporate protocol of small metal desks for underlings and large wooden desks for overlords.

At Intel, Noyce decided to eliminate the notion of levels of management altogether. He and Moore ran the show; that much was clear. But below them there were only the strategic business segments, as they called them. They were comparable to the major departments in an orthodox corporation, but they had far more autonomy. Each was run like a separate corporation. Middle managers at Intel had more responsibility than most vice-presidents back East. They were also much younger and got lower-back pain and migraines earlier. At Intel, if the marketing division had to make a major decision that would affect the engineering division, the problem was not routed up a hierarchy to a layer of executives who oversaw both departments. Instead, "councils," made up of people already working on the line in the divisions that were affected, would meet and work it out themselves. The councils moved horizontally, from problem to problem. They had no vested power. They were not governing bodies but coordinating councils.

Noyce was a great believer in meetings. The people in each department or work unit were encouraged to convene meetings whenever the spirit moved them. There were rooms set aside for meetings at Intel, and they were available on a first come, first served basis, just like the parking spaces. Often meetings were held at lunchtime. That was not a policy; it was merely an example set by Noyce. There were no executive lunches at Intel. Back East, in New York, executives treated lunch as a daily feast of the nobility, a sumptuous celebration of their eminence, in the Lucullan expense-account restaurants of Manhattan. The restaurants in the East and West Fifties of Manhattan were like something out of a dream. They recruited chefs from all over Europe and the Orient. Pasta primavera, saucisson, sorrel mousse, homard cardinal, terrine de légumes Montesquieu, paillard de pigeon, medallions of beef Chinese Gordon, veal Valdostana, Verbena roast turkey with Hayman sweet potatoes flown in from the eastern shore of Virginia, raspberry soufflé, baked Alaska, zabaglione, pear torte, crème brûlée—and the wines! and the brandies! and the port! the Sambucca! the cigars! and the decor!—walls with lacquered woodwork and winking mirrors and sconces with little pleated peach-colored shades, all of it designed by the very same decorators who walked duchesses to parties for Halston on Eaton Square!—and captains and maître d's who made a fuss over you in movie French in front of your clients and friends and fellow overlords!—it was Mount Olympus in mid-Manhattan every day from 12:30 to 3 p.m., and you emerged into the pearl-gray light of the city with such ambrosia pumping through your veins that even the clotted streets with the garbagemen backing up their grinder trucks and yelling, " 'Mon back, 'mon back, 'mon back, 'mon back," as if talking Urban Chippewa—even this became part of the bliss of one's eminence in the corporate world! There were many chief executive officers who kept their headquarters in New York long after the last rational reason for doing so had vanished . . . because of the ineffable experience of being a CEO and having lunch five days a week in Manhattan!

At Intel lunch had a different look to it. You could tell when it was noon at Intel because at noon men in white aprons arrived at the front entrance gasping from the weight of the trays they were carrying. The trays were loaded down with deli sandwiches and waxed cups full of drinks with clear plastic tops, with globules of Sprite or Diet Shasta sliding around the tops on the inside. That was your lunch. You ate some sandwiches made of roast beef or chicken sliced into translucent rectangles by a machine in a processing plant and then reassembled on the bread in layers that gave off dank whiffs of hormones and chemicals, and you washed it down with Sprite or Diet Shasta, and you sat amid the particle-board partitions and metal desktops, and you kept your mind on your committee meeting. That was what Noyce did, and that was what everybody else did.

If Noyce called a meeting, then he set the agenda. But after that, everybody was an equal. If you were a young engineer and you had an idea you wanted to get across, you were supposed to speak up and challenge Noyce or anybody else who didn't get it right away. This was a little bit of heaven. You were face-to-face with the inventor, or the co-inventor, of the very road to El Dorado, and he was only forty-one years old, and *he* was listening to *you*. He had his head down and his eyes beamed up at you, and he was absorbing it all. He wasn't a boss. He was

Gary Cooper! He was here to help you be self-reliant and do as much as you could on your own. This wasn't a corporation . . . it was a congregation.

By the same token, there were sermons and homilies. At Intel everyone—Noyce included—was expected to attend sessions on "the Intel Culture." At these sessions the principles by which the company was run were spelled out and discussed. Some of the discussions had to do specifically with matters of marketing or production. Others had to do with the broadest philosophical principles of Intel and were explained via the Socratic method at management seminars by Intel's number-three man, Andrew Grove.

Grove would say, "How would you sum up the Intel approach?"

Many hands would go up, and Grove would choose one, and the eager communicant would say, "At Intel you don't wait for someone else to do it. You take the ball yourself and you run with it."

And Grove would say, "Wrong. At Intel you take the ball yourself and you let the air out and you fold the ball up and put it in your pocket. Then you take another ball and run with it, and when you've crossed the goal you take the second ball out of your pocket and reinflate it and score twelve points instead of six."

Grove was the most colorful person at Intel. He was a thin man in his mid-thirties with tight black curls all over his head. The curls ran down into a pair of muttonchops that seemed to run together like goulash with his mustache. Every day he wore either a turtleneck jersey or an open shirt with an ornamental chain dangling from his neck. He struck outsiders as the epitome of a style of the early 1970s known as California Groovy. In fact, Grove was the epitome of the religious principle that the greater the freedom—for example, the freedom to dress as you pleased—the greater the obligation to exercise discipline. Grove's own groovy outfits were neat and clean. The truth was, he was a bit of a bear on the subject of neatness and cleanliness. He held what he called "Mr. Clean inspections," showing up in various work areas wearing his muttonchops and handlebar mustache and his Harry Belafonte shirt and the gleaming chainwork, inspecting offices for books stacked too high, papers strewn over desktops, doing everything short of running a white glove over the shelves, as if this were some California Groovy Communal version of Parris Island. Grove was also the inspiration for such items as the performance ratings and the Late List. Each employee received a report card periodically with a grade based on certain presumably objective standards. The grades were *superior, exceeds requirements, meets requirements, marginally meets requirements*, and *does not meet requirements*. This was the equivalent of A, B, C, D, and F in school. Noyce was all for it. "If you're ambitious and hardworking," he would say, "you *want* to be told how you're doing." In Noyce's view, most of the young hotshots who were coming to work for Intel had never had the benefit of honest grades in their lives. In the late 1960s and early 1970s college faculties had been under pressure to give all students passing marks so they wouldn't have to go off to Vietnam, and they had caved in, until the entire grading system was meaningless. At Intel they would learn what measuring up meant. The Late List was also like something from a strict school. Everyone was expected at work at 8 a.m. A record was kept of how many employees arrived after 8:10 a.m. If 7 percent or more were late for three months, then everybody in the section had to start signing in. There was no inevitable penalty for being late, however. It was up to each department head to make of the Late List what he saw fit. If he knew a man was working overtime every night on a certain project, then his presence on the Late List would probably be regarded as nothing more than that, a line on a piece of paper. At bottom—and this was part of the Intel Culture—Noyce and Grove knew that penalties were very nearly useless. Things like report cards and Late Lists worked only if they stimulated self-discipline.

The worst form of discipline at Intel was to be called on the Antron II carpet before Noyce himself. Noyce insisted on ethical behavior in all dealings within the company and between companies. That was the word people used to describe his approach, "ethical"; that and "moral." Noyce was known as a very aggressive businessman, but he stopped short of cutting throats—and he never talked about revenge.

He would not tolerate peccadilloes such as little personal I'll-reimburse-it-on-Monday dips into the petty cash. Noyce's Strong Silent stare, his Gary Cooper approach, could be mortifying as well as inspiring. When he was angry, his baritone voice never rose. He seemed like a powerful creature that only through the greatest self-control was refraining from an attack. He somehow created the impression that if pushed one more inch, he would fight. As a consequence he seldom had to. No one ever trifled with Bob Noyce.

Noyce managed to create an ethical universe within an inherently amoral setting: the American business corporation in the second half of the twentieth century. At Intel there was good and there was evil, and there was freedom and there was discipline, and to an extraordinary degree employees internalized these matters, like members of Cromwell's army. As the workforce grew at Intel, and the profits soared, labor unions, chiefly the International Association of Machinists and Aerospace Workers, the Teamsters, and the Stationary Engineers Union, made several attempts to organize Intel. Noyce made it known, albeit quietly, that he regarded unionization as a death threat to Intel, and to the semiconductor industry generally. Labor-management battles were part of the ancient terrain of the East. If Intel was divided into workers and bosses, with the implication that each side had to squeeze its money out of the hides of the other, the enterprise would be finished. Motivation would no longer be internal; it would be objectified in the deadly form of work rules and grievance procedures. The one time it came down to a vote, the union lost out by the considerable margin of four to one. Intel's employees agreed with Noyce. Unions were part of the dead hand of the past . . . Noyce and Intel were on the road to El Dorado.

By the early 1970s Noyce and Moore's 1103 memory chip had given this brand-new company an entire corner of the semiconductor market. But that was only the start. Now a thirty-two-year-old Intel engineer named Ted Hoff came up with an invention as important as Noyce's integrated circuit had been a decade earlier: the microprocessor. The microprocessor was known as "the computer on a chip," because it put all the arithmetic and logic functions of a computer on a chip the size of the head of a tack. The possibilities for creating and using small computers now surpassed most people's imagining, even within the industry. One of the more obvious possibilities was placing a small computer in the steering and braking mechanisms of a car that would take over for the driver in case of a skid or excessive speed on a curve.

In Ted Hoff, Noyce was looking at proof enough of his hypothesis that out here on the electrical frontier the great flashes came to the young. Hoff was about the same age Noyce had been when he invented his integrated circuit. The glory was now Hoff's. But Noyce took Hoff's triumph as proof of a second hypothesis: If you created the right type of corporate community, the right type of autonomous congregation, genius would flower. Certainly the corporate numbers were flowering. The news of the microprocessor, on top of the success of the 1103 memory chip, nearly trebled the value of Intel stock from 1971 to 1973. Noyce's own holdings were now worth $18.5 million. He was in roughly the same position as Josiah Grinnell a hundred years before, when Grinnell brought the Rock Island Railroad into Iowa.

Noyce continued to live in the house in the Los Altos hills that he had bought in 1960. He was not reluctant to spend his money; he was merely reluctant to show it. He spent a fortune on landscaping, but you could do that and the world would be none the wiser. Gradually the house disappeared from view behind an enormous wall of trees, tropical bushes, and cockatoo flowers. Noyce had a pond created on the back lawn, a waterscape elaborate enough to put on a bus tour, but nobody other than guests ever saw it. The lawn stretched on for several acres and had a tennis court, a swimming pool, and more walls of boughs and hot-pastel blossoms, and the world saw none of that, either.

Noyce drove a Porsche roadster, and he didn't mind letting it out for a romp. Back East, when men made a great deal of money, they tended to put a higher and higher value on their own hides. Noyce, on the other hand, seemed to enjoy finding new ways to hang his out over the edge. He took up paragliding over the ski slopes at Aspen on a Rogolla wing. He built a Quicksilver hang glider and flew it off cliffs until a friend of his, a champion at the sport, fractured his pelvis and a leg flying a Quicksilver. He also took up scuba diving, and now he had his Porsche. The high-performance foreign sports car became one of the signatures of the successful Silicon Valley entrepreneur. The sports car was perfect. Its richness consisted of something small, dense, and hidden: the engineering beneath the body shell. Not only that, the very luxury of a sports car was the experience of driving it yourself. A sports car didn't even suggest a life with servants. Porsches and Ferraris became the favorites. By 1975 the Ferrari agency in Los Gatos was the second biggest Ferrari agency on the West Coast. Noyce also bought a 1947 Republic Seabee amphibious airplane, so that he could take the family for weekends on the lakes in northern California. He now had two aircraft, but he flew the ships himself.

Noyce was among the richest individuals on the San Francisco Peninsula, as well as the most important figure in the Silicon Valley, but his name seldom appeared in the San Francisco newspapers. When it did, it was in the business section, not on the society page. That, too, became the pattern for the new rich of the Silicon Valley. San Francisco was barely forty-five minutes up the Bayshore Freeway from Los Altos, but psychologically San Francisco was an entire continent away. It was a city whose luminaries kept looking back East, to New York, to see if they were doing things correctly.

In 1974 Noyce wound up in a situation that to some seemed an all-too-typical midlife in the Silicon Valley story. He and Betty, his wife of twenty-one years, were divorced, and the following year he "intramarried." Noyce, who was forty-seven, married Intel's personnel director, Ann Bowers, who was thirty-seven. The divorce was mentioned in the *San Francisco Chronicle*, but not as a social note. It was a major business story. Under California law, Betty received half the family's assets. When word got out that she was going to sell off $6 million of her Intel stock in the interest of diversifying her fortune, it threw the entire market in Intel stock into a temporary spin. Betty left California and went to live in a village on the coast of Maine. Noyce kept the house in Los Altos.

By this time, the mid-1970s, the Silicon Valley had become the late-twentieth-century-California version of a new city, and Noyce and other entrepreneurs began to indulge in some introspection. For ten years, thanks to racial hostilities and the leftist politics of the antiwar movement, the national press had dwelled on the subject of ethnic backgrounds. This in itself tended to make the engineers and entrepreneurs of the Silicon Valley conscious of how similar most of them were. Most of the major figures, like Noyce himself, had grown up and gone to college in small towns in the Middle West and the West. John Bardeen had grown up in and gone to college in Madison, Wisconsin. Walter Brattain had grown up in and gone to college in Washington. Shockley grew up in Palo Alto at a time when it was a small college town and went to the California Institute of Technology. Jack Kilby was born in Jefferson City, Missouri, and went to college at the University of Illinois. William Hewlett was born in Ann Arbor and went to school at Stanford. David Packard grew up in Pueblo, Colorado, and went to Stanford. Oliver Buckley grew up in Sloane, Iowa, and went to college at Grinnell. Lee De Forest came from Council Bluffs, Iowa (and went to Yale). And Thomas Edison grew up in Port Huron, Michigan, and didn't go to college at all.

Some of them, such as Noyce and Shockley, had gone East to graduate school at MIT, since it was the most prestigious engineering school in the United States. But MIT had proved to be a backwater . . . the sticks . . . when it came to the most advanced form of engineering, solid-state electronics. Grinnell College, with its one thousand students, had been years ahead of MIT. The picture had been the same on the other great frontier of technology in the second half of the twentieth century, namely, the space program. The engineers who fulfilled one of man's most ancient dreams, that of traveling to the moon, came from the same background, the small towns of the Midwest and the West. After the triumph of Apollo 11, when Neil Armstrong and "Buzz"

Aldrin became the first mortals to walk on the moon, NASA's administrator, Tom Paine, happened to remark in conversation, "This was the triumph of the squares." A reporter overheard him—and did the press ever have a time with that! But Paine had come up with a penetrating insight. As it says in the Book of Matthew, the last shall be first. It was engineers from the supposedly backward and narrow-minded boondocks who had provided not only the genius but also the passion and the daring that won the space race and carried out John F. Kennedy's exhortation, back in 1961, to put a man on the moon "before this decade is out." The passion and the daring of these engineers was as remarkable as their talent. Time after time they had to shake off the meddling hands of timid souls from back East. The contribution of MIT to Project Mercury was minus one. The minus one was Jerome Wiesner of the MIT electronic research lab, who was brought in by Kennedy as a special adviser to straighten out the space program when it seemed to be faltering early in 1961. Wiesner kept flinching when he saw what NASA's boondockers were preparing to do. He tried to persuade Kennedy to forfeit the manned space race to the Soviets and concentrate instead on unmanned scientific missions. The boondockers of Project Mercury, starting with the project's director, Bob Gilruth, an aeronautical engineer from Nashwauk, Minnesota, dodged Wiesner for months, like moonshiners evading a roadblock, until they got astronaut Alan Shepard launched on the first Mercury mission. Who had time to waste on players as behind the times as Jerome Wiesner and the Massachusetts Institute of Technology . . . out here on technology's leading edge?

Just why was it that small-town boys from the Middle West dominated the engineering frontiers? Noyce concluded it was because in a small town you became a technician, a tinker, an engineer, and an inventor, by necessity.

"In a small town," Noyce liked to say, "when something breaks down, you don't wait around for a new part, because it's not coming. You make it yourself."

Yet in Grinnell necessity had been the least of the mothers of invention. There had been something else about Grinnell, something people Noyce's age could feel but couldn't name. It had to do with the fact that Grinnell had once been a religious community; not merely a town with a church but a town that was inseparable from the church. In Josiah Grinnell's day most of the townspeople were devout Congregationalists, and the rest were smart enough to act as if they were. Anyone in Grinnell who aspired to the status of feedstore clerk or better joined the First Congregational Church. By the end of the Second World War educated people in Grinnell, and in all the Grinnells of the Middle West, had begun to drop this side of their history into a lake of amnesia. They gave in to the modern urge to be urbane. They themselves began to enjoy sniggering over Grant Wood's *American Gothic* and Sherwood Anderson's and Sinclair Lewis's prose portraits of the Middle West. Once the amnesia set in, all they remembered from the old days was the austere moral codes, which in some cases still hung on. Josiah Grinnell's real estate covenants prohibiting drinking, for example . . . Just imagine! How absurd it was to see these unburied bones of something that had once been strong and alive.

That something was Dissenting Protestantism itself. Oh, it had once been quite strong and very much alive! The passion—the exhilaration!—of those early days was what no one could any longer recall. To be a believing Protestant in a town such as Grinnell in the middle of the nineteenth century was to experience a spiritual ecstasy greater than any that the readers of *Main Street* or the viewers of *American Gothic* were likely to know in their lifetimes. Josiah Grinnell had gone to Iowa in 1854 to create nothing less than a City of Light. He was a New Englander who had given up on the East. He had founded the first Congregational church in Washington, D.C., and then defected from it when the congregation, mostly Southerners, objected to his antislavery views. He went to New York and met the famous editor of the *New York Herald*, Horace Greeley. It was while talking to Josiah Grinnell, who was then thirty-two and wondering what to do with his life, that Greeley uttered the words for which he would be remembered forever after: "Go west, young man, go west." So Grinnell went to Iowa, and he and three friends bought up five thousand acres of land in order to start up a Congregational community the way he thought it should be done. A City of Light! The first thing he organized was the congregation. The second was the college. Oxford and Cambridge had started banning Dissenting Protestants in the seventeenth century; Dissenters founded their own schools and colleges. Grinnell became a champion of "free schools," and it was largely thanks to him that Iowa had one of the first and best public school systems in the West. To this day Iowa has the highest literacy rate of any state. In the 1940s a bright youngster whose parents were not rich—such as Bob Noyce or his brother Donald—was far more likely to receive a superior education in Iowa than in Massachusetts.

And if he was extremely bright, if he seemed to have the quality known as genius, he was infinitely more likely to go into engineering in Iowa, or Illinois or Wisconsin, than anywhere in the East. Back East engineering was an unfashionable field. The East looked to Europe in matters of intellectual fashion, and in Europe the ancient aristocratic bias against manual labor lived on. Engineering was looked upon as nothing more than manual labor raised to the level of a science. There was "pure" science and there was engineering, which was merely practical. Back East engineers ranked, socially, below lawyers, doctors, Army colonels, Navy captains, English, history, biology, chemistry, and physics professors; and business executives. This piece of European snobbery had never reached Grinnell, Iowa, however.

Neither had the corollary piece of snobbery that said a scientist was lowering himself by going into commerce. Dissenting Protestants looked upon themselves as secular saints, men and women of God who did God's work not as penurious monks and nuns but as successful workers in the everyday world. To be rich and successful was even better, and just as righteous. One of Josiah Grinnell's main projects was to bring the Rock Island Railroad into Iowa. Many in his congregation became successful farmers of the gloriously fertile soil around Grinnell. But there was no sense of rich and poor. All the congregation opened up the virgin land in a common struggle out on the frontier. They had given up the comforts of the East . . . in order to create a City of Light in the name of the Lord. Every sacrifice, every privation, every denial of the pleasures of the flesh, brought them closer to that state of bliss in which the light of God shines forth from the apex of the soul. What were the momentary comforts and aristocratic poses of the East . . . compared to this? Where would the fleshpots back East be on that day when the heavens opened up and a light fell 'round about them and a voice from on high said: "Why mockest thou me?" The light! The light! Who, if he had ever known that glorious light, if he had ever let his soul burst forth into that light, could ever mock these, my very seed, with a *Main Street* or an *American Gothic*! There, in Grinnell, reigned the passion that enabled men and women to settle the West in the nineteenth century against the most astonishing odds and in the face of overbearing hardships.

By the standards of St. Francis of Assisi or St. Jerome, who possessed nothing beyond the cloak of righteousness, Josiah Grinnell was a very secular saint indeed. He died a rich man. And Robert Noyce's life was a great deal more secular than Josiah Grinnell's. In a single decade, 1973–1983, Intel's sales grew from $64 million a year to almost one billion. Noyce's own holdings were worth an estimated four billion dollars. Noyce had wandered away from the church itself. He smoked. He smoked a lot. He took a drink when he felt like it. He had gotten a divorce. Nevertheless, when Noyce went west, he brought Grinnell with him . . . unaccountably sewn into the lining of his coat!

In the last stage of his career Josiah Grinnell had turned from the building of his community to broader matters affecting Iowa and the Middle West. In 1863 he became one of midland Iowa's representatives in Congress. Likewise, in 1974 Noyce turned over the actual running of Intel to Gordon Moore and Andrew Grove and kicked himself upstairs to become chairman of the board. His major role became that of spokesman for the Silicon Valley and the electronic frontier itself. He became chairman of the Semiconductor Industry Association. He led the industry's campaign to deal with the mounting competition from Japan. He was awarded the National Medal of Science in a White

House ceremony in 1980. He was appointed to the University of California Board of Regents and inducted into the National Inventors Hall of Fame and the American Academy of Arts and Sciences. In 1988 he moved to Austin, Texas, to assume a national role, just the way Josiah Grinnell had gone to Washington. He headed up Sematech, a consortium of fourteen semiconductor manufacturers who would work with the federal government to create an overwhelming and impregnable might for the United States in the age of computers—and put the Japanese in their place. Only Noyce had the stature—and the Gary Cooper gaze of command—to make so many VIPs fall in line at Sematech. He was hardly a famous man in the usual sense, however. He was practically unknown to the general public. But among those who followed the semiconductor industry he was a legend. He was certainly famous back East on Wall Street. When a reporter asked James Magid of the underwriting firm of L. F. Rothschild, Unterberg, Towbin about Noyce, he said, "Noyce is a national treasure."

Oh yes! What a treasure indeed was the moral capital of the nineteenth century! Noyce happened to grow up in a family in which the long-forgotten light of Dissenting Protestantism still burned brightly. The light!—the light at the apex of every human soul! Ironically, it was that long-forgotten light . . . from out of the churchy, blue-nosed sticks . . . that led the world into the twenty-first century, across the electronic grid and into space.

Surely the moral capital of the nineteenth century is by now all but completely spent. Robert Noyce's was the last generation to have grown up in families where the light of Dissenting Protestantism existed in anything approaching a pure state. Noyce had an ineffable Dissenting Protestant charisma—charisma means literally a gift from God—but, like Josiah Grinnell, he was also mortal, although he didn't look it. In 1988, when he went to Austin, he was sixty but still had the build of the Grinnell College intercollegiate swimmer he used to be. He had turned his back yards in Los Gatos and Austin into Olympic swimming venues where he worked out regularly. Every hair he ever had in his head was still nailed in, and none dared turn white. He also had tennis courts both places. He also still smoked. A lot. On Saturday evening, June 2, 1990, at home in Austin, he played his usual hard round of tennis. Sunday morning he woke up and dove into the pool for his morning swim. His left main heart artery closed forever, and he died within the hour. There was no funeral, no religious ceremony; his body was cremated. Huge nonreligious "memorial celebrations of his life"—the favorite secular sentimentalism of the day—were held in Austin and in San Jose, California, but they took on an inexplicably religious overtone. As the San Jose "celebration" ended, a pilot with a special FAA dispensation flew Noyce's own Cessna Citation jet down low over the crowd, a moment that reminded everybody of some heroic military aviator's funeral. Workmen released thousands of gas-filled red, white, and blue balloons that ascended from this earth to—where?—Heaven? The swarms of people on hand left with the mournful feeling that some sort of profound—dared they utter the word "spiritual"?—force had gone out of the life of the Silicon Valley.

Over the next ten years, as the Valley swelled with new people and new wealth, the name Noyce was quickly forgotten, and people who could expound upon algorithms and on-line trachoma would have drawn a blank on the term Congregationalist. And yet out in the Silicon Valley *some* sort of light shines still. People who run even the newest companies in the Valley repeat Noycisms with conviction and with relish—and without a clue as to where they came from. The young CEOs all say, "Datadyne is not a corporation, it's a *cul*ture," or "iLinx is not a corporation, it's a *so*ciety," or "honeybear.com's assets"—the latest vogue is for down-home nontech names—"honeybear.com's assets aren't hardware, they're the software of the three hundred souls who work here." They talk about the soul and spiritual vision as if it were the most natural subject in the world for a well-run company to be concerned about.

The day one of the Valley's new firms, Eagle Computer, Inc., sprang its IPO, investors went for it like the answer to a dream. At the close of trading on the stock market, the company's forty-year-old CEO, Dennis Barnhart, was suddenly worth 9 million. Four and a half hours later he and a pal took his Ferrari out for a little romp, hung their hides out over the edge, lost control on a curve in Los Gatos, and went through a guardrail, and Barnhart was killed. Naturally, that night people in the business could talk of very little else. One of the best-known CEOS in the Valley said, "It's the dark side of the Force." He said it without a trace of irony, and his friends nodded in contemplation. They had no term for it, but they knew exactly what Force he meant.

Digibabble, Fairy Dust, and the Human Anthill

The scene was the Suntory Museum, Osaka, Japan, in an auditorium so postmodern it made your teeth vibrate. In the audience were hundreds of Japanese art students. The occasion was the opening of a show of the work of four of the greatest American illustrators of the twentieth century: Seymour Chwast, Paul Davis, Milton Glaser, and James McMullan, the core of New York's fabled Pushpin Studio. The show was titled *Pushpin and Beyond: The Celebrated Studio That Transformed Graphic Design*. Up on the stage, aglow with global fame, the Americans had every reason to feel terrific about themselves.

Seated facing them was an interpreter. The Suntory's director began his introduction in Japanese, then paused for the interpreter's English translation:

"Our guests today are a group of American artists from the Manual Age."

Now the director was speaking again, but his American guests were no longer listening. They were too busy trying to process his opening line. *The Manual Age . . . the Manual Age . . .* The phrase ricocheted about inside their skulls . . . bounced off their pyramids of Betz, whistled through their corpora callosa, and lodged in the Broca's and Wernicke's areas of their brains.

All at once they got it. The hundreds of young Japanese staring at them from the auditorium seats saw them not as visionaries on the cutting edge . . . but as woolly old mammoths who had somehow wandered into the Suntory Museum from out of the mists of a Pliocene past . . . a lineup of relics unaccountably still living, still breathing, left over from . . . *the Manual Age!*

Marvelous. I wish I had known Japanese and could have talked to all those students as they scrutinized the primeval spectacle before them. They were children of the dawn of—need one spell it out?—the Digital Age. Manual, "freehand" illustrations? How brave of those old men to have persevered, having so little to work with. Here and now in the Digital Age illustrators used—what else?—the digital computer. Creating images from scratch? What a quaint old term, "from scratch," and what a quaint old notion . . . In the Digital Age, illustrators "morphed" existing pictures into altered forms on the digital screen. The very concept of postmodernity was based on the universal use of the digital computer . . . whether one was morphing illustrations or synthesizing music or sending rocket probes into space or achieving, on the Internet, instantaneous communication and information retrieval among people all over the globe. The world had shrunk, shrink-wrapped in an electronic membrane. No person on earth was more than six mouse clicks away from any other. The Digital Age was fast rendering national boundaries and city limits and other old geographical notions obsolete. Likewise, regional markets, labor pools, and industries. The world was now unified . . . online. There remained only one "region," and its name was the Digital Universe.

Out of that fond belief has come the concept of convergence.

Or perhaps I should say out of that *faith*, since the origin of the concept is religious; Roman Catholic, to be specific. The term itself, "convergence," as used here in the Digital Age, was coined by a Jesuit priest, Pierre Teilhard de Chardin. Another ardent Roman Catholic, Marshall McLuhan, broadcast the message throughout the intellectual world and gave the Digital Universe its first and most memorable name: "the global village." Thousands of dot-com dreamers are now busy amplifying the message without the faintest idea where it came from.

Teilhard de Chardin—usually referred to by the first part of his last name, Teilhard, pronounced TAY-yar—was one of those geniuses who, in Nietzsche's phrase (and as in Nietzsche's case), were doomed to be understood only after their deaths. Teilhard died in 1955. It has taken the current Web mania, nearly half a century later, for this romantic figure's theories to catch fire. Born in 1881, he was the second son among eleven children in the family of one of the richest landowners in France's Auvergne region. As a young man he experienced three passionate callings: the priesthood, science, and Paris. He was the sort of worldly priest European hostesses at the turn of the century died for: tall, dark, and handsome, and aristocratic on top of that, with beautifully tailored black clerical suits and masculinity to burn. His athletic body and ruddy complexion he came by honestly, from the outdoor life he led as a paleontologist in archaeological digs all over the world. And the way that hard, lean, weathered face of his would break into a confidential smile when he met a pretty woman—by all accounts, every other woman in *le monde* swore she would be the one to separate this glamorous Jesuit from his vows.

For Teilhard also had glamour to burn, three kinds of it. At the age of thirty-two he had been the French star of the most sensational archaeological find of all time, the Piltdown man, the so-called missing link in the evolution of ape to man, in a dig near Lewes, England, led by the Englishman Charles Dawson. One year later, when World War I broke out, Teilhard refused the chance to serve as a chaplain in favor of going to the front as a stretcher bearer rescuing the wounded in the midst of combat. He was decorated for bravery in that worst-of-all-infantry-wars' bloodiest battles: Ypres, Artois, Verdun, Villers-Cotterêts, and the Marne. Meantime, in the lulls between battles he had begun writing the treatise with which he hoped to unify all of science and all of religion, all of matter and all of spirit, heralding God's plan to turn all the world, from inert rock to humankind, into a single sublime Holy Spirit.

"With the evolution of Man," he wrote, "a new law of Nature has come into force—that of convergence." Biological evolution had created step one, "expansive convergence." Now, in the twentieth century, by means of technology, God was creating "compressive convergence." Thanks to technology, "the hitherto scattered" species *Homo sapiens* was being united by a single "nervous system for humanity," a "living membrane," a single "stupendous thinking machine," a unified consciousness that would cover the earth like "a thinking skin," a "noösphere," to use Teilhard's favorite neologism. And just what technology was going to bring about this convergence, this noösphere? On this point, in later years, Teilhard was quite specific: radio, television, the telephone, and "those astonishing electronic computers, pulsating with signals at the rate of hundreds of thousands a second."

One can think whatever one wants about Teilhard's theology, but no one can deny his stunning prescience. When he died in 1955, television was in its infancy and there was no such thing as a computer you could buy ready-made. Computers were huge, hellishly expensive, made-to-order machines as big as a suburban living room and bristling with vacuum tubes that gave off an unbearable heat. Since the microchip and the microprocessor had not yet been invented, no one was even speculating about a personal computer in every home, much less about combining the personal computer with the telephone to create an entirely new medium of communication. Half a century ago, only Teilhard foresaw what is now known as the Internet.

What Teilhard's superiors in the Society of Jesus and the Church hierarchy thought about it all in the 1920s, however, was not much. The plain fact was that Teilhard accepted the Darwinian theory of evolution. He argued that biological evolution had been nothing more than God's first step in an infinitely grander design. Nevertheless, he accepted it. When Teilhard had first felt his call to the priesthood, it had been during the intellectually liberal papacy of Leo XIII. But by the 1920s the pendulum had swung back within the Church, and evolutionism was not acceptable in any guise. At this point began the central dilemma, the great sorrow—the tragedy, I am tempted to say—of this remarkable man's life. A priest was not allowed to put anything into public print without his superiors' approval. Teilhard's dilemma was precisely the fact that science and religion were not unified. As a scientist, he could not bear to disregard scientific truth; and in his opinion, as a man who had devoted decades to paleontology, the theory of evolution was indisputably correct. At the same time he could not envision a life lived outside the Church.

God knew there were plenty of women who were busy envisioning it for him. Teilhard's longest, closest, tenderest relationship was with an American sculptress named Lucile Swan. Lovely little Mrs. Swan was in her late thirties and had arrived in Peking in 1929 on the China leg of a world tour aimed at diluting the bitterness of her recent breakup with her husband. Teilhard was in town officially to engage in some major archaeological digs in China and had only recently played a part in discovering the second great "missing link," the Peking man. In fact, the Church had exiled him from Europe for fear he would ply his evolutionism among priests and other intellectuals. Lucile Swan couldn't get over him. He was the right age, forty-eight, a celebrated scientist, a war hero, and the most gorgeous white man in Peking. The crowning touch of glamour was his brave, doomed relationship with his own church. She had him over to her house daily "for tea." In addition to her charms, which were many, she seems also to have offered an argument aimed at teasing him out of the shell of celibacy. In effect, the Church was forsaking him because he had founded his own new religion. Correct? Since it was his religion, couldn't he have his priests do anything he wanted them to do? When she was away, he wrote her letters of great tenderness and longing. "For the very reason that you are such a treasure to me, dear Lucile," he wrote at one point, "I ask you not to build too much of your life on me . . . Remember, whatever sweetness I force myself not to give you, I do in order to be worthy of you."

The final three decades of his life played out with the same unvarying frustration. He completed half a dozen books, including his great work, *The Phenomenon of Man.* The Church allowed him to publish none of it and kept him in perpetual exile from Europe and his beloved Paris. His only pleasure and ease came from the generosity of women, who remained attracted to him even in his old age. In 1953, two years before his death, he suffered one especially cruel blow. It was discovered that the Piltdown man had been, in fact, a colossal hoax pulled off by Charles Dawson, who had hidden various doctored ape and human bones like Easter eggs for Teilhard and others to find. He was in an acute state of depression when he died of a cerebral hemorrhage at the age of seventy-four, still in exile. His final abode was a dim little room in the Hotel Fourteen on East Sixtieth Street in Manhattan, with a single window looking out on a filthy air shaft composed, in part, of a blank exterior wall of the Copacabana nightclub.

Not a word of his great masterwork had ever been published, and yet Teilhard had enjoyed a certain shady eminence for years. Some of his manuscripts had circulated among his fellow Jesuits, *sub rosa, sotto voce,* in a Jesuit *samizdat.* In Canada he was a frequent topic of conversation at St. Michael's, the Roman Catholic college of the University of Toronto. Immediately following his death, his Paris secretary, Jeanne Mortier, to whom he had left his papers, began publishing his writings in a steady stream, including *The Phenomenon of Man.* No one paid closer attention to this gusher of Teilhardiana than a forty-four-year-old St. Michael's teaching fellow named Marshall McLuhan, who taught English literature. McLuhan was already something of a campus star at the University of Toronto when Teilhard died. He had dreamed up an extracurricular seminar on popular culture and was drawing packed houses as he held forth on topics such as the use of sex in advertising, a discourse that had led to his first book, *The Mechanical Bride*, in 1951. He was a tall, slender man, handsome in a lairdly Scottish way, who played the droll don to a T, popping off deadpan three-liners—not one-liners but three-liners—people couldn't forget.

One time I asked him how it was that Pierre Trudeau managed to stay in power as Prime Minister through all the twists and turns of Canadian politics. Without even the twitch of a smile McLuhan responded, "It's simple. He has a French name, he thinks like an Englishman, and he looks like an Indian. We all feel very guilty about the Indians here in Canada."

Another time I was in San Francisco doing stories on both McLuhan and topless restaurants, each of which was a new phenomenon. So I got the bright idea of taking the great communications theorist to a topless restaurant called the Off Broadway. Neither of us had ever seen such a thing. Here were scores of businessmen in drab suits skulking at tables in the dark as spotlights followed the waitresses, each of whom had astounding silicone-enlarged breasts and wore nothing but high heels, a G-string, and the rouge on her nipples. Frankly, I was shocked and speechless. Not McLuhan.

"Very interesting," he said.

"What is, Marshall?"

He nodded at the waitresses. "They're wearing . . . us."

"What do you mean, Marshall?"

He said it very slowly, to make sure I got it:

"They're . . . putting . . . us . . . on."

But the three-liners and the pop culture seminar were nothing compared to what came next, in the wake of Teilhard's death: namely, McLuhanism.

McLuhanism was Marshall's synthesis of the ideas of two men. One was his fellow Canadian, the economic historian Harold Innis, who had written two books arguing that new technologies were primal, fundamental forces steering human history. The other was Teilhard. McLuhan was scrupulous about crediting scholars who had influenced him, so much so that he described his first book of communications theory, *The Gutenberg Galaxy*, as "a footnote to the work of Harold Innis." In the case of Teilhard, however, he was caught in a bind. McLuhan's "global village" was nothing other than Teilhard's "noösphere," but the Church had declared Teilhard's work heterodox, and McLuhan was not merely a Roman Catholic, he was a convert. He had been raised as a Baptist but had converted to Catholicism while in England studying at Cambridge during the 1930s, the palmy days of England's great Catholic literary intellectuals, G. K. Chesterton and Hilaire Belloc. Like most converts, he was highly devout. So in his own writings he mentioned neither Teilhard nor the two-step theory of evolution that was the foundation of Teilhard's worldview. Only a single reference, a mere *obiter dictum*, attached any religious significance whatsoever to the global village: "The Christian concept of the mystical body—all men as members of the body of Christ—this becomes technologically a fact under electronic conditions."

I don't have the slightest doubt that what fascinated him about television was the possibility it might help make real Teilhard's dream of the Christian unity of all souls on earth. At the same time, he was well aware that he was publishing his major works, *The Gutenberg Galaxy* (1962) and *Understanding Media* (1964), at a moment when even the slightest whiff of religiosity was taboo, if he cared to command the stage in the intellectual community. And that, I assure you, he did care to do. His father had been an obscure insurance and real estate salesman, but his mother, Elsie, had been an actress who toured Canada giving dramatic readings, and he had inherited her love of the limelight. So he presented his theory in entirely secular terms, arguing that a new, dominant medium such as television altered human consciousness by literally changing what he called the central nervous system's "sensory balance." For reasons that were never clear to me—although I did question him on the subject—McLuhan regarded television as not a visual but an "aural and tactile" medium that was thrusting the new television generation back into what he termed a "tribal" frame of mind. These are matters that today fall under the purview of neuroscience, the study of the brain and the central nervous system. Neuroscience has made spectacular progress over the past twenty-five years and is now the hottest field in science and, for that matter, in all of academia. But neuroscientists are not even remotely close to being able to determine something such as the effect of television upon one individual, much less an entire generation.

That didn't hold back McLuhan, or the spread of McLuhanism, for a second. He successfully established the concept that new media such as television have the power to alter the human mind and thereby history itself. He died in 1980 at the age of sixty-nine after a series of strokes, more than a decade before the creation of the Internet. Dear God—if only he were alive today! What heaven the present moment would have been for him! How he would have loved the Web! What a shimmering Oz he would have turned his global village into!

But by 1980 he had spawned swarms of believers who were ready to take over where he left off. It is they, entirely secular souls, who dream up our fin de siècle notions of convergence for the Digital Age, never realizing for a moment that their ideas are founded upon Teilhard's and McLuhan's faith in the power of electronic technology to alter the human mind and unite all souls in a seamless Christian web, the All-in-One. Today you can pick up any organ of the digital press, those magazines for dot-com lizards that have been spawned thick as shad since 1993, and close your eyes and riffle through the pages and stab your forefinger and come across evangelical prose that sounds like a hallelujah! for the ideas of Teilhard or McLuhan or both.

I did just that, and in *Wired* magazine my finger landed on the name Danny Hillis, the man credited with pioneering the concept of massively parallel computers, who writes: "Telephony, computers, and CD-ROMs are all specialized mechanisms we've built to bind us together. Now evolution takes place in microseconds . . . We're taking off. We're at that point analogous to when single-celled organisms were turning into multicelled organisms. We are amoebas and we can't figure out what the hell this thing is that we're creating . . . We are not evolution's ultimate product. There's something coming after us, and I imagine it is something wonderful. But we may never be able to comprehend it, any more than a caterpillar can comprehend turning into a butterfly."

Teilhard seemed to think the phase-two technological evolution of man might take a century or more. But you will note that Hillis has it reduced to microseconds. Compared to Hillis, Bill Gates of Microsoft seems positively tentative and cautious as he rhapsodizes in *The Road Ahead*: "We are watching something historic happen, and it will affect the world seismically." He's "thrilled" by "squinting into the future and catching that first revealing hint of revolutionary possibilities." He feels "incredibly lucky" to be playing a part "in the beginning of an epochal change . . ."

We can only appreciate Gates's self-restraint when we take a stab at the pages of the September 1998 issue of *Upside* magazine and come across its editor in chief, Richard L. Brandt, revealing just how epochally revolutionary Gates's Microsoft really is: "I expect to see the overthrow of the U.S. government in my lifetime. But it won't come from revolutionaries or armed conflict. It won't be a quick-and-bloody coup; it will be a gradual takeover . . . Microsoft is gradually taking over everything. But I'm not suggesting that Microsoft will be the upstart that will gradually make the U.S. government obsolete. The culprit is more obvious. It's the Internet, damn it. The Internet is a global phenomenon on a scale we've never witnessed."

In less able hands such speculations quickly degenerate into what all who follow the digital press have become accustomed to: Digibabble. All of our digifuturists, even the best, suffer from what the philosopher Joseph Levine calls "the explanatory gap." There is never an explanation of just why or how such vast changes, such evolutionary and revolutionary great leaps forward, are going to take place. McLuhan at least recognized the problem and went to the trouble of offering a neuroscientific hypothesis, his theory of how various media alter the human nervous system by changing the "sensory balance." Everyone after him has succumbed to what is known as the "Web-mind fallacy," the purely magical assumption that as the Web, the Internet, spreads over the globe, the human mind expands with it. Magical beliefs are leaps of logic based on proximity or resemblance. Many primitive tribes have associated the waving of the crops or tall grass in the wind with the rain that follows. During a drought the tribesmen get together and create harmonic waves with their bodies in the belief that it is the waving that brings on the rain. Anthropologists have posited these tribal hulas as the origin of dance. Similarly, we have the current magical Web euphoria. A computer is a computer, and the human brain is a computer. Therefore, a computer is a brain, too, and if we get a sufficient number of them, millions, billions, operating all over the world, in a single seamless Web, we will have a superbrain that converges on a plane far above such old-fashioned concerns as nationalism and racial and ethnic competition.

I hate to be the one who brings this news to the tribe, to the magic Digikingdom, but the simple truth is that the Web, the Internet, does one thing. It speeds up the retrieval and dissemination of information, partially eliminating such chores as going outdoors to the mailbox or the adult bookstore, or having to pick up the phone to get hold of your stockbroker or some buddies to shoot the breeze with. That one thing the Internet does, and only that. All the rest is Digibabble.

May I log on to the past for a moment? Ever since the 1830s, people in the Western Hemisphere have been told that technology was making the world smaller, the assumption being that only good could come of the shrinkage. When the railroad locomotive first came into use, in the 1830s, people marveled and said it made the world smaller by bringing widely separated populations closer together. When the telephone was invented, and the transoceanic cable and the telegraph and the radio and the automobile and the airplane and the television and the fax, people marveled and said it all over again, many times. But if these inventions, remarkable as they surely are, have improved the human mind or reduced the human beast's zeal for banding together with his blood brethren against other human beasts, it has escaped my notice. One hundred and seventy years after the introduction of the locomotive, the Balkans today are a cluster of virulent spores more bloody-minded than ever. The former Soviet Union is now fifteen nations split up along ethnic bloodlines. The very Zeitgeist of the twenty-first century is summed up in the cry "Back to blood!" The thin crust of nationhoods the British established in Asia and Africa at the zenith of their imperial might has vanished, and it is the tribes of old that rule. What has made national boundaries obsolete in so much of Eastern Europe, Africa, and Asia? Not the Internet but the tribes. What have the breathtaking advances in communications technology done for the human mind? Beats me. SAT scores among the top tenth of high-school students in the United States, that fraction who are prime candidates for higher education in any period, are lower today than they were in the early 1960s. Believe, if you wish, that computers and the Internet in the classroom will change all that, but I assure you, it is sheer Digibabble.

Since so many theories of convergence were magical assumptions about the human mind in the Digital Age, notions that had no neuroscientific foundation whatsoever, I wondered what was going on in neuroscience that might bear upon the subject. This quickly led me to neuroscience's most extraordinary figure, Edward O. Wilson.

Wilson's own life is a good argument for his thesis, which is that among humans, no less than among racehorses, inbred traits will trump upbringing and environment every time. In its bare outlines his childhood biography reads like a case history for the sort of boy who today winds up as the subject of a tabloid headline: DISSED DORK SNIPERS JOCKS. He was born in Alabama to a farmer's daughter and a railroad engineer's son who became an accountant and an alcoholic. His parents separated when Wilson was seven years old, and he was sent off to the Gulf Coast Military Academy. A chaotic childhood was to follow. His father worked for the federal Rural Electrification Administration, which kept reassigning him to different locations, from the Deep South to Washington, D.C., and back again, so that in eleven years Wilson attended fourteen different public schools. He grew up shy and introverted and liked the company only of other loners, preferably those who shared his enthusiasm for collecting insects. For years he was a skinny runt, and then for years after that he was a beanpole. But no matter what ectomorphic shape he took and no matter what school he went to, his life had one great center of gravity: He could be stuck anywhere on God's green earth and he would always be the smartest person in his class. That remained true after he graduated with a bachelor's degree and a master's in biology from the University of Alabama and became a doctoral candidate and then a teacher of biology at Harvard for the next half century. He remained the best in his class every inch of the way. Seething Harvard savant after seething Harvard savant, including one Nobel laureate, has seen his reputation eclipsed by this terribly reserved, terribly polite Alabamian, Edward O. Wilson.

Wilson's field within the discipline of biology was zoology; and within zoology, entomology, the study of insects; and within entomology, myrmecology, the study of ants. Year after year he studied his ants, from Massachusetts to the wilds of Suriname. He made major discoveries about ants, concerning, for example, their system of communicating via the scent of sticky chemical substances known as pheromones—all this to great applause in the world of myrmecology, considerable applause in the world of entomology, fair-to-middling applause in the world of zoology, and polite applause in the vast world of biology generally. The consensus was that quiet Ed Wilson was doing precisely what quiet Ed Wilson had been born to do, namely, study ants, and God bless him. Apparently none of them realized that Wilson had experienced that moment of blazing revelation all scientists dream of having. It is known as the "Aha!" phenomenon.

In 1971 Wilson began publishing his now-famous sociobiology trilogy. Volume I, *The Insect Societies,* was a grand picture of the complex social structure of insect colonies in general, starring the ants, of course. The applause was well nigh universal, even among Harvard faculty members, who kept their envy and resentment on a hair trigger. So far Ed Wilson had not tipped his hand.

The Insect Societies spelled out in great detail just how extraordinarily diverse and finely calibrated the career paths and social rankings of insects were. A single ant queen gave birth to a million offspring in an astonishing variety of sizes, with each ant fated for a particular career. Forager ants went out to find and bring back food. Big army ants went forth as marauders, "the Huns and Tartars of the insect world," slaughtering other ant colonies, eating their dead victims, and even bringing back captured ant larvae to feed the colony. Still other ants went forth as herdsmen, going up tree trunks and capturing mealybugs and caterpillars, milking them for the viscous ooze they egested (more food), and driving them down into the underground colony for the night, i.e., to the stables. Livestock!

But what steered the bugs into their various, highly specialized callings? Nobody trained them, and they did not learn by observation. They were born, and they went to work. The answer, as every entomologist knew, was genetics, the codes imprinted (or hardwired, to use another metaphor) at birth. So what, if anything, did this have to do with humans, who in advanced societies typically spent twelve or thirteen years, and often much longer, going to school, taking aptitude tests, talking to job counselors, before deciding upon a career?

The answer, Wilson knew, was to be found in the jungles of a Caribbean island. Fifteen years earlier, in 1956, he had been a freshly minted Harvard biology instructor accompanying his first graduate student, Stuart Altmann, to Cayo Santiago, known among zoologists as "monkey island," off the coast of Puerto Rico. Altmann was studying rhesus macaque monkeys in their own habitat. This was four years before Jane Goodall began studying chimpanzees in the wild in East Africa. Wilson, as he put it later in his autobiography, was bowled over by the monkeys' "sophisticated and often brutal world of dominance orders, alliances, kinship bonds, territorial disputes, threats and displays, and unnerving intrigues." In the evenings, teacher and student, both in their twenties, talked about the possibility of finding common characteristics among social animals, even among those as outwardly different as ants and rhesus macaques. They decided they would have to ignore glib surface comparisons and find deep principles, statistically demonstrable principles. Altmann already had a name for such a discipline, "sociobiology," which would cover all animals that lived within social orders, from insects to primates. Wilson thought about that—

Aha!

—human beings were primates, too. It took him nineteen years and excursions into such esoteric and highly statistical disciplines as population biology and allometry ("relative growth of a part in relation to an entire organism") to work it out to the point of a compelling synthesis grounded in detailed observation, in the wild and in the laboratory, and set forth in terms of precise measurements. *The Insect Societies* had been merely the groundwork. In 1975 he published the central thesis itself: *Sociobiology: The New Synthesis.* Not, as everyone in the world of biology noticed, A new synthesis but *The* new synthesis. *The* with a capital *T*.

In the book's final chapter, the now famous Chapter 27, he announced that man and all of man's works were the products of deep patterns running throughout the story of evolution, from ants one-tenth of an inch long to the species *Homo sapiens.* Among *Homo sapiens,* the division of roles and work assignments between men and women, the division of labor between the rulers and the ruled, between the great pioneers and the lifelong drudges, could not be explained by such superficial, external approaches as history, economics, sociology, or anthropology. Only sociobiology, firmly grounded in genetics and the Darwinian theory of evolution, could do the job.

During the furor that followed, Wilson compressed his theory into one sentence during an interview. Every human brain, he said, is born not as a blank slate waiting to be filled in by experience but as "an exposed negative waiting to be slipped into developer fluid." The negative might be developed well or it might be developed poorly, but all you were going to get was what was already on the negative at birth.

In one of the most remarkable displays of wounded Marxist chauvinism in American academic history (and there have been many), two of Wilson's well-known colleagues at Harvard's Museum of Comparative Zoology, paleontologist Stephen Jay Gould and geneticist Richard Lewontin, joined a group of radical activists called Science for the People to form what can only be called an "antiseptic squad." The goal, judging by their public statements, was to demonize Wilson as a reactionary eugenicist, a Nazi in embryo, and exterminate sociobiology as an approach to the study of human behavior. After three months of organizing, the cadre opened its campaign with a letter, signed by fifteen faculty members and students in the Boston area, to the leading American organ of intellectual etiquette and deviation sniffing, *The New York Review of Books*. Theories like Wilson's, they charged, "tend to provide a genetic justification of the status quo and of existing privileges for certain groups according to class, race, or sex." In the past, vile Wilson-like intellectual poisons had "provided an important basis for the enactment of sterilization laws . . . and also for the eugenics policies which led to the establishment of gas chambers in Nazi Germany." The campaign went on for years. Protesters picketed Wilson's sociobiology class at Harvard (and the university and the faculty kept mum and did nothing). Members of INCAR, the International Committee Against Racism, a group known for its violent confrontations, stormed the annual meeting of the American Association for the Advancement of Science in Washington and commandeered the podium just before Wilson was supposed to speak. One goony seized the microphone and delivered a diatribe against Wilson while the others jeered and held up signs with swastikas—whereupon a woman positioned behind Wilson poured a carafe of ice water, cubes and all, over his head, and the entire antiseptic squad joined in the chorus: "You're all wet! You're all wet! You're all wet!"

The long smear campaign against Edward O. Wilson was one of the most sickening episodes in American academic history—and it could not have backfired more completely. As Freud once said, "Many enemies, much honor." Overnight, Ed Wilson became the most famous biologist in the United States. He was soon adorned with the usual ribbons of celebrity: appearances on the *Today* show, the *Dick Cavett*

Show, Good Morning America, and the covers of *Time* and *The New York Times Magazine* . . . while Gould and Lewontin seethed . . . and seethed . . . and contemplated their likely place in the history of science in the twentieth century: a footnote or two down in the *ibid.* thickets of the biographies of Edward Osborne Wilson.

In 1977 Wilson won the National Medal for Science. In 1979 he won the Pulitzer Prize for nonfiction for the third volume of his sociobiology trilogy, *On Human Nature.* Eleven years later he and his fellow myrmecologist, Bert Hölldobler, published a massive (7½ pounds), highly technical work, *The Ants*, meant as the last word on these industrious creatures who had played such a big part in Wilson's career. The book won the two men Pulitzer Prizes. It was Wilson's second.

His smashing success revived Darwinism in a big way. Sociobiology had presented evolution as the ultimate theory, the convergence of all knowledge. Darwinists had been with us always, of course, ever since the days of the great man himself. But in the twentieth century the Darwinist story of human life—natural selection, sexual selection, survival of the fittest, and the rest of it—had been overshadowed by the Freudian and Marxist stories. Marx said social class determined a human being's destiny; Freud said it was the Oedipal drama within the family. Both were forces external to the newborn infant. Darwinists, Wilson foremost among them, turned all that upside down and proclaimed that the genes the infant was born with determined his destiny.

A field called evolutionary psychology became all the rage, attracting many young biologists and philosophers who enjoyed the naughty and delicious thrill of being Darwinian fundamentalists. The influence of genes was absolute. Free will among humans, no less than among ants, was an illusion. The "soul" and the "mind" were illusions, too, and so was the very notion of a "self." The quotation marks began spreading like dermatitis over all the commonsense beliefs about human nature. The new breed, the fundamentalists, hesitated to use Wilson's term, "sociobiology," because there was always the danger that the antiseptic squads, the Goulds and the Lewontins and the INCAR goonies and goonettes, might come gitchoo. But all the bright new fundamentalists were Ed Wilson's offspring, nevertheless.

They soon ran into a problem that Wilson had largely finessed by offering only the broadest strokes. Darwin's theory provided a wonderfully elegant story of how the human beast evolved from a single cell in the primordial ooze and became the fittest beast on earth—but offered precious little to account for what man had created once he reached the level of the wheel, the shoe, and the toothbrush. Somehow the story of man's evolution from the apes had not set the stage for what came next. Religions, ideologies, scholarly disciplines, aesthetic experiences such as art, music, literature, and the movies, technological wonders such as the Brooklyn Bridge and breaking the bonds of Earth's gravity with spaceships, not to mention the ability to create words and grammars and record such extraordinary accomplishments—there was nothing even remotely homologous to be found among gorillas, chimpanzees, or any other beasts. So was it really just Darwinian evolution? Anthropologists had always chalked such things up to culture. But it had to be Darwinian evolution! Genetics had to be the answer! Otherwise, fundamentalism did not mean much.

In 1976, a year after Wilson had lit up the sky with *Sociobiology: The New Synthesis*, a British zoologist and Darwinian fundamentalist, Richard Dawkins, published a book called *The Selfish Gene* in which he announced the discovery of memes. Memes were viruses in the form of ideas, slogans, tunes, styles, images, doctrines, anything with sufficient attractiveness or catchiness to infect the brain—"infect," like "virus," became part of the subject's earnest, wannabe-scientific terminology—after which they operated like genes, passing along what had been naïvely thought of as the creations of culture.

Dawkins's memes definitely infected the fundamentalists, in any event. The literature of Memeland began pouring out: Daniel C. Dennett's *Darwin's Dangerous Idea*, William H. Calvin's *How Brains Think*, Steven Pinker's *How the Mind Works*, Robert Wright's *The Moral Animal*, *The Meme Machine* by Susan Blackmore (with a foreword by

Richard Dawkins), and on and on. Dawkins has many devout followers precisely because his memes are seen as the missing link in Darwinism as a theory, a theoretical discovery every bit as important as the skull of the Peking man. One of Bill Gates's epigones at Microsoft, Charles Simonyi, was so impressed with Dawkins and his memes and their historic place on the scientific frontier, he endowed a chair at Oxford University titled the Charles Simonyi Professor of the Public Understanding of Science and installed Dawkins in it. This makes Dawkins the postmodern equivalent of the Archbishop of Canterbury. Dawkins is now Archbishop of Darwinian Fundamentalism and Hierophant of the Memes.

There turns out to be one serious problem with memes, however. They don't exist. A neurophysiologist can use the most powerful and sophisticated brain imaging now available—and still not find a meme. The Darwinian fundamentalists, like fundamentalists in any area, are ready for such an obvious objection. They will explain that memes operate in a way analogous to genes, i.e., through natural selection and survival of the fittest memes. But in science, unfortunately, "analogous to" just won't do. The tribal hula is analogous to the waving of a wheat field in the wind before the rain, too. Here the explanatory gap becomes enormous. Even though some of the fundamentalists have scientific credentials, not one even hazards a guess as to how, in physiological, neural terms, the meme "infection" is supposed to take place. Although no scientist, McLuhan at least offered a neuroscientific hypothesis for McLuhanism.

So our fundamentalists find themselves in the awkward position of being like those Englishmen in the year 1000 who believed quite literally in the little people, the fairies, trolls, and elves. To them, Jack Frost was not merely a twee personification of winter weather. Jack Frost was one of the little people, an elf who made your fingers cold, froze the tip of your nose like an icicle, and left the ground too hard to plow. You couldn't see him, but he was there. Thus also with memes. Memes are little people who sprinkle fairy dust on genes to enable them to pass along so-called cultural information to succeeding generations in a proper Darwinian way.

Wilson, who has a lot to answer for, transmitted more than fairy dust to his progeny, however. He gave them the urge to be popular. After all, he was a serious scientist who had become a celebrity. Not only that, he had made the bestseller lists. As they say in scholarly circles, much of his work has been really quite accessible. But there is accessible . . . and there is cute. The fundamentalists have developed the habit of cozying up to the reader or, as they are likely to put it, "cozying up." When they are courting the book-buying public, they use quotation marks as friendly winks. They are quick to use the second-person singular in order to make you ("you") feel right at home ("right at home") and italicized words to make sure you *get it* and lots of conversational contractions so you *won't* feel intimidated by a lot of big words such as "algorithms," which *you're* not likely to tolerate unless *there's* some way to bring you closer to your wise friend, the author, by a just-between-us-pals approach. Simple, *I'd* say! One fundamentalist book begins with the statement that "intelligence is what you use when you don't know what to do (an apt description of my present predicament as I attempt to write about intelligence). If you're good at finding the one right answer to life's multiple-choice questions, you're *smart*. But there's more to being *intelligent*—a creative aspect, whereby you invent something new 'on the fly' " (*How Brains Think* by William H. Calvin, who also came up with a marvelously loopy synonym for fairy dust: "Darwinian soft-wiring").

Meantime, as far as Darwin II himself is concerned, he has nice things to say about Dawkins and his Neuro Pop brood, and he wishes them well in their study of the little people, the memes, but he is far too savvy to buy the idea himself. He theorizes about something called "culturgens," which sound suspiciously like memes, but then goes on to speak of the possibility of a "gene-culture coevolution." I am convinced that in his heart Edward O. Wilson believes just as strongly as Dawkins in Darwinian fundamentalism. I am sure he believes just as absolutely in the idea that human beings, for all their extraordinary works, consist solely of matter and water, of strings of molecules containing DNA that are connected to a chemical analog computer known as the brain, a mechanism that creates such illusions as "free will" and . . . "me." But Darwin II is patient, and he is a scientist. He is not going to engage in any such sci-fi as meme theory. To test meme theory it would be necessary first to fill in two vast Saharas in the field of brain research: memory and consciousness itself. Memory has largely defied detailed neural analysis, and consciousness has proven totally baffling. No one can even define it. Anaesthesiologists who administer drugs and gases to turn their patients' consciousness off before surgery have no idea why they work. Until memory and consciousness are understood, meme theory will remain what it is today: amateur night.

But Wilson is convinced that in time the entire physics and chemistry, the entire neurobiology of the brain and the central nervous system will be known, just as the 100,000-or-so genes are now being identified and located one by one in the Human Genome Project. When the process is completed, he believes, then all knowledge of living things will converge . . . under the umbrella of biology. All mental activity, from using allometry to enjoying music, will be understood in biological terms.

He actually said as much a quarter of a century ago in the opening paragraph of *Sociobiology*'s incendiary Chapter 27. The humanities and social sciences, he said, would "shrink to specialized branches of biology." Such venerable genres as history, biography, and the novel would become "the research protocols," i.e., preliminary reports of the study of human evolution. Anthropology and sociology would disappear as separate disciplines and be subsumed by "the sociobiology of a single primate species," *Homo sapiens*. There was so much else in Chapter 27 to outrage the conventional wisdom of the Goulds and the Lewontins of the academic world that they didn't pay much attention to this convergence of all human disciplines and literary pursuits.

But in 1998 Wilson spelled it out at length and so clearly that no one inside or outside of academia could fail to get the point. He published an entire book on the subject, *Consilience,* which immediately became a bestseller despite the theoretical nature of the material. The term "consilience" was an obsolete word referring to the coming together, the confluence, of different branches of knowledge.

The ruckus *Consilience* kicked up spread far beyond the fields of biology and evolutionism. *Consilience* was a stick in the eye of every novelist, every historian, every biographer, every social scientist—every intellectual of any stripe, come to think of it. They were all about to be downsized, if not terminated, in a vast intellectual merger. The counterattack began. Jeremy Bernstein, writing in *Commentary*, drew first blood with a review titled "E. O. Wilson's Theory of Everything." It began: "It is not uncommon for people approaching the outer shores of middle age to go slightly dotty." Oh Lord, another theory of everything from the dotty professor. This became an intellectual drumbeat—"just another theory of everything"—and Wilson saw himself tried and hanged on a charge of hubris.

As for me, despite the prospect of becoming a mere research protocol drudge for evolutionism, I am willing to wait for the evidence. I am skeptical, but like Wilson, I am willing to wait. If Wilson is right, what interests me is not so much what happens when all knowledge flows together as what people will do with it once every nanometer and every action and reaction of the human brain has been calibrated and made manifest in predictable statistical formulas. I can't help thinking of our children of the dawn, the art students we last saw in the Suntory Museum, Osaka, Japan. Not only will they be able to morph illustrations on the digital computer, they will also be able to predict, with breathtaking accuracy, the effect that certain types of illustrations will have on certain types of brains. But, of course, the illustrators' targets will be able to dial up the same formulas and information and diagnose the effect that any illustration, any commercial, any speech, any flirtation, any bill, any coo has been crafted to produce. Life will become one incessant, colossal round of the match game or liar's poker or one-finger–two-finger or rock-paper-scissors.

Something tells me, mere research protocol drudge though I may be, that I will love it all, cherish it, press it to my bosom. For I already have a working title, *The Human Comedy*, and I promise you, you will laugh your head off . . . your head and that damnable, unfathomable chemical analog computer inside of it, too.

Sorry, but Your Soul Just Died

Being a bit behind the curve, I had only just heard of the digital revolution when Louis Rossetto, co-founder of *Wired* magazine, wearing a shirt with no collar and his hair as long as Felix Mendelssohn's, looking every inch the young California visionary, gave a speech before the Cato Institute announcing the dawn of the twenty-first century's digital civilization. As his text, he chose Teilhard de Chardin's prediction fifty years ago that radio, television, and computers would create a "noösphere," an electronic membrane covering the earth and wiring all humanity together in a single nervous system. Geographic locations, national boundaries, the old notions of markets and political processes—all would become irrelevant. With the Internet spreading over the globe at an astonishing pace, said Rossetto, that marvelous modem-driven moment is almost at hand.

Could be. But something tells me that within ten years, by 2010, the entire digital universe is going to seem like pretty mundane stuff compared to a new technology that right now is but a mere glow radiating from a tiny number of American and Cuban (yes, Cuban) hospitals and laboratories. It is called brain imaging, and anyone who cares to get up early and catch a truly blinding twenty-first-century dawn will want to keep an eye on it.

Brain imaging refers to techniques for watching the human brain as it functions, in real time. The most advanced forms currently are three-dimensional electroencephalography using mathematical models; the more familiar PET scan (positron-emission tomography); the new fMRI (functional magnetic resonance imaging), which shows brain blood-flow patterns, and MRS (magnetic resonance spectroscopy), which measures biochemical changes in the brain; and the even newer PET reporter gene/PET reporter probe, which is, in fact, so new that it still has that length of heavy lumber for a name. Used so far only in animals and a few desperately sick children, the PET reporter gene/PET reporter probe pinpoints and follows the activity of specific genes. On a scanner screen you can actually see the genes light up inside the brain.

By the standards of the year 2000, these are sophisticated devices. Ten years from now, however, they may seem primitive compared to the stunning new windows into the brain that will have been developed.

Brain imaging was invented for medical diagnosis. But its far greater importance is that it may very well confirm, in ways too precise to be disputed, current neuroscientific theories about "the mind," "the self," "the soul," and "free will." Granted, all those skeptical quotation marks are enough to put anybody on the *qui vive* right away, but Ultimate Skepticism is part of the brilliance of the dawn I have promised.

Neuroscience, the science of the brain and the central nervous system, is on the threshold of a unified theory that will have an impact as powerful as that of Darwinism a hundred years ago. Already there is a new Darwin, or perhaps I should say an updated Darwin, since no one ever believed more religiously in Darwin the First than does he: Edward O. Wilson.

As we have seen, Wilson has created and named the new field of sociobiology, and he has compressed its underlying premise into a single sentence. Every human brain, he says, is born not as a blank tablet (a *tabula rasa*) waiting to be filled in by experience but as "an exposed negative waiting to be slipped into developer fluid." (See page 81, above.) You can develop the negative well or you can develop it poorly, but either way you are going to get precious little that is not already imprinted on the film. The print is the individual's genetic history, over thousands of years of evolution, and there is not much anybody can do about it. Furthermore, says Wilson, genetics determine not only things such as temperament, role preferences, emotional responses, and levels of aggression but also many of our most revered moral choices, which are not choices at all in any free-will sense but tendencies imprinted in the hypothalamus and limbic regions of the brain, a concept expanded upon in 1993 in a much-talked-about book, *The Moral Sense*, by James Q. Wilson (no kin to Edward O.).

This, the neuroscientific view of life, has become the strategic high ground in the academic world, and the battle for it has already spread well beyond the scientific disciplines and, for that matter, out into the general public. Both liberals and conservatives without a scientific bone in their bodies are busy trying to seize the terrain. The gay rights movement, for example, has fastened onto a study, published in July 1993 by the highly respected Dean Hamer of the National Institutes of Health, announcing the discovery of "the gay gene." Obviously, if homosexuality is a genetically determined trait, like left-handedness or hazel eyes, then laws and sanctions against it are attempts to legislate against Nature. Conservatives, meantime, have fastened upon studies indicating that men's and women's brains are wired so differently, thanks to the long haul of evolution, that feminist attempts to open up traditionally male roles to women are the same thing: a doomed violation of Nature.

Wilson himself has wound up in deep water on this score; or cold water, if one need edit. In his personal life Wilson is a conventional liberal, PC, as the saying goes—he *is*, after all, a member of the Harvard faculty—concerned about environmental issues and all the usual things. But he has said that "forcing similar role identities" on both men and women "flies in the face of thousands of years in which mammals demonstrated a strong tendency for sexual division of labor. Since this division of labor is persistent from hunter-gatherer through agricultural and industrial societies, it suggests a genetic origin. We do not know when this trait evolved in human evolution or how resistant it is to the continuing and justified pressures for human rights."

"Resistant" was Darwin II, the neuroscientist, speaking. "Justified" was the PC Harvard liberal. He was not PC or liberal enough. As we have already seen, protesters invaded the annual meeting of the American Academy for the Advancement of Science, where Wilson was appearing, dumped a pitcher of ice water, cubes and all, over his head, and began chanting, "You're all wet! You're all wet!" The most prominent feminist in America, Gloria Steinem, went on television and, in an interview with John Stossel of ABC, insisted that studies of genetic differences between male and female nervous systems should cease forthwith.

But that turned out to be mild stuff in the current political panic over neuroscience. In February 1992, Frederick K. Goodwin, a renowned psychiatrist, head of the federal Alcohol, Drug Abuse, and Mental Health Administration, and a certified yokel in the field of public relations, made the mistake of describing, at a public meeting in Washington, the National Institute of Mental Health's ten-year-old Violence Initiative. This was an experimental program whose hypothesis was that, as among monkeys in the jungle—Goodwin was noted for his monkey studies—much of the criminal mayhem in the United States was caused by a relatively few young males who were genetically predisposed to it; who were hardwired for violent crime, in short. Out in the jungle, among mankind's closest animal relatives, the chimpanzees, it seemed that a handful of genetically twisted young males were the ones who committed practically *all* the wanton murders of other males and the physical abuse of females. What if the same were true among human beings? What if, in any given community, it turned out to be a handful of young males with toxic DNA who were pushing statistics for violent crime up to such high levels? The Violence Initiative envisioned identifying these individuals in childhood, somehow, some way, someday, and treating them therapeutically with drugs. The notion that crime-ridden urban America was a "jungle," said Goodwin, was perhaps more than just a tired old metaphor.

That did it. That may have been the stupidest single word uttered by an American public official in the year 1992. The outcry was immediate. Senator Edward Kennedy of Massachusetts and Representative John Dingell of Michigan (who, it became obvious later, suffered from hydrophobia when it came to science projects) not only condemned Goodwin's remarks as racist but also delivered their scientific verdict: Research among primates "is a preposterous basis" for analyzing anything as complex as "the crime and violence that plagues our country today." (This came as surprising news to NASA scientists who had first trained and sent a chimpanzee called Ham up on top of a Redstone rocket into suborbital space flight and then trained and sent another one, called Enos, which is Greek for "man," up on an Atlas rocket and around the earth in orbital space flight and had thereby accurately and completely predicted the physical, psychological, and task-motor responses of the human astronauts Alan Shepard and John Glenn, who repeated the chimpanzees' flights and tasks months later.) The Violence Initiative was compared to Nazi eugenic proposals for the extermination of undesirables. Dingell's Michigan colleague, Representative John Conyers, then chairman of the Government Operations Committee and senior member of the Congressional Black Caucus, demanded Goodwin's resignation—and got it two days later, whereupon the government, with the Department of Health and Human Services now doing the talking, denied that the Violence Initiative had ever existed. It disappeared down the memory hole, to use Orwell's term.

A conference of criminologists and other academics interested in the neuroscientific studies done so far for the Violence Initiative—a conference underwritten in part by a grant from the National Institutes of Health—had been scheduled for May 1993 at the University of Maryland. Down went the conference, too; the NIH drowned it like a kitten. A University of Maryland legal scholar named David Wasserman tried to reassemble the troops on the Q.T., as it were, in a hall all but hidden from human purview in a hamlet called Queenstown in the foggy, boggy boondocks of Queen Annes County on Maryland's Eastern Shore. (The Clinton administration tucked Elian Gonzalez away in this same county while waiting for the Cuban-American vote to chill before the Feds handed the boy over to Fidel Castro.) The NIH, proving it was a hard learner, quietly provided $133,000 for the event, but only after Wasserman promised to fireproof the proceedings by also inviting scholars who rejected the notion of a possible genetic genesis of crime and scheduling a cold-shower session dwelling on the evils of the eugenics movement of the early twentieth century. No use, boys! An army of protesters found the poor cringing devils anyway and stormed into the auditorium chanting, "Maryland conference, you can't hide—we know you're pushing genocide!" It took two hours for them to get bored enough to leave, and the conference ended in a complete muddle, with the specially recruited fireproofing PC faction issuing a statement that said: "Scientists as well as historians and sociologists must not allow themselves to provide academic respectability for racist pseudoscience." Today, at the NIH, the term Violence Initiative is a synonym for *taboo*. The present moment resembles that moment in the Middle Ages when the Catholic Church forbade the dissection of human bodies, for fear that what was discovered inside might cast doubt on the Christian doctrine that God created man in his own image.

Even more radioactive is the matter of intelligence, as measured by IQ tests. Privately—not many care to speak out—the vast majority of neuroscientists believe the genetic component of an individual's intelligence is remarkably high. Your intelligence can be improved upon, by skilled and devoted mentors, or it can be held back by a poor upbringing—i.e., the negative can be well developed or poorly developed—but your genes are what really make the difference. The recent ruckus over

Charles Murray and Richard Herrnstein's *The Bell Curve* is probably just the beginning of the bitterness the subject is going to create.

Not long ago, according to two neuroscientists I interviewed, a firm called Neurometrics sought out investors and tried to market an amazing but simple invention known as the IQ Cap. The idea was to provide a way of testing intelligence that would be free of "cultural bias," one that would not force anyone to deal with words or concepts that might be familiar to people from one culture but not to people from another. The IQ Cap recorded only brain waves; and a computer, not a potentially biased human test-giver, analyzed the results. It was based on the work of neuroscientists such as E. Roy John,* who is now one of the major pioneers of electroencephalographic brain imaging; Duilio Giannitrapani, author of *The Electrophysiology of Intellectual Functions*; and David Robinson, author of *The Wechsler Adult Intelligence Scale and Personality Assessment: Toward a Biologically Based Theory of Intelligence and Cognition* and many other monographs famous among neuroscientists. I spoke to one researcher who had devised an IQ Cap himself by replicating an experiment described by Giannitrapani in *The Electrophysiology of Intellectual Functions.* It was not a complicated process. You attached sixteen electrodes to the scalp of the person you wanted to test. You had to muss up his hair a little, but you didn't have to cut it, much less shave it. Then you had him stare at a marker on a blank wall. This particular researcher used a raspberry-red thumbtack. Then you pushed a toggle switch. In sixteen seconds the Cap's computer box gave you an accurate prediction (within one-half of a standard deviation) of what the subject would score on all eleven subtests of the Wechsler Adult Intelligence Scale or, in the case of chil-

*The term "neurometric" is closely identified with John, who has devised both the Neurometric Battery, a comprehensive system for analyzing brain functions, and the Neurometric Analyzer, a patented instrument for making use of the Battery; but John had nothing to do with Neurometrics, Inc. He describes the Battery in *Neurometric Evaluation of Brain Function in Normal and Learning Disabled Children* (Ann Arbor: University of Michigan Press, 1989).

dren, the Wechsler Intelligence Scale for Children—all from sixteen seconds' worth of brain waves. There was nothing culturally biased about the test whatsoever. What could be cultural about staring at a thumbtack on a wall? The savings in time and money were breathtaking. The conventional IQ test took two hours to complete; and the overhead, in terms of paying test-givers, test-scorers, test-preparers, and the rent, was $100 an hour at the very least. The IQ Cap required about fifteen minutes and sixteen seconds—it took about fifteen minutes to put the electrodes on the scalp—and about a tenth of a penny's worth of electricity. Neurometrics's investors were rubbing their hands and licking their chops. They were about to make a killing.

In fact—*nobody wanted their damnable IQ Cap!*

It wasn't simply that no one *believed* you could derive IQ scores from brain waves—it was that nobody *wanted* to believe it could be done. Nobody *wanted* to believe that human brainpower is . . . *that hardwired.* Nobody wanted to learn in a flash that . . . *the genetic fix is in.* Nobody wanted to learn that he was . . . *a hardwired genetic mediocrity* . . . and that the best he could hope for in this Trough of Mortal Error was to live out his mediocre life as a stress-free dim bulb. Barry Sterman of UCLA, chief scientist for a firm called Cognitive Neurometrics, who has devised his own brain-wave technology for market research and focus groups, regards brain-wave IQ testing as possible—but in the current atmosphere you "wouldn't have a Chinaman's chance of getting a grant" to develop it.

Here we begin to sense the chill that emanates from the hottest field in the academic world. The unspoken and largely unconscious premise of the wrangling over neuroscience's strategic high ground is: We now live in an age in which science is a court from which there is no appeal. And the issue this time around, at the beginning of the twenty-first century, is not the evolution of the species, which can seem a remote business, but the nature of our own precious inner selves.

The elders of the field, such as Wilson, are well aware of all this and are cautious, or cautious compared to the new generation. Wilson still holds out the possibility—I think he doubts it, but he still holds out the possibility—that at some point in evolutionary history culture began to influence the development of the human brain in ways that cannot be explained by strict Darwinian theory. But the new generation of neuroscientists are not cautious for a second. In private conversations, the bull sessions, as it were, that create the mental atmosphere of any hot new science—and I love talking to these people—they express an uncompromising determinism.

They start with the second most famous statement in all of modern philosophy, Descartes's "*Cogito ergo sum*," "I think, therefore I am," which they regard as the essence of "dualism," the old-fashioned notion that the mind is something distinct from its mechanism, the brain and the body. (I will get to the most famous statement in a moment.) This is also known as the "ghost in the machine" fallacy, the quaint belief that there is a ghostly "self" somewhere inside the brain that interprets and directs its operations. Neuroscientists involved in three-dimensional electroencephalography will tell you that there is not even any one place in the brain where consciousness or self-consciousness (*Cogito ergo sum*) is located. This is merely an illusion created by a medley of neurological systems acting in concert. The young generation takes this yet one step further. Since consciousness and thought are entirely physical products of your brain and nervous system—and since your brain arrived fully imprinted at birth—what makes you think you have free will? Where is it going to come from? What "ghost," what "mind," what "self," what "soul," what anything that will not be immediately grabbed by those scornful quotation marks is going to bubble up your brain stem to give it to you? I have heard neuroscientists theorize that, given computers of sufficient power and sophistication, it would be possible to predict the course of any human being's life moment by moment, including the fact that the poor devil was about to shake his head over the very idea. I doubt that any Calvinist of the sixteenth century ever believed so completely in predestination as these, the hottest and most intensely rational young scientists in the United States in the twenty-first.

Since the late 1970s, in the Age of Wilson, college students have been heading into neuroscience in job lots. The Society for Neuroscience was founded in 1970 with 1,100 members. Today, one generation later, its membership exceeds 26,000. The society's latest convention, in Miami, drew more than 20,000 souls, making it one of the biggest professional conventions in the country. In the venerable field of academic philosophy, young faculty members are jumping ship in embarrassing numbers and shifting into neuroscience. They are heading for the laboratories. Why wrestle with Kant's God, Freedom, and Immortality when it is only a matter of time before neuroscience, probably through brain imaging, reveals the actual physical mechanism that fabricates these mental constructs, these illusions?

Which brings us to the most famous statement in all of modern philosophy: Nietzsche's "God is dead." The year was 1882. The book was *Die Fröhliche Wissenschaft* (*The Gay Science*). Nietzsche said this was not a declaration of atheism, although he was in fact an atheist, but simply the news of an event. He called the death of God a "tremendous event," the greatest event of modern history. The news was that educated people no longer believed in God, as a result of the rise of rationalism and scientific thought, including Darwinism, over the preceding 250 years. But before you atheists run up your flags of triumph, he said, think of the implications. "The story I have to tell," wrote Nietzsche, "is the history of the next two centuries." He predicted (in *Ecce Homo*) that the twentieth century would be a century of "wars such as have never happened on earth," wars catastrophic beyond all imagining. And why? Because human beings would no longer have a god to turn to, to absolve them of their guilt; but they would still be racked by guilt, since guilt is an impulse instilled in children when they are very young, before the age of reason. As a result, people would loathe not only one another but themselves. The blind and reassuring faith they formerly poured into their belief in God, said Nietzsche, they would now pour into a belief in barbaric nationalistic brotherhoods: "If the doctrines . . . of the lack of any cardinal distinction between man and animal, doctrines I consider true but deadly"—he says in an allusion to Darwinism in *Untimely Meditations*—"are hurled into the people for another generation . . . then nobody should be surprised when . . . brotherhoods with the aim of the robbery and exploitation of the non-brothers . . . will appear in the arena of the future."

Nietzsche's view of guilt, incidentally, is also that of neuroscientists a century later. They regard guilt as one of those tendencies imprinted in the brain at birth. In some people the genetic work is not complete, and they engage in criminal behavior without a twinge of remorse—thereby intriguing criminologists, who then want to create Violence Initiatives and hold conferences on the subject.

Nietzsche said that mankind would limp on through the twentieth century "on the mere pittance" of the old decaying God-based moral codes. But then, in the twenty-first, would come a period more dreadful than the great wars, a time of "the total eclipse of all values" (in *The Will to Power*). This would also be a frantic period of "revaluation," in which people would try to find new systems of values to replace the osteoporotic skeletons of the old. But you will fail, he warned, because you cannot believe in moral codes without simultaneously believing in a god who points at you with his fearsome forefinger and says "Thou shalt" or "Thou shalt not."

Why should we bother ourselves with a dire prediction that seems so far-fetched as "the total eclipse of all values"? Because of man's track record, I should think. After all, in Europe, in the peaceful decade of the 1880s, it must have seemed even more far-fetched to predict the world wars of the twentieth century and the barbaric brotherhoods of Nazism and Communism. Ecce vates! *Ecce vates!* Behold the prophet! How much more proof can one demand of a man's powers of prediction?

A hundred years ago those who worried about the death of God could console one another with the fact that they still had their own bright selves and their own inviolable souls for moral ballast and the marvels of modern science to chart the way. But what if, as seems likely, the greatest marvel of modern science turns out to be brain imaging? And what if, ten years from now, brain imaging has proved, beyond any doubt, that not only Edward O. Wilson but also the young generation are, in fact, correct?

The elders, such as Wilson himself and Daniel C. Dennett, the author of *Darwin's Dangerous Idea: Evolution and the Meanings of Life*, and Richard Dawkins, author of *The Selfish Gene* and *The Blind Watchmaker*, insist that there is nothing to fear from the truth, from the ultimate extension of Darwin's dangerous idea. They present elegant arguments as to why neuroscience should in no way diminish the richness of life, the magic of art, or the righteousness of political causes, including, if one need edit, political correctness at Harvard or Tufts, where Dennett is Director of the Center for Cognitive Studies, or Oxford, where Dawkins is something called Professor of Public Understanding of Science. (Dennett and Dawkins, every bit as much as Wilson, are earnestly, feverishly, politically correct.) Despite their best efforts, however, neuroscience is not rippling out into the public on waves of scholarly reassurance. But rippling out it is, rapidly. The conclusion people out beyond the laboratory walls are drawing is: *The fix is in! We're all hardwired!* That, and: *Don't blame me! I'm wired wrong!*

This sudden switch from a belief in Nurture, in the form of social conditioning, to Nature, in the form of genetics and brain physiology, is the great intellectual event, to borrow Nietzsche's term, of the late twentieth century. Up to now the two most influential ideas of the century have been Marxism and Freudianism (see page 82). Both were founded upon the premise that human beings and their "ideals"—Marx and Freud knew about quotation marks, too—are completely molded by their environment. To Marx, the crucial environment was one's social class; "ideals" and "faiths" were notions foisted by the upper orders upon the lower as instruments of social control. To Freud, the crucial environment was the Oedipal drama, the unconscious sexual plot that was played out in the family early in a child's existence. The "ideals" and "faiths" you prize so much are merely the parlor furniture you feature for receiving your guests, said Freud; I will show you the cellar, the furnace, the pipes, the sexual steam that actually runs the house. By the mid-1950s even anti-Marxists and anti-Freudians had come to assume the centrality of class domination and Oedipally conditioned sexual drives. On top of this came Pavlov, with his "stimulus-response bonds," and B. F. Skinner, with his "operant conditioning," turning the supremacy of conditioning into something approaching a precise form of engineering.

So how did this brilliant intellectual fashion come to so screeching and ignominious an end?

The demise of Freudianism can be summed up in a single word: lithium. In 1949 an Australian psychiatrist, John Cade, gave five days of lithium therapy—for entirely the wrong reasons—to a fifty-one-year-old mental patient who was so manic-depressive, so hyperactive, unintelligible, and uncontrollable, he had been kept locked up in asylums for twenty years. By the sixth day, thanks to the lithium buildup in his blood, he was a normal human being. Three months later he was released and lived happily ever after in his own home. This was a man who had been locked up and subjected to two decades of Freudian logorrhea to no avail whatsoever. Over the next twenty years antidepressant and tranquillizing drugs completely replaced Freudian talk-talk as treatment for severe mental disturbances. By the mid-1980s, neuroscientists looked upon Freudian psychiatry as a quaint relic based largely upon superstition (such as dream analysis—*dream* analysis!), like phrenology or mesmerism. In fact, among neuroscientists, phrenology now has a higher reputation than Freudian psychiatry, since phrenology was in a certain crude way a precursor of electroencephalography. Freudian psychiatrists are now regarded as quacks with sham medical degrees, as ears that people with more money than sense can hire to talk into.

Marxism was finished off even more suddenly—in a single year, 1973—with the smuggling out of the Soviet Union and the publication in France of the first of the three volumes of Aleksandr Solzhenitsyn's

The Gulag Archipelago. Other writers, notably the British historian Robert Conquest, had already exposed the Soviet Union's vast network of concentration camps, but their work was based largely on the testimony of refugees, and refugees were routinely discounted as biased and bitter observers. Solzhenitsyn, on the other hand, was a Soviet citizen, still living on Soviet soil, a *zek* himself for eleven years, *zek* being Russian slang for concentration-camp prisoner. His credibility had been vouched for by none other than Nikita Khrushchev, who in 1962 had permitted the publication of Solzhenitsyn's novella of the gulag, *One Day in the Life of Ivan Denisovich,* as a means of cutting down to size the daunting shadow of his predecessor Stalin. "Yes," Khrushchev had said in effect, "what this man Solzhenitsyn has to say is true. Such were Stalin's crimes." Solzhenitsyn's brief fictional description of the Soviet slave labor system was damaging enough. But *The Gulag Archipelago,* a two-thousand-page, densely detailed, nonfiction account of the Soviet Communist Party's systematic extermination of its enemies, real and imagined, of its own countrymen, *by the tens of millions,* through an enormous, methodical, bureaucratically controlled "human sewage disposal system," as Solzhenitsyn called it—*The Gulag Archipelago* was devastating. After all, this was a century in which there was no longer any possible ideological detour around the concentration camp. Among European intellectuals, even French intellectuals, Marxism collapsed as a spiritual force immediately. Ironically, it survived longer in the United States before suffering a final, merciful *coup de grâce* on November 9, 1989, with the breaching of the Berlin Wall, which signaled in an unmistakable fashion what a debacle the Soviets' seventy-two-year field experiment in socialism had been. (Marxism still hangs on, barely, acrobatically, in American universities in a Mannerist form known as Deconstruction, a literary doctrine that depicts language itself as an insidious tool used by the powers that be to deceive the proles and peasants.)

Freudianism and Marxism—and with them, the entire belief in social conditioning—were demolished so swiftly, so suddenly, that neuroscience has surged in, as if into an intellectual vacuum. Nor do you have to be a scientist to detect the rush.

Anyone with a child in school knows the signs all too well. I am intrigued by the faith parents now invest—the craze began about 1990—in psychologists who diagnose their children as suffering from a defect known as attention deficit disorder, or ADD. Of course, I have no way of knowing whether this "disorder" is an actual, physical, neurological condition or not, but neither does anybody else in this early stage of neuroscience. The symptoms of this supposed malady are always the same. The child or, rather, the boy—forty-nine out of fifty cases are boys—fidgets around in school, slides off his chair, doesn't pay attention, distracts his classmates during class, and performs poorly. In an earlier era he would have been pressured to pay attention, work harder, show some self-discipline. To parents caught up in the new intellectual climate of the 1990s, that approach seems cruel, because my little boy's problem is . . . *he's wired wrong!* The poor little tyke—*the fix has been in since birth!* Invariably the parents complain, "All he wants to do is sit in front of the television set and watch cartoons and play Sega Genesis." For how long? "How long? For hours at a time." Hours at a time; as even any young neuroscientist will tell you, that boy may have a problem, but it is not an attention deficit.

Nevertheless, all across America we have the spectacle of an entire generation of little boys, by the tens of thousands, being dosed up on ADD's magic bullet of choice, Ritalin, the CIBA-Geneva Corporation's brand name for the stimulant methylphenidate. I first encountered Ritalin in 1966, when I was in San Francisco doing research for a book on the psychedelic or hippie movement. A certain species of the genus hippie was known as the Speed Freak, and a certain strain of Speed Freak was known as the Ritalin Head. The Ritalin Heads *loved* Ritalin. You'd see them in the throes of absolute Ritalin raptures . . . Not a wiggle, not a peep . . . They would sit engrossed in *anything at all* . . . a manhole cover, their own palm wrinkles . . . indefinitely . . . through shoulda-been mealtime after mealtime . . . through raging insomnias . . . Pure methylphenidate nirvana . . . From 1990 to 1995, CIBA-Geneva's sales of Ritalin rose 600 percent; and not because of the appetites of subsets of the species Speed Freak in San Francisco, either. It was because an entire generation of American boys, from the best private schools of the Northeast to the worst sludge-trap public schools of Los Angeles and San Diego, was now strung out on methylphenidate, diligently doled out to them every day by their connection, the school nurse. America is a wonderful country! I mean it! No honest writer would challenge that statement! The human comedy never runs out of material! It never lets you down!

Meantime, the notion of a self—a self who exercises self-discipline, postpones gratification, curbs the sexual appetite, stops short of aggression and criminal behavior—a self who can become more intelligent and lift itself to the very peaks of life by its own bootstraps through study, practice, perseverance, and refusal to give up in the face of great odds—this old-fashioned notion (what's a *boot*strap, for God's sake?) of success through enterprise and true grit is already slipping away, slipping away . . . slipping away . . . The peculiarly American faith in the power of the individual to transform himself from a helpless cypher into a giant among men, a faith that ran from Emerson ("Self-Reliance") to Horatio Alger's *Luck and Pluck* stories to Dale Carnegie's *How to Win Friends and Influence People* to Norman Vincent Peale's *The Power of Positive Thinking* to Og Mandino's *The Greatest Salesman in the World*—that faith is now as moribund as the god for whom Nietzsche wrote an obituary in 1882. It lives on today only in the decrepit form of the "motivational talk," as lecture agents refer to it, given by retired football stars such as Fran Tarkenton to audiences of businessmen, most of them woulda-been athletes (like the author of this article), about how life is like a football game. "It's late in the fourth period and you're down by thirteen points and the Cowboys got you hemmed in on your own one-yard line and it's third and twenty-three. Whaddaya do? . . ."

Sorry, Fran, but it's third and twenty-three and the genetic fix is in, and the new message is now being pumped out into the popular press and onto television at a stupefying rate. Who are the pumps? They are a new breed who call themselves "evolutionary psychologists." You can be sure that twenty years ago the same people would have been calling themselves Freudian; but today they are genetic determinists, and the press has a voracious appetite for whatever they come up with.

The most popular study currently—it is *still* being featured on television news shows—is David Lykken and Auke Tellegen's study at the University of Minnesota of two thousand twins that shows, according to these two evolutionary psychologists, that an individual's happiness is largely genetic. Some people are hardwired to be happy and some are not. Success (or failure) in matters of love, money, reputation, or power is transient stuff; you soon settle back down (or up) to the level of happiness you were born with genetically. *Fortune* devoted a long takeout, elaborately illustrated, of a study by evolutionary psychologists at Britain's University of Saint Andrews showing that you judge the facial beauty or handsomeness of people you meet not by any social standards of the age you live in but by criteria hardwired in your brain from the moment you were born. Or, to put it another way, beauty is not in the eye of the beholder but embedded in his genes. In fact, today, in the year 2000, if your appetite for newspapers, magazines, and television is big enough, you will quickly get the impression that there is nothing in your life, including the fat content of your body, that is not genetically predetermined. If I may mention just a few things the evolutionary psychologists have illuminated for me recently:

One widely publicized study found that women are attracted to rich or powerful men because they are genetically hardwired to sense that alpha males will be able to take better care of their offspring. So if her current husband catches her with somebody better than he is, she can say in all sincerity, "I'm just a lifeguard in the gene pool, honey." Personally, I find that reassuring. I used to be a cynic. I thought the reason so many beautiful women married ugly rich men was that they were schemers, connivers, golddiggers. Another study found that the male of the human species is genetically hardwired to be polygamous, i.e., unfaithful to his legal mate, so that he will cast his seed as widely as humanly possible. Well . . . men can read, too! "Don't blame me, honey.

Four hundred thousand years of evolution made me do it." Another study showed that most murders are the result of genetically hardwired compulsions. Well . . . convicts can read, too, and hoping for parole, they report to the prison psychiatrist: "Something came over me . . . and then the knife went in."* Another showed that teenage girls, being in the prime of their fecundity, are genetically hardwired to be promiscuous and are as helpless to stop themselves as minks or rabbits. Some public school systems haven't had to be told twice. They provide not only condoms but also special elementary, junior high, and high schools where teenage mothers can park their offspring in nursery rooms while they learn to read print and do sums.

Where does that leave "self-control"? In quotation marks, like many old-fashioned notions—once people believe that this ghost in the machine, "the self," does not even exist and brain imaging proves it, once and for all.

So far, neuroscientific theory is based largely on indirect evidence, from studies of animals or of how a normal brain changes when it is invaded (by accidents, disease, radical surgery, or experimental needles). Darwin II himself, Edward O. Wilson, has only limited direct knowledge of the human brain. He is a zoologist, not a neurologist, and his theories are extrapolations from the exhaustive work he has done in his specialty, the study of insects. The French surgeon Paul Broca discovered Broca's area, one of the two speech centers of the left hemisphere of the brain, only after one of his patients suffered a stroke. Even the PET scan and the PET reporter gene/PET reporter probe are technically medical invasions, since they require the injection of chemicals or viruses into the body. But they offer glimpses of what the noninvasive imaging of the future will probably look like. A neuroradiologist can read a list of topics out loud to a person being given a PET scan, topics pertaining to sports, music, business, history, whatever, and when he finally hits one the person is interested in, a particular area of the

*Recounted by the British prison psychiatrist Theodore Dalrymple in the magazine *City Journal*.

cerebral cortex actually lights up on the screen. Eventually, as brain imaging is refined, the picture may become as clear and complete as those see-through exhibitions, at auto shows, of the inner workings of the internal combustion engine. At that point it may become obvious to everyone that all we are looking at is a piece of machinery, an analog chemical computer, that processes information from the environment. "All," since you can look and look and you will not find any ghostly self inside, or any mind, or any soul.

Thereupon, in the year 2010 or 2030, some new Nietzsche will step forward to announce: "The self is dead"—except that being prone to the poetic, like Nietzsche the First, he will probably say: "The soul is dead." He will say that he is merely bringing the news, the news of the greatest event of the millennium: "The soul, that last refuge of values, is dead, because educated people no longer believe it exists." Unless the assurances of the Wilsons and the Dennetts and the Dawkinses also start rippling out, the madhouse that will ensue may make the phrase "the total eclipse of all values" seem tame.

If I were a college student today, I don't think I could resist going into neuroscience. Here we have the two most fascinating riddles of the twenty-first century: the riddle of the human mind and the riddle of what happens to the human mind when it comes to know itself absolutely. In any case, we live in an age in which it is impossible and pointless to avert your eyes from the truth.

Ironically, said Nietzsche, this unflinching eye for truth, this zest for skepticism, is the legacy of Christianity (for complicated reasons that needn't detain us here). Then he added one final and perhaps ultimate piece of irony in a fragmentary passage in a notebook shortly before he lost his mind (to the late nineteenth century's great venereal scourge, syphilis). He predicted that eventually modern science would turn its juggernaut of skepticism upon itself, question the validity of its own foundations, tear them apart, and self-destruct. I thought about that in the summer of 1994, when a group of mathematicians and computer scientists held a conference at the Santa Fe Institute on "Limits to Scientific Knowledge." The consensus was that since the human mind is, after all, an entirely physical apparatus, a form of computer, the product of a particular genetic history, it is finite in its capabilities. Being finite, hardwired, it will probably never have the power to comprehend human existence in any complete way. It would be as if a group of dogs were to call a conference to try to understand The Dog. They could try as hard as they wanted, but they wouldn't get very far. Dogs can communicate only about forty notions, all of them primitive, and they can't record anything. The project would be doomed from the start. The human brain is far superior to the dog's, but it is limited nonetheless. So any hope of human beings arriving at some final, complete, self-enclosed theory of human existence is doomed, too.

This, science's Ultimate Skepticism, has been spreading ever since then. Over the past two years even Darwinism, a sacred tenet among American scientists for the past seventy years, has been beset by . . . doubts. Scientists—not religiosi—notably the mathematician David Berlinski ("The Deniable Darwin," *Commentary*, June 1996) and the biochemist Michael Behe (*Darwin's Black Box*, 1996) have begun attacking Darwinism as a mere theory, not a scientific discovery, a theory woefully unsupported by fossil evidence and featuring, at the core of its logic, sheer mush. (Dennett and Dawkins, for whom Darwin is the Only Begotten, the Messiah, are already screaming. They're beside themselves, utterly apoplectic. Wilson, the giant, keeping his cool, has remained above the battle.) Noam Chomsky has made things worse by pointing out that there is nothing even in the highest apes remotely comparable to human speech, which is in turn the basis of recorded memory and, therefore, everything from skyscrapers and missions to the moon to Islam and little matters such as the theory of evolution. He says it's not that there is a missing link; there is nothing to link up *with*. By 1990 the physicist Petr Beckmann of the University of Colorado had already begun going after Einstein. He greatly admired Einstein for his famous equation of matter and energy, $E=mc^2$, but called his theory of relativity mostly absurd and grotesquely untestable. Beckmann died in

1993. His Fool Killer's cudgel has been taken up by Howard Hayden of the University of Connecticut, who has many admirers among the up-coming generation of Ultimately Skeptical young physicists. The scorn the new breed heaps upon quantum mechanics ("has no real-world applications" . . . "depends entirely on goofball equations"), Unified Field Theory ("Nobel worm bait"), and the Big Bang Theory ("creationism for nerds") has become withering. If only Nietzsche were alive! He would have relished every minute of it!

Recently I happened to be talking to a prominent California geologist, and she told me: "When I first went into geology, we all thought that in science you create a solid layer of findings, through experiment and careful investigation, and then you add a second layer, like a second layer of bricks, all very carefully, and so on. Occasionally some adventurous scientist stacks the bricks up in towers, and these towers turn out to be insubstantial and they get torn down, and you proceed again with the careful layers. But we now realize that the very first layers aren't even resting on solid ground. They are balanced on bubbles, on concepts that are full of air, and those bubbles are being burst today, one after the other."

I suddenly had a picture of the entire astonishing edifice collapsing and modern man plunging headlong back into the primordial ooze. He's floundering, sloshing about, gulping for air, frantically treading ooze, when he feels something huge and smooth swim beneath him and boost him up, like some almighty dolphin. He can't see it, but he's much impressed. He names it God.

VITA ROBUSTA, ARS ANOREXICA

In the Land of the Rococo Marxists

Where was *I*? On the wrong page? The wrong channel? Outside the bandwidth? As building managers here in New York shut down the elevators at 11:30 p.m. on December 31, 1999, so that citizens would not be trapped between floors by Y2K microchip failures—and licensed pyrotechnicians launched EPA-sanctioned fireworks from cordoned-off Central Park "venues" at precisely 12:00:01 a.m., January 1, 2000, to mark the arrival of the twenty-first century and the third millennium—did a single solitary savant note that the First American Century had just come to an end and the Second American Century had begun?—and that there might well be five, six, eight more to come?—resulting in a Pax Americana lasting a thousand years? Or did I miss something?

Did a single historian mention that America now dominates the world to an extent that would have made Julius Caesar twitch with envy?—would have made Alexander the Great, who thought there were no more worlds to conquer, get down on all fours and beat his fists on the ground in despair because he was merely a warrior and had never heard of international mergers and acquisitions, rock and rap, fireball movies, TV, the NBA, the World Wide Web, and the "globalization" game?

Was a single bard bestirred to write a mighty anthem—along the lines of James Thomson's "Rule, Britannia! Britannia rule the waves! Britons never, never, never shall be slaves!"—for America, the nation that in the century just concluded had vanquished two barbaric nationalistic brotherhoods, the German Nazis and the Russian Communists, two hordes of methodical slave-hunting predators who made the Huns and Magyars look whimsical by comparison? Or had the double A's in my Discman died on me?

Did anybody high or low look for a Frédéric-Auguste Bartholdi to create a new tribute on the order of the Statue of Liberty for the nation that in the twentieth century, even more so than in the nineteenth, opened her arms to people from all over the globe—to Vietnamese, Thais, Cambodians, Laotians, Hmong, Ethiopians, Albanians, Senegalese, Guyanese, Eritreans, Cubans, as well as everybody else—and made sure they enjoyed full civil rights, including the means to take political power in a city the size of Miami if they could muster the votes? Did anybody even wistfully envision such a monument to America the International Haven of Democracy? Or had my *Flash Art* subscription run out?

Did any of the America-at-century's-end network TV specials strike the exuberant note that Queen Victoria's Diamond Jubilee struck in 1897? All I remember are voice-overs saying that for better or worse . . . hmm, hmm . . . McCarthyism, racism, Vietnam, right-wing militias, Oklahoma City, Heaven's Gate, Doctor Death . . . on balance, hmm, we're not entirely sure . . . for better or worse, America had won the Cold War . . . hmm, hmm, hmm . . .

My impression was that one American Century rolled into another with all the pomp and circumstance of a mouse pad. America's great triumph inspired all the patriotism and pride (or, if you'd rather, chauvinism), all the yearning for glory and empire (or, if you'd rather, the spirit of Manifest Destiny), all the martial jubilee music of a mouse click.

Such was my impression; but it was only that, my impression. So I drew upon the University of Michigan's fabled public-opinion survey resources. They sent me the results of four studies, each approaching the matter from a different angle. Chauvinism? The spirit of Manifest Destiny? According to one survey, 74 percent of Americans don't want the United States to intervene abroad unless in cooperation with other nations, presumably so that we won't get all the blame. Excitement? Americans have no strong feelings about their country's supremacy one way or the other. They are lacking in affect, as the clinical psychologists say.

There were seers who saw this coming even at the unabashedly pompous peak (June 22) of England's 1897 Jubilee. One of them was Rudyard Kipling, the empire's de facto poet laureate, who wrote a poem for the Jubilee, "Recessional," warning: "Lo, all our pomp of yesterday/Is one with Nineveh and Tyre!" He and many others had the uneasy feeling that the foundations of European civilization were already shifting beneath their feet, a feeling indicated by the much used adjectival compound fin-de-siècle. Literally, of course, it meant nothing more than "end-of-the-century," but it connoted something modern, baffling, and troubling in Europe. Both Nietzsche and Marx did their greatest work seeking to explain the mystery. Both used the term "decadence."

But if there was decadence, what was decaying? Religious faith and moral codes that had been in place since time was, said Nietzsche, who in 1882 made the most famous statement in modern philosophy—"God is dead"—and three startlingly accurate predictions for the twentieth century. He even estimated when they would begin to come true: about 1915. (1) The faith men formerly invested in God they would now invest in barbaric "brotherhoods with the aim of the robbery and exploitation of the non-brothers." Their names turned out, in due course, to be the German Nazis and the Russian Communists. (2) There would be "wars such as have never been waged on earth." Their names turned out to be World War I and World War II. (3) There no longer would be Truth but, rather, "truth" in quotation marks, depending upon which concoction of eternal verities the modern barbarian found most useful at any given moment. The result would be universal skepticism, cynicism, irony, and contempt. World War I began in 1914 and ended in 1918. On cue, as if Nietzsche were still alive to direct the drama, an entirely new figure, with an entirely new name, arose in Europe: that embodiment of skepticism, cynicism, irony, and contempt, the Intellectual.

The word "intellectual," used as a noun referring to the "intellectual laborer" who assumes a political stance, did not exist until Georges Clemenceau used it in 1898 during the Dreyfus case, congratulating those "intellectuals," such as Marcel Proust and Anatole France, who had joined Dreyfus's great champion, Emile Zola. Zola was an entirely new form of political eminence, a popular novelist. His famous *J'accuse* was published on the front page of a daily newspaper, *L'Aurore* ("The Dawn"), which printed 300,000 copies and hired hundreds of extra newsboys, who sold virtually every last one by midafternoon.

Zola and Clemenceau provided a wholly unexpected leg up in life for the ordinary worker ants of "pure intellectual labor" (Clemenceau's term): your fiction writers, playwrights, poets, history and lit profs, that whole cottage industry of poor souls who scribble, scribble, scribble. Zola was an extraordinary reporter (or "documenter," as he called himself) who had devoured the details of the Dreyfus case to the point where he knew as much about it as any judge, prosecutor, or law clerk. But that inconvenient detail of Zola's biography was soon forgotten. The new hero, the intellectual, didn't need to burden himself with the irksome toil of reporting or research. For that matter, he needed no particular education, no scholarly training, no philosophical grounding, no conceptual frameworks, no knowledge of academic or scientific developments other than the sort of stuff you might pick up in Section 9 of the Sunday newspaper. Indignation about the powers that be and the bourgeois fools who did their bidding—that was all you needed. Bango! You were an intellectual.

From the very outset the eminence of this new creature, the intellectual, who was to play such a tremendous role in the history of the twentieth century, was inseparable from his *necessary* indignation. It was his indignation that elevated him to a plateau of moral superiority. Once up there, he was in a position to look down at the rest of humanity. And it hadn't cost him any effort, intellectual or otherwise. As Marshall McLuhan would put it years later: "Moral indignation is a technique used to endow the idiot with dignity." Precisely which intellectuals of the twentieth century were or were not idiots is a debatable point, but it is hard to argue with the definition I once heard a French diplomat offer at a dinner party: "An intellectual is a person knowledgeable in one field who speaks out only in others."

After World War I, American writers and scholars had the chance to go to Europe in large numbers for the first time. They got an eyeful of the Intellectual up close. That sneer, that high-minded aloofness from the mob, those long immaculate alabaster forefingers with which he pointed down at the rubble of a botched civilization—it was irresistible. The only problem was that when our neophyte intellectuals came back to the United States to strike the pose, there was no rubble to point at. Far from being a civilization in ruins, the United States had emerged from the war as the new star occupying the center of the world stage. Far from reeking of decadence, the United States had the glow of a young giant: brave, robust, innocent, and unsophisticated.

But young scribblers roaring drunk (as Nietzsche had predicted) on skepticism, cynicism, irony, and contempt were in no mood to let such . . . circumstances . . . stand in the way. From the very outset the attempt of this country cousin, the American intellectual, to catch up with his urbane European model was touching, as only the strivings of a colonial subject can be. Throughout the twentieth century, the picture would never change (and today, a hundred years later, the sweaty little colonial still trots along at the heels of . . . sahib). In the 1920s the first job was to catch up with the European intellectuals' mockery of the "bourgeoisie," which had begun a full forty years earlier. H. L. Mencken, probably the most brilliant American essayist of the twentieth century, led the way by pie-ing the American version of same with his term "the booboisie." In fiction the solution was to pull back the covers from this apple-cheeked, mom's-cooking country of ours and say, "There! Take a good look at what's underneath! Get a whiff of the rot just below the surface!"—the way Sinclair Lewis did it in *Main Street*, *Babbitt*, *Elmer Gantry*, and *Arrowsmith*, for which he became the first American to win the Nobel Prize in Literature, and Sherwood Anderson did it in *Winesburg, Ohio*. Anderson's specialty was exposing the Middle American hypocrite, such as the rigidly proper, sexually twisted Peeping Tom Midwestern preacher. He created a stock character and a stock plot that others have been laboriously cranking out ever since in books, TV, and movies, from *Peyton Place* to *American Beauty*.

The Great Depression of the 1930s gave our version of this new breed, the intellectual, plenty of material to get wholesomely indignant about. For a change, America did look dreadful. But even then things weren't as blissfully vile as they were in Europe, the birthplace of the intellectual. Europe, after all, now had the Depression plus fascism. The solution was what became the specialty of our colonial intellectuals: the adjectival catch-up. Europe had real fascism? Well, we had "social fascism." And what was that? That was the name Left intellectuals gave to Roosevelt's New Deal. Roosevelt's "reforms" merely masked the fascism whose dark night would soon descend upon America.

"Fascism" was, in fact, a Marxist coinage. Marxists borrowed the name of Mussolini's Italian party, the Fascisti, and applied it to Hitler's Nazis, adroitly papering over the fact that the Nazis, like Marxism's standard-bearers, the Soviet Communists, were revolutionary socialists. In fact, "Nazi" was (most annoyingly) shorthand for the National Socialist German Workers' Party. European Marxists successfully put over the idea that Nazism was the brutal, decadent last gasp of "capitalism." Few of their colonial cousins in America became doctrinaire, catechism-drilled Marxists, but most were soon enveloped in a heavy Marxist mist. The Marxist fable of the "capitalists" and the "bourgeoisie" oppressing "the masses"—"the proletariat"—took hold even among intellectuals who were anti-Marxist. Prior to the Nazi-Soviet pact of 1939, the American Communist Party had great success mobilizing the colonials on behalf of "anti-fascist" causes, such as the Loyalists' battle against the "fascist" Franco in the Spanish Civil War. "Anti-fascism" became a universal ray gun, good for zapping anybody, anywhere, from up here . . . on the intellectuals' Everest of Indignation.

After World War II, this mental atmosphere led to a curious anomaly. By objective standards, the United States quickly became the most powerful, prosperous, and popular nation of all time. Militarily we developed the power to blow the entire planet to smithereens by turning a couple of keys in a missile silo; but even if it all blew, we also developed the power to escape, breaking the bonds of Earth's gravity and flying to the moon in history's most amazing engineering feat. And there was something still more amazing. The country turned into what the utopian socialists of the nineteenth century, the Saint-Simons and Fouriers, had dreamed about: an El Dorado where the average workingman would have the political freedom, the personal freedom, the money, and the free time to fulfill his potential in any way he saw fit. It got to the point where if you couldn't reach your tile mason or your pool cleaner, it was because he was off on a Royal Caribbean cruise with his third wife. And as soon as American immigration restrictions were relaxed in the 1960s, people of every land, every color, every religion, people from Africa, Asia, South America, and the Caribbean, began pouring into the United States.

But our intellectuals dug in like terriers. Just as they had after World War I, they refused to buckle under to . . . circumstances. They saw *through* El Dorado and produced the most inspired adjectival catch-ups of the twentieth century. Real fascism and genocide were finished after World War II, but the intellectuals used the Rosenberg case, the Hiss case, McCarthyism—the whole Communist Witch Hunt—and, above all, the war in Vietnam to come up with . . . "incipient fascism" (Herbert Marcuse, much prized as a bona-fide European "Frankfurt School" Marxist who had moved to our shores), "preventive fascism" (Marcuse again), "local fascism" (Walter Lippmann), "brink of" fascism (Charles Reich), "informal Fascism" (Philip Green), "latent fascism" (Dotson Rader), not to mention the most inspired catch-up of all: "cultural genocide." Cultural genocide referred to the refusal of American universities to have open admissions policies, so that any minority applicant could enroll without regard to GPAs and SATs and other instruments of latent-incipient-brink-of-fascist repression.

"Cultural genocide" was inspired, but in this entire *opéra bouffe* of fascism, racism, and fascist-racist genocide, the truly high note was hit by one Susan Sontag. In a 1967 article for *Partisan Review* entitled "What's Happening to America," she wrote: "The white race *is* the cancer of human history; it is the white race and it alone—its ideologies and inventions—which eradicates autonomous populations wherever it spreads, which has upset the ecological balance of the planet, which now threatens the very existence of life itself."

The white race *is* the cancer of human history? Who *was* this woman? Who and what? An anthropological epidemiologist? A renowned authority on the history of cultures throughout the world, a synthesizer of the magnitude of a Max Weber, a Joachim Wach, a Sir James Frazer, an Arnold Toynbee? Actually, she was just another scribbler who spent her life signing up for protest meetings and lumbering to the podium encumbered by her prose style, which had a handicapped parking sticker valid at *Partisan Review*. Perhaps she was exceptionally hell-bent on illustrating McLuhan's line about indignation endowing the idiot with dignity, but otherwise she was just a typical American intellectual of the post–World War II period.

After all, having the faintest notion of what you were talking about was irrelevant. Any scholar or scientist who merely possessed profound knowledge in his or her own field did not qualify as an intellectual. The prime example was Noam Chomsky, a brilliant linguist who on his own figured out that language is a structure built into the very central nervous system of *Homo sapiens*, a theory that neuroscientists, lacking the instruments to do so heretofore, have only recently begun to verify. But Chomsky was not known as an intellectual until he denounced the war in Vietnam, something he knew absolutely nothing about—thereby qualifying for his new eminence.

American intellectuals of the Adjectival Fascism phase had a terrible year in 1989. In June, Chinese students in Beijing rebelled against the *ancien* Maoist *régime*, defied the tanks, and brought out into Tiananmen Square a plaster statue, the *Goddess of Democracy*, who, with her arms lifted to the heavens, looked suspiciously like the Statue of Liberty in New York Harbor. Who among the intellectuals ever would have suspected that Chinese dissidents had been looking to America as their model of freedom all along? Then on November 9 the Berlin Wall came down, and in no time the Soviet Union collapsed and its Eastern European empire disintegrated.

It was a mess, all right—no two ways about that. It made it damned hard to express your skepticism, your cynicism, your contempt, in Marxist terms. "Capitalism," "proletariat," "the masses," "the means of production," "infantile leftism," "the dark night of fascism," or even "anti-fascism"—all these things suddenly sounded, well, not so much *wrong* . . . as *old* . . . "Vulgar Marxism" it came to be called, vulgar in the sense of . . . unsophisticated.

The important thing was not to admit you were wrong in any fundamental way. You couldn't let anybody get away with the notion that just because the United States had triumphed, and just because some unfortunate things had come out after the Soviet archives were opened up—I mean, damn!—it looks like Hiss and the Rosenbergs actually *were* Soviet agents—and even the Witch Hunt, which was one of the bedrocks of our beliefs—damn again!—these books by Klehr and

Haynes, in the Yale series on American Communism, and Radosh and Weinstein make it pretty clear that while Joe McCarthy was the despicable liar we always knew he was, the American Communist Party really was devoted primarily to Soviet propaganda and espionage, and their spies really did penetrate the U.S. government at high levels. Yale!—so respectable, too!—how could they give their imprimatur to these renegade right-wing scholars who do this kind of stuff? Not to mention the Spanish Civil War—*archives*! Turns out the Loyalists secretly called in the Soviets at the very outset of hostilities—and if they'd won, Spain would have been the first Soviet puppet state!

And now Vietnam, our other bedrock, the holiest of all our causes—those damnable archives again! How could anybody be so perfidious as to open up secret records? They make it look like the Soviets and the Chinese, in concert with the North Vietnamese Communists, were manipulating the Vietcong all along! They make it look like America's intervention in Vietnam was some kind of idealistic crusade, fought solely to stop the onslaught of Communism's slave-hunting Magyar hordes in Southeast Asia!

The main thing is to make sure we don't let them use this stuff to invalidate the way we ascended the Olympian peaks of aloofness for seven decades, from November 11, 1918, the end of World War I, to November 9, 1989, the day the Wall fell. The fact that America won the Cold War does not wash away the stains America left during the Cold War, does it? We've still got the devil himself, the brute, Joe McCarthy, and Richard Nixon and the House Committee on Un-American Activities and all that crowd, who cost a lot of people in Hollywood and academia their jobs, don't we? And racism? The mere fact that the powers that be gave everybody all these so-called civil rights and voting rights doesn't mean that virulent and peculiarly American disease has been eliminated, does it? Not by any means!

This urge to expose the fallacy of "American triumphalism" has led to a poignant moment here in the year 2000. For eleven years now, ever since Tiananmen Square and the fall of the Wall, people in the former empire of the Soviet Union have been looking to the United States for the very principles of living in a condition of freedom. East European college students will startle you with their knowledge of America's own struggle for freedom two and a quarter centuries ago. In 1993, in New York, I happened to meet a Hungarian student who knew speeches by the great orator of the American Revolution, Patrick Henry, by heart, and not just his famous "Give me liberty or give me death" speech of 1775, either, but also his 1765 Stamp Act speech, the one before the colonial House of Burgesses in Williamsburg. He could recite it verbatim:

" 'Caesar had his Brutus; Charles the First, his Cromwell; and George the Third—'

" 'Treason!' cried out the Speaker of the House. 'Treason!'

" '—may profit by their example,' said Patrick Henry. 'If *this* be treason . . . make the most of it!' "

Young people like him in Eastern Europe, where writers such as Solzhenitsyn and Václav Havel were the very keepers of the flame of freedom, have naturally sought out American literary figures to learn of the great democratic principles of the freest nation on earth. But almost without exception, American writers are . . . intellectuals. If our young Hungarian were to walk up to an American intellectual and recite Patrick Henry's Stamp Act speech, he would receive in response only (in Thomas Mann's phrase) a hollow silence.

Where else can the millions recently freed from the late Soviet tyranny turn? To America's clergy? Alas, except for the rare brave Roman Catholic padre, America's clergy have become irrelevant to public opinion, unless they yield to the temptation—and many have—to become intellectuals themselves.

That leaves our academic philosophers, our year 2000 versions of Immanuel Kant, John Stuart Mill, and David Hume. Here we come upon one of the choicest chapters in the human comedy. Today, at any leading American university, a Kant, with all his dithering about God, freedom, and immortality, or even a Hume, wouldn't survive a year in graduate school, much less get hired as an instructor. The philosophy departments, history departments, English and comparative literature departments, and, at many universities, anthropology, sociology, and even psychology departments are now divided, in John L'Heureux's delicious terminology (*The Handmaid of Desire*), into the Young Turks and the Fools. Most Fools are old, mid-fifties, early sixties, but a Fool can be any age, twenty-eight as easily as fifty-eight, if he is one of that minority on the faculty who still believe in the old nineteenth-century Germanic modes of so-called objective scholarship. Today the humanities faculties are hives of abstruse doctrines such as structuralism, poststructuralism, postmodernism, deconstruction, reader-response theory, commodification theory . . . The names vary, but the subtext is always the same: Marxism may be dead, and the proletariat has proved to be hopeless. They're all at sea with their third wives. But we can find new proletariats whose ideological benefactors we can be—women, non-whites, put-upon white ethnics, homosexuals, transsexuals, the polymorphously perverse, pornographers, prostitutes (sex workers), hardwood trees—which we can use to express our indignation toward the powers that be and our aloofness to their bourgeois stooges, to keep the flame of skepticism, cynicism, irony, and contempt burning. This will not be Vulgar Marxism; it will be . . . Rococo Marxism, elegant as a Fragonard, sly as a Watteau. We won't get too hung up on political issues, which never seem to work out right anyway. Instead, we will expose the stooges' so-called truths, which the Fools ignorantly cultivate, and deconstruct their self-deluding concoctions of eternal verities. We will show how the powers that be manipulate, with poisonous efficiency, the very language we speak in order to imprison us in an "invisible panopticon," to use the late French "poststructuralist" Michel Foucault's term.

Foucault and another Frenchman, Jacques Derrida, are the great idols of Rococo Marxism in America. Could it be otherwise? Today, as throughout the twentieth century, our intellectuals remain sweaty little colonials, desperately trotting along, trying to catch up, catch up, catch up with the way the idols do it in France, which is through Theory, Theory, Theory. In this pursuit, some colonials inevitably run faster than others, and leading the pack currently are two academicians, Stanley Fish and Judith Butler. Before the Wall came down, the archetypal American intellectual was a mere scribbler who joyfully hoisted himself up to the status of intellectual. Since the Wall came down, the archetypal American intellectual is the scholar who has joyfully lowered himself to the status of mere intellectual. If Nietzsche's already fabulous powers of prophecy had been specific enough to dream up a couple of characters to dramatize the deconstruction of Truth with a capital T that he foresaw, he would have dreamed up Fish and Butler and thrust them into *Thus Spake Zarathustra*. Fish is a sixty-one-year-old Milton scholar with a Ph.D. from Yale. Or a lapsed Milton scholar; he achieved stardom as the Rococo head of the English Department at Duke and now has been commissioned by the University of Illinois at Chicago, for $230,000 a year plus perks (big-time stuff in academia), to assemble a stable of Rococo stars in para-proletariat studies, not excluding, he says, study of "body parts, excretory functions, the sex trade, dildos, bisexuality, transvestism, and lesbian pornography." Fish says such things with a true Swiftian gusto, relishing the inevitable alarm that ensues. As colonial Rococovists go, he cuts a uniquely dashing figure, driving a vintage Jaguar, a long scarf furled about his neck, à la Théophile Gautier. In his rakishness and mischievous gleam, he differs markedly from the cranky deconstruction crews who follow him. He does wear sweaters with no shirt visible underneath, however, just as nearly all Young Turks, male or female, affect some sort of Generation X garb—sweatshirts, T-shirts, jeans, sneakers, all-black Young Artists outfits—in order to out-casual and out-Young the Fools, who are still stuck back in the Tweedy Prof mode.

On the conceptual level, Fish is best known for his "reader-response theory," which holds that literary texts mean nothing in themselves, that meaning is only a mental construct concocted by the reader. It is a short step from this premise to the argument that the powers that be have had a picnic loading the language with terminology calculated to make you concoct the mental constructs they want you to concoct in order to manipulate your mind.

May I offer an arch and perhaps familiar but clear example? Recently I came across a woman at one of our top universities who taught a course in Feminist Theory and gave her students F's if they spelled the plural of the female of the species "women" on a test or in a paper. She insisted on "womyn," since the powers that be, at some point far back in the mists of history, had built male primacy into the very language itself by making "women" 60 percent "men." How did the students react? They shrugged. They have long since learned the futility of objecting to Rococo Marxism. They just write "womyn" and go about the business of grinding out a credit in the course.

One student told me the only problem was that when she wrote her papers on her word processor and used spell check, all hell broke loose. "You get these little wavy red lines all over the screen, under 'womyn.' Spell check doesn't have 'womyn.'" Then she shrugged. "Or at least mine doesn't."

The undisputed queen of feminist theory is Judith Butler, a forty-four-year-old Hegel scholar with (like Fish) a Ph.D. from Yale, who is also known as the diva of Queer Studies. She is small and not very prepossessing, but graduate students all over the country say "diva" at the mere mention of her name. A group of them put out a fan magazine called *Judy!* devoted to chronicling the way she rams home her "performativity" theory of speech and sexual behavior as forms of anarchy.

"All gender roles are an imitation for which there is no original," runs her most famous paradox. She is even more famous for her convoluted Theoryese. In 1998 the journal *Philosophy and Literature* named her winner of their Bad Writing Contest for a sentence that began "The move from a structuralist account in which capital is understood to structure social relations in relatively homologous ways to a view of hegemony in which power relations are subject to repetition, convergence, and rearticulation . . ."—and went on for fifty-nine words more.

Her zine fans love the insouciant yet erudite way she dismisses such attacks. "Ponderousness," she says, referring to Hegel, "is part of the phenomenological challenge of his text."

The battle of the Fools versus the Young Turks has escalated beyond words, however. In 1987 the traditionalists formed a self-defense organization called the National Association of Scholars; 1,000 joined. In a public statement, Fish, while at Duke, branded them with the *R* word, the *S* word, and the *H* word—racist, sexist, and homophobic—and sent a memo to Duke's provost recommending that no member of the tainted organization be allowed on key university committees. The provost refused. The Scholars accused Fish of trying to blacklist them. At more than one major university, Young Turks roamed about in Gen X clothes, red ballpoint pens at the ready, sniffing out deviationists . . . sexists . . . racists . . . classists (*sic*) . . . homophobes . . . ethnophobes . . . The stories of Young Turks nudging and whispering to keep graduate students away from Fool courses, to the point where some Fool ends up with zero students for the year, would make a fairly grisly chapter in a book.

In the face of such confidence and aggressiveness on the part of the Young Turks and such devotion on the part of their graduate-student T.A. followers, who is left to support a student in her misgivings about "womyn" or any other manifestation of Rococo Marxism? Her other teachers? Some dean? The university's president? The most unlikely of all, believe me, is the president.

Recently I met a student who told me he was taking a cross-disciplinary course entitled Civilizations of North America. "Cross-disciplinary" is a fashionable term in academia just now, not to be confused with the old (Fool) term "interdisciplinary," which refers to the use of concepts from two or more conventional scholarly disciplines to study a particular subject, such as using the concepts of sociology and economics to write history. No, "cross-disciplinary" refers to crossing all disciplines . . . much the way a 747 crosses the North Pole at

40,000 feet above an impenetrable cloud cover . . . on the way to a single destination: Rococo Marxism. So the instructor informs the class that while Americans might have more money, possessions, technological advantages, and conveniences than Mexicans or Canadians, when it comes to "social cleavages"—along the lines of race, gender, class, ethnicity, and regional imbalances—Americans are the primitives. On this subject—life's fundamentals—we need to take lessons at the knees of the Mexicans and the Canadians.

The Canadians? The Mexicans? No kidding? . . . Didn't the French of Quebec province get so bitter about the British majority that they almost seceded from Canada just five years ago? And just six years ago didn't the Indians in Mexico's southernmost province, Chiapas, rise up in an armed rebellion? And gender . . . gosh . . . isn't it an open secret that foreign corporations like to employ women on their assembly lines in Mexico because Mexican women are taught all their lives to submit to male authority? Or am I dreaming?

Shrugging: "Hey, I don't know. That's what he told us."

By now, in the year 2000, that's what anyone is apt to do . . . shrug and go on about his business. For eighty-two years now, America's intellectuals, right on time, as Nietzsche predicted it, have expressed their skepticism toward American life. And, as the French say, "Skepticism soon hardens into contempt." As any Fool sociologist could tell you, there are only two objectively detectable social classes in America: people above the bachelor's-degree line—i.e., people who have graduated from four-year colleges—and people below it, who haven't. By now people above it have learned to shrug and acquiesce to "political correctness," to Rococo Marxism, because they know that to oppose it out loud is in poor taste. It is a . . . breach of the etiquette you must observe to establish yourself as an educated person.

Meanwhile, in the ranks of people below that sheerly dividing line, the bachelor's degree, all those limo drivers and cable TV linesmen on the cruises, there are plenty who voice their opposition—at night, over cigarettes, in the ship's Palais Doré cocktail lounge . . . muttering, grousing, grousing, muttering . . . all the while doubting their own common sense. Is it any wonder, then, when survey after survey shows Americans entering the Second American Century, the Pax Americana, in a state of . . . whatever . . .

We are left, finally, with one question. What exactly do the intellectuals want out of their Rococo Marxist mental acrobatics? Is it change they want, change for all the para-proletariats whose ideological benefactors they proclaim themselves to be? Of course not. Actual change would involve irksome toil. So what do they want?

It's a simple business, at bottom. All the intellectual wants, in his heart of hearts, is to hold on to what was magically given to him one shining moment a century ago. He asks for nothing more than to remain aloof, removed, as Revel once put it, from the mob, the philistines . . . "the middle class."

Just think of the fun Nietzsche could have had, if only God were not dead! Think of what it would have been like for him if he could have lolled for the past hundred years—he died in 1900—on a king-size cloud in Heaven, with angels playing Richard Strauss (he had given up on Wagner) in harp quartets as he gazed down upon the creatures only he had been brilliant enough to foresee . . . the barbaric brethren . . . the world warriors . . . the Truth demolition crews prowling about in children's clothes . . . A prophet, I presume, enjoys seeing his prophecies come true, but I have the feeling Nietzsche would have become bored by a hundred years of . . . "the intellectual" . . . I can almost hear that hortatory and apostrophic voice of his: How could you writers and academics have settled for such an easy, indolent role—for so long! How could you have chosen a facile snobbery over the hard work, the endless work, the Herculean work of gaining knowledge? I think he would have shaken his head over their ponderous, amateurish theories of cognition and sexuality. I think he would have grown weary of their dogged skepticism, cynicism, irony, and contempt and would have said, Why don't you admit it to me (no one need know—after all, I'm dead): if you must rate nations, at this moment in history your "accursed" America is the very micrometer by which all others must be measured.

And he would have been right.

The Marxists of the Soviets' East European empire had their Havel; the Marxists of the Soviet Union itself, their Solzhenitsyn; and the Rococo Marxists of America—

"Chauvinism!" cry the intellectuals. "Patriotism!"

—may profit by their example. If *this* be patriotism . . . make the most of it!

The Invisible Artist

Frederick Hart died at the age of fifty-five on August 13, 1999, two days after a team of doctors at Johns Hopkins discovered he had lung cancer, abruptly concluding one of the most bizarre stories in the history of twentieth-century art. While still in his twenties Hart consciously, pointedly, aimed for the ultimate in the Western tradition of sculpture, achieved it in a single stroke, then became invisible, and remained as invisible as Ralph Ellison's invisible man, who was invisible "simply because people refused to see me."

Not even Giotto, the twelve-year-old shepherd boy who was out in the meadow with the flock one day circa 1280, using a piece of flint to draw a picture of sheep on the face of a boulder, when the vacationing Florentine artist Cimabue happened to stroll by and discover the baby genius—not even Giotto could match Frederick Hart's storybook rise from obscurity.

Hart was born in Atlanta to a failed actress and a couldn't-be-bothered newspaper reporter. He was only three when his mother died, whereupon he was packed off to an aunt in a part of rural South Carolina where people ate peanuts boiled in salty water. He developed into an incorrigible Conway, South Carolina, juvenile delinquent, failed the ninth grade on his first try, and got thrown out of school on his second. Yet at the age of sixteen, by then a high-school dropout, he managed, to universal or at least Conway-wide amazement, to gain admission to the University of South Carolina by scoring a composite 35 out of a maximum 36 on an ACT college entrance test, the equivalent of a 1,560 on the College Boards.

He lasted six months. He became the lone white student to join 250 black students in a civil rights protest, was arrested, then expelled from the university. Informed that the Ku Klux Klan was looking for him, he fled to Washington.

In Washington he managed to get a job as a clerk at the Washington National Cathedral, a stupendous stone structure built in the Middle English Gothic style. The cathedral employed a crew of Italian masons full-time, and Hart became intrigued with their skill at stone carving. Several times he asked the master carver, an Italian named Roger Morigi, to take him on as an apprentice, but got nowhere. There was no one on the job but experienced Italians. By and by, Hart got to know the crew and took to borrowing tools and having a go at discarded pieces of stone. Morigi was so happily surprised by his aptitude, he made him an apprentice, after all, and soon began urging him to become a sculptor. Hart turned out to have Giotto's seemingly God-given genius—Giotto was a sculptor as well as a painter—for pulling perfectly formed human figures out of stone and clay at will and rapidly.

In 1971, Hart learned that the cathedral was holding an international competition to find a sculptor to adorn the building's west façade with a vast and elaborate spread of deep bas-reliefs and statuary on the theme of the Creation. Morigi urged Hart to enter. He entered and won. A working-class boy nobody had ever heard of, an apprentice stone carver, had won what would turn out to be the biggest and most prestigious commission for religious sculpture in America in the twentieth century.

The project brought him unimaginable dividends. The erstwhile juvenile delinquent from Conway, South Carolina, was a creature of hot passions, a handsome, slender boy with long, wavy, light brown hair, an artist by night with a rebellious hairdo and a rebellious attitude who was a big hit with the girls. In the late afternoons he had taken to hanging about Dupont Circle in Washington, which had become something of a bohemian quarter. Afternoon after afternoon he saw the same ravishing young woman walking home from work down Connecticut Avenue. His hot Hart flame lit, he introduced himself and asked her if she would pose for his rendition of the Creation, an array of idealized young men and women rising nude from out of the chaotic swirl of Creation's dawn. She posed. They married. Great artists and the models they fell in love with already accounted for the most romantic part of art history. But probably no model in all that lengthy, not to say lubricious, lore was ever so stunningly beautiful as Lindy Lain Hart. Her face and figure were to recur in his work throughout his career.

The hot-blooded boy's passion, as Hart developed his vision of the Creation, could not be consummated by Woman alone. He fell in love with God. For Hart, the process began with his at first purely pragmatic research into the biblical story of the Creation in the Book of Genesis. He had been baptized in the Presbyterian Church, and he was working for the Episcopal Church at the Washington National Cathedral. But by the 1970s, neither of these proper, old-line, in-town Protestant faiths offered the strong wine a boy who was in love with God was looking for. He became a Roman Catholic and began to regard his talent as a charisma, a gift from God. He dedicated his work to the idealization of the possibilities God offered man.

From his conception of *Ex Nihilo,* as he called the centerpiece of his huge Creation design (literally, "out of nothing"; figuratively, out of the chaos that preceded Creation), to the first small-scale clay model, through to the final carving of the stone—all this took eleven years.

In 1982, *Ex Nihilo* was unveiled in a dedication ceremony. The next day, Hart scanned the newspapers for reviews . . . *The Washington Post* . . . *The New York Times* . . . nothing . . . nothing the next day, either . . . nor the next week nor the week after that. The one mention of any sort was an obiter dictum in the *Post's* Style (read: Women's) section indicating that the west façade of the cathedral now had some new but earnestly traditional (read: old-fashioned) decoration. So Hart started monitoring the art magazines. Months went by . . . nothing. It reached the point that he began yearning for a single paragraph by an art critic who would say how much he loathed *Ex Nihilo* . . . anything, anything at all . . . to prove there was someone out there in the art world who in some way, however slightly or rudely, cared.

The truth was, no one did, not in the least. *Ex Nihilo* never got *ex nihilo* simply because art worldlings refused to see it.

Hart had become so absorbed in his "triumph" that he had next to no comprehension of the American art world as it existed in the 1980s. In fact, the art world was strictly the New York art world, and it was scarcely a world, if world was meant to connote a great many people. In the one sociological study of the subject, *The Painted Word*, the author estimated the entire art "world" consisted of some three thousand curators, dealers, collectors, scholars, critics, and artists in New York. Art critics, even in the most remote outbacks of the heartland, were perfectly content to be obedient couriers of the word as received from New York. And the word was that School of Renaissance sculpture like Hart's was nonart. Art worldlings just couldn't see it.

The art magazines opened Hart's eyes until they were bleary with bafflement. Classical statues were "pictures in the air." They used a devious means—skill—to fool the eye into believing that bronze or stone had turned into human flesh. Therefore, they were artificial, false, meretricious. By 1982, no ambitious artist was going to display skill, even if he had it. The great sculptors of the time did things like have unionized elves put arrangements of rocks or bricks flat on the ground, objects they, the artists, hadn't laid a finger on (Carl Andre), or prop up slabs of Cor-Ten steel straight from the foundry, edgewise (Richard Serra); or they took G.E. fluorescent light tubes straight out of the box from the hardware store and arranged them this way and that (Dan Flavin); or they welded I-beams and scraps of metal together (Anthony

Caro). This expressed the material's true nature, its "gravity" (no stone pictures floating in the air), its "objectness."

This was greatness in sculpture. As Tom Stoppard put it in his play *Artist Descending a Staircase*, "Imagination without skill gives us contemporary art."

Hart lurched from bafflement to shock, then to outrage. He would force the art world to see what great sculpture looked like.

By 1982, he was already involved in another competition for a huge piece of public sculpture in Washington. A group of Vietnam veterans had just obtained congressional approval for a memorial that would pay long-delayed tribute to those who had fought in Vietnam with honor and courage in a lost and highly unpopular cause. They had chosen a jury of architects and art worldlings to make a blind selection in an open competition; that is, anyone could enter, and no one could put his name on his entry. Every proposal had to include something—a wall, a plinth, a column—on which a hired engraver could inscribe the names of all 57,000-plus members of the American military who had died in Vietnam. Nine of the top ten choices were abstract designs that could be executed without resorting to that devious and accursed bit of trickery: skill. Only the number-three choice was representational. Up on one end of a semicircular wall bearing the 57,000 names was an infantryman on his knees beside a fallen comrade, looking about for help. At the other end, a third infantryman had begun to run along the top of the wall toward them. The sculptor was Frederick Hart.

The winning entry was by a young Yale undergraduate architectural student named Maya Lin. Her proposal was a V-shaped wall, period, a wall of polished black granite inscribed only with the names; no mention of honor, courage, or gratitude; not even a flag. Absolutely skill-proof, it was.

Many veterans were furious. They regarded her wall as a gigantic pitiless tombstone that said, "Your so-called service was an absolutely pointless disaster." They made so much noise that a compromise was struck. An American flag and statue would be added to the site. Hart was chosen to do the statue. He came up with a group of three soldiers, realistic down to the aglets of their boot strings, who appear to have just emerged from the jungle into a clearing, where they are startled to see Maya Lin's V-shaped black wall bearing the names of their dead comrades.

Naturally enough, Maya Lin was miffed at the intrusion, and so a make-peace get-together was arranged in Plainview, New York, where the foundry had just completed casting the soldiers. Doing her best to play the part, Maya Lin asked Hart—as Hart recounted it—if the young men used as models for the three soldiers had complained of any pain when the plaster casts were removed from their faces and arms. Hart couldn't imagine what she was talking about. Then it dawned on him. She assumed that he had followed the lead of the ingenious art worldling George Segal, who had contrived a way of sculpturing the human figure without any skill whatsoever: by covering the model's body in wet plaster and removing it when it began to harden. No artist of her generation (she was twenty-one) could even conceive of a sculptor starting out solely with a picture in his head, a stylus, a brick of moist clay and some armature wire. No artist of her generation could even speculate about . . . skill.

President Ronald Reagan presided at a dedication ceremony unveiling Hart's *Three Soldiers* on Veterans Day, 1984. The next day Hart looked for the art reviews . . . in *The Washington Post* . . . *The New York Times* . . . and, as time went by, in the magazines. And once more, nothing . . . not even the inside-out tribute known as savaging. *Three Soldiers* received only so-called civic reviews, the sort of news or feature items or picture captions that say, in effect, "This thing is big, it's outdoors, and you may see it on the way to work, and so we should probably tell you what it is." Civic reviews of outdoor representational sculpture often don't even mention the name of the sculptor. Why mention the artist, since it's nonart by definition?

Hart was by no mention alone. In 1980, a sculptor named Eric Parks completed a statue of Elvis Presley for downtown Memphis. It was unveiled before a crowd of thousands of sobbing women; it became, and remains, a tremendous tourist attraction; civic reviews only. And who remembers the name Eric Parks? In 1985, a sculptor named Raymond J. Kaskey completed the second-biggest copper sculpture in America—the Statue of Liberty is the biggest—an immense Classical figure of a goddess in a toga with her right hand outstretched toward the multitudes. *Portlandia*, she was called. Tens of thousands of citizens of Portland, Oregon, turned out on a Sunday to see her arrive on a barge on the Willamette River and get towed downtown. Parents lifted their children so they could touch her fingertips as she was hoisted up to her place atop the porte cochere of the new Portland Public Services Building; civic reviews only. In 1992, Audrey Flack completed *Civitas*, four Classical goddesses, one for each corner of a highway intersection just outside a moribund mill town, Rock Hill, South Carolina. It has been a major tourist attraction ever since; cars come from all directions to see the goddesses lit up at night; a nearby fallow cotton field claiming to be an "industrial park" suddenly a sellout; Rock Hill comes alive; civic reviews only.

Over the last fifteen years of his life Hart did something that, in art-world terms, was even more infra dig than *Ex Nihilo* and *Three Soldiers*: he became America's most popular living sculptor. He developed a technique for casting sculpture in acrylic resin. The result resembled Lalique glass. Many of his smaller pieces were nudes, using Lindy as a model, so lyrical and sensual that Hart's Classicism began to take on the contours of Art Nouveau. The gross sales of his acrylic castings had gone well over $100 million. None was ever reviewed.

Art worldlings regarded popularity as skill's live-in slut. Popularity meant shallowness. Rejection by the public meant depth. And truly hostile rejection very likely meant greatness. Richard Serra's *Titled Arc*, a leaning wall of rusting steel smack in the middle of Federal Plaza in New York, was so loathed by the building's employees that 1,300 of them, including many federal judges, signed a petition for its removal. They were angry and determined, and eventually the wall was cut apart and hauled away. Serra thereby achieved an eminence of immaculate purity: his work involved absolutely no skill and was despised by everyone outside the art world who saw it. Today many art worldlings regard him as America's greatest sculptor.

In 1987, Hart moved seventy-five miles northwest of Washington to a 135-acre estate in the Virginia horse country and built a Greek Revival mansion featuring double-decked porches with twelve columns each; bought horses for himself, Lindy, and their two sons, Lain and Alexander; stocked the place with tweeds, twills, tack, and bench-made boots; grew a beard like the King of Diamonds'; and rode to the hounds—all the while turning out new work at a prolific rate.

In his last years he began to summon to his estate a cadre of like-minded souls, a handful of artists, poets, and philosophers, a dedicated little derrière-garde (to borrow a term from the composer Stefania de Kenessey), to gird for the battle to take art back from the Modernists. They called themselves the Centerists.

It wasn't going to be easy to get a new generation of artists to plunge into the fray yodeling, "Onward! To the Center!" Nevertheless, Hart persevered. Since his death certain . . . signs . . . have begun, as a sixties song once put it, blowing in the wind: the suddenly serious consideration, by the art world itself, of Norman Rockwell as a Classical artist dealing in American mythology . . . the "edgy buzz," to use two nineties words, over a sellout show at the Hirschl & Adler Gallery of six young representational painters known as the "Paint Group," five of them graduates of America's only Classical, derrière-garde art school, the New York Academy of Art . . . the tendency of a generation of serious young collectors, flush with new Wall Street money, to discard the tastes of their elders and to collect "pleasant" and often figurative art instead of the abstract, distorted, or "wounded" art of the Modern tradition . . . the soaring interest of their elders in the work of the once-ridiculed French "academic" artists Bougereau, Meissonier, and Gérôme and the French "fashion painter" Tissot. The art historian Gregory Hedberg, Hirschl & Adler's director for European art, says that with metronomic regularity the dawn of each new century has seen a collapse of one reigning taste and the establishment of another. In the early 1600s the Mannerist giants (for example, El Greco) came down off fashionable walls and the Baroque became all the rage; in the early 1700s, the Baroque giants (Rembrandt) came down and the Rococo went up; in the early 1800s the Rococo giants (Watteau) came down and the Neoclassicists went up; and in the early twentieth century, the modern movement turned the Neoclassical academic giants Bougereau, Meissonier, and Gérôme into joke figures in less than twenty-five years.

And at the dawn of the twenty-first? In the summer of 1985 the author of *The Painted Word* gave a lecture at the Parrish Museum in Southampton, New York, entitled "Picasso: The Bougereau of the Year 2020." Should such turn out to be the case, Frederick Hart will not have been the first major artist to have died ten minutes before history absolved him and proved him right.

The Great Relearning

In 1968, in San Francisco, I came across a curious footnote to the hippie movement. At the Haight-Ashbury Free Clinic there were doctors who were treating diseases no living doctor had ever encountered before, diseases that had disappeared so long ago they had never even picked up Latin names, diseases such as the mange, the grunge, the itch, the twitch, the thrush, the scroff, the rot. And how was it that they had now returned? It had to do with the fact that thousands of young men and women had migrated to San Francisco to live communally in what I think history will record as one of the most extraordinary religious fevers of all time.

The hippies sought nothing less than to sweep aside all codes and restraints of the past and start out from zero. At one point the novelist Ken Kesey, leader of a commune called the Merry Pranksters, organized a pilgrimage to Stonehenge with the idea of returning to Anglo-Saxon civilization's point zero, which he figured was Stonehenge, and heading out all over again to do it better. Among the codes and restraints that people in the communes swept aside—quite purposely—were those that said you shouldn't use other people's toothbrushes or sleep on other people's mattresses without changing the sheets or, as was more likely, without using any sheets at all, or that you and five other people shouldn't drink from the same bottle of Shasta or take tokes from the same cigarette. And now, in 1968, they were relearning . . . the laws of hygiene . . . by getting the mange, the grunge, the itch, the twitch, the thrush, the scroff, the rot.

This process, namely the relearning—following a Promethean and unprecedented start from zero—seems to me to be the *leitmotif* of the twenty-first century in America.

"Start from zero" was the slogan of the Bauhaus School. The story of how the Bauhaus, a tiny artists' movement in Germany in the 1920s, swept aside the architectural styles of the past and created the glass-box face of the modern American city during the twentieth century is a familiar one, and I won't retell it. But I should mention the soaring spiritual exuberance with which the movement began, the passionate conviction of the Bauhaus's leader, Walter Gropius, that by starting from zero in architecture and design man could free himself from the dead hand of the past. By the late 1970s, however, architects themselves were beginning to complain of the dead hand of the Bauhaus: the flat roofs, which leaked from rain and collapsed from snow; the tiny bare beige office cubicles, which made workers feel like component parts; the glass walls, which let in too much heat, too much cold, too much glare, and no air at all. The relearning is now under way in earnest. The architects are busy rummaging about in what the artist Richard Merkin calls the Big Closet. Inside the Big Closet, in promiscuous heaps, are the abandoned styles of the past. The current favorite rediscoveries: Classical, Georgian, Secession, and Moderne (Art Deco). Relearning on the wing, the architects are off on a binge of eclecticism comparable to the Victorian period's 125 years ago.

In politics the twentieth century's great start from zero was one-party socialism, also known as Communism or Marxism-Leninism. Given that system's bad reputation in the West today, it is instructive to read John Reed's *Ten Days That Shook the World*—before turning to Aleksandr Solzhenitsyn's *Gulag Archipelago*. The old strike-hall poster of a Promethean worker in a blue shirt breaking his chains across his mighty chest was in truth the vision of ultimate human freedom the movement believed in at the outset. For intellectuals in the West the painful dawn began with the publication of *The Gulag Archipelago* in 1973. (See above, pp. 101–2.) Solzhenitsyn insisted that the villain behind the Soviet concentration-camp network was not Stalin or Lenin (who invented the term "concentration camp") or even Marxism. It was instead the Soviets' peculiarly twentieth-century notion that they could sweep aside not only the old social order but also its religious ethic, which had been millennia in the making ("common decency," Orwell called it) and reinvent morality . . . here . . . now . . . "at the point of a gun," in the famous phrase of the Maoists. Well before the sudden breaching of the Berlin Wall on November 9, 1989, the relearning had reached the point where even ruling circles in the Soviet Union and China had begun to wonder how best to convert Communism into something other than, in Bernard Henri-Levy's memorable phrase, "barbarism with a human face."

The great American contribution to the twentieth century's start from zero was in the area of manners and mores, especially in what was rather primly called "the sexual revolution." In every hamlet, even in the erstwhile Bible Belt, may be found the village brothel, no longer hidden in a house of blue lights or red lights or behind a green door but openly advertised by the side of the road with a thousand-watt backlit plastic sign: TOTALLY ALL-NUDE GIRL SAUNA MASSAGE AND MARATHON ENCOUNTER SESSIONS INSIDE. Up until 1985 pornographic movie theaters were as ubiquitous as the 7-Eleven, including outdoor drive-ins with screens six, seven, eight stories high, the better to beam all the moistened folds and glistening nodes and stiffened giblets to a panting American countryside. In 1985 the pornographic theater began to be replaced by the pornographic videocassette, which could be brought into any home. Up on the shelf in the den, next to the *World Book Encyclopedia* and the Modern Library Classics, one now finds the cassettes: *Sally's Alley*; *Young and Hung*; *Yo! Rambette!*; *Latin Teacher: She Sucks, She Has Sucked, She Will Have Sucked*. In the fall of 1987, a twenty-five-year-old Long Island church secretary named Jessica Hahn provoked a tittering flurry in the tabloid press when the news broke that she had posed nude for *Playboy* magazine. Her punishment? A triumphal tour of the nation's television talk and variety shows. As far as I was concerned, the high point came when a ten-year-old girl, a student at a private school, wearing a buttercup blouse, a cardigan sweater, and her school uniform skirt, approached her outside a television studio with a stack of *Playboy* magazines featuring the church secretary with breasts bare and thighs ajar and asked her to autograph them. With the school's blessing, she intended to take the signed copies back to the campus and hold a public auction. The proceeds would go to the poor.

But in the sexual revolution, too, a painful dawn broke in the 1980s, and the relearning, in the form of prophylaxis, began. All may be summed up in a single term requiring no amplification: AIDS.

The Great Relearning—if anything so prosaic as remedial education can be called great—should be thought of not so much as the end point of the twentieth century as the theme of the twenty-first. There is no law of history that says a new century must start ten or twenty years beforehand, but two times in a row it has worked out that way. The nineteenth century began with the American and French Revolutions of the late eighteenth. The twentieth century began with the formulation of Marxism, Freudianism, and Modernism in the late nineteenth. And the twenty-first began with the Great Relearning—in the form of the destruction of the Berlin Wall in a single day, dramatizing the utter failure of the most momentous start-from-zero of all.

The twenty-first century, I predict, will confound the twentieth-century notion of the Future as something exciting, novel, unexpected, or radiant; as Progress, to use an old word. It is already clear that the large cities, thanks to the Relearning, will not even look new. Quite the opposite: the cities of the year 2000 are already beginning to look more like the cities of 1900 than the cities of 1980. From the South Bronx in New York to Southeast in Atlanta, no longer is public housing ("the projects") built to look like commercial towers. The new look: the twee ground-hugging suburban garden villas of London's Hampstead Heath. The twenty-first century will have a retrograde look and a retrograde mental atmosphere. People of our craven new world, snug in their Neo-Georgian apartment complexes, will gaze back with awe upon the century just ended. They will regard the twentieth as the century in which wars became so enormous they were known as World Wars, the century in which technology leapt forward so rapidly man developed the capacity to destroy the planet itself—but also the capacity to escape to the stars on spaceships if it blew—and to jigger with his own genes. But above all, they will look back upon the twentieth as the century in which their forebears had the amazing confidence, the Promethean brass, to defy the gods and try to push man's power and freedom to limitless, godlike extremes. They will look back in awe . . . without the slightest temptation to emulate the daring of those who swept aside all rules and tried to start from zero. Instead, they will sink ever deeper into their Neo-Louis bergères, idly twirling information about on the Internet, killing time like Victorian matrons doing their crocheting, knitting, tatting, needlepoint, and quilting, content to live in what will be known as the Somnolent Century or the Twentieth Century's Hangover.

My Three Stooges

I can tell you, taking eleven years to write one book is a killer financially, a blow to the base of the skull mentally and physically, hell for your family, a slovenly imposition upon all concerned—in short, an inexcusable performance verging on shameful. Nevertheless, that was how long it took me to write one book, a novel called *A Man in Full*. Eleven years. My children grew up thinking that was all I did: write, and never finish, a book called *A Man in Full*.

Why did it take me so long? Not having access to Dr. Freud's emergency night-line number, I won't try to get into matters I don't understand. I will only mention one thing I *know* cost me years. I committed the sin of hubris. I was going to cram the *world* into that novel, *all* of it.

Off I went to Japan on the most expensive trip of my life, because this book was going to embrace the entire globe. I returned with only two bits of information that I think might add to my fellow Americans' knowledge of the Far East. First, living in a house with shoji screens for walls is even more beautiful than looking at one in a coffee-table book, but you can hear everything. *Everything.* Second, never try to treat two Japanese businessmen to three hours of whiskey and small talk in a Tokyo hostess bar, the updated version of the geisha house, with only $900 in your pocket. When the check comes, you will be, by American standards, horribly embarrassed and, by Japanese standards, terminally humiliated. *Terminally.*

This book was also going to tell you everything you could possibly want to know about the American art world, from the still-booming (it was 1988 when I started out) art market at the top to the life of all the wretched, squirming, wriggling, desperate unknown artists at the bottom. I spent months—*months!*—in the lower depths. It seems that all the art schools, from the Rhode Island School of Design on the East Coast to the California Institute of the Arts on the West Coast, tell their students, quite accurately, that first they must catch on with a gallery in New York. After that, they can go be artists anywhere they want; but unless they first get their tickets punched in New York, their careers will go nowhere. So they come pouring into New York's nether reaches literally by the tens of thousands, succeeding mainly in driving up each other's rents in filthy, airless, treeless, grassless, rotting old sweatshop districts with names like SoHo, NoHo, Dumbo, TriBeCa, and Wevar, the only slums in the world inhabited chiefly by young white people with masters of fine arts degrees. Interesting . . . and completely irrelevant to the story of *A Man in Full.*

The book was also going to go behind the TV screen and lay bare the world of television news; and in due course I developed a plot twist in which a network magazine show would undertake an elaborate sting operation in order to trap three soldiers at Fort Bragg, North Carolina, who are suspects in a murder case. So now I spent another eternity busying myself with network-news practices in New York and Army life at Fort Bragg and on the gaudy strip outside it, Bragg Boulevard. Eventually I did get something out of all this effort, a novella called *Ambush at Fort Bragg* that may be found elsewhere in these pages (175–245). But what did it have to do with *A Man in Full*, whose action takes place in Georgia and California? Nothing.

God knows it took me long enough to do the reporting on matters that *did* turn out to bear directly upon *A Man in Full*: Southern plantation life today, commercial real estate development, banking and bankruptcy, the modern working class, prison life, Asian immigrants, black professional and political life in Atlanta, Atlanta's social structure, manners, and mores, plus those of the 7-Eleven Land east of Oakland, California. I went to see the Santa Rita jail in Alameda County, California; duet apartments in Pittsburg, California; Sikhs and Eritreans in Oakland; and Vietnamese in Oakland and in Chamblee, Georgia, which is an old, erstwhile-rural town just east of Atlanta now swollen with Asian and Mexican immigrants. My Vietnamese did all right, but my Sikhs made it into only four paragraphs in the entire book; my Eritreans, only one.

I emphasize these reporting stints for a reason beyond trying to explain why the novel took me so long. In 1973, while I was still exclusively a writer of nonfiction, fourteen years before I published my first novel, I wrote an essay on what was known back then as "the New Journalism." In it, I said that the American novel was in bad shape, languishing from an otherworldly preciousness, but that there was "a tremendous future for a sort of novel that will be called the journalistic novel or perhaps documentary novel," a novel "of intense social realism based upon the same painstaking reporting that goes into the New Journalism."

In 1987 I published my first novel, *The Bonfire of the Vanities*, with the hope of proving my point. Did I? Only others can answer that question. All I can say is that I was sufficiently emboldened by the novel's reception to write an essay for *Harper's* entitled "Stalking the Billion-footed Beast." I argued that by now the American novel had deteriorated into a "weak, pale, tabescent" condition so grave, its very survival depended on somehow sending "a battalion, a brigade, of Zolas"—I had already identified Zola as the giant of the journalistic or documentary novel—"out into this wild, bizarre, unpredictable, Hog-stomping Baroque country of ours to reclaim it as a literary property." Since that was precisely what I had done in "documenting" (Zola's term) and then writing *The Bonfire of the Vanities*, I shouldn't have been surprised when some people found my words self-serving. Nevertheless, that was what I believed, and, in any case, I was already deep into the reporting for what I hoped would be another novel of Zolaesque realism, *A Man in Full*.

As the years went by—two, four, five, eight, ten, and, finally, eleven—the suspense intensified. Not, I hasten to add, in the world outside, which seems to be able to successfully contain its excitement, if any, in such matters, but in me; the suspense down in my solar plexus, I assure you, was terrific. The years had been mounting, and given my own preaching about realism or "naturalism" (another of Zola's terms), so had the stakes. My publishers, Farrar, Straus and Giroux, upped them a bit more by announcing a first printing of 1.2 million for my new book when it finally came out in November 1998.

My first inkling of how *A Man in Full* might be received by critics came when *Vanity Fair* assigned the writer David Kamp to do a story on The Man Who Spent Eleven Years Writing One Book and got hold of a Xeroxed copy of most of the 2,300-page manuscript. Kamp's lead went:

"He strides through the vestibule, a lean, courtly figure resplendent in—

"*No, no no!* No scene setting! To the chase: is the book any good?

"Relax, it is. The 11-year wait since *The Bonfire of the Vanities* was worrisome, but the new one, which is called *A Man in Full*, works quickly to allay fears that Tom Wolfe had only one decent novel in him . . . Lovely to have you back, sir."

So I relaxed, for the first time in weeks. What ensued was all that a man who had just spent eleven years writing one book could dare hope for.

Before I continue with this story—and it *is* a story with a plot—and the plot soon thickens—please let me assure you of one thing: I realize as clearly as anyone else how unseemly it is for a writer to be anything but insouciant about book reviews, publicity, and sales figures. Rimbaud set the bar for insouciance about as high as it is ever likely to go when, in his early thirties, finding himself hailed by critics as the most important poet in France, he replied, "*Merde pour la poésie.*" But Arnold Bennett, the British novelist, author of a wildly successful book, *The Old Wives' Tale* (1908), wasn't half bad, either, when he said, "I don't read my reviews, I measure them." So please believe me when I say I am only going into these crass matters—reviews, publicity, sales—in the case of *A Man in Full* because they are essential to understanding our story.

First, the reviews. Every publication that people immediately check to gauge a new book's success or failure was generous with praise, more generous, to tell the truth, than I could have ever hoped, starting with gauge number one, the all-important *New York Times Book Review*. Over the years I've come off well in the *Times* now and then, and I've taken my drubbings, but this round, I must say, went my way. The reviewer, Michael Lewis, wrote: "The novel contains passages as powerful and as beautiful as anything written—not merely by a contemporary American novelist but by *any* American novelist"; and he added: "The book is as funny as anything Wolfe has ever written; at the same time it is also deeply, strangely affecting." In *The Wall Street Journal* Andrew Ferguson called it "a masterpiece" and "a greater achievement than 'Bonfire': richer, deeper, more touching and more humane." In *Newsweek* Malcolm Jones said: "Right now, no writer—reporter or novelist—is getting it [the Zeitgeist] on paper better than Tom Wolfe." In the daily *New York Times*, Michiko Kakutani didn't care for the book's ending, but in light of what she had to say about the rest of *A Man in Full*, I certainly couldn't complain. The *pièce de résistance*, however, was a long review and profile by the highly respected Paul Gray in *Time*, not to mention my picture, which was on the magazine's cover. "No summary of *A Man in Full*," wrote Gray, "can do justice to the novel's ethical nuances and hell-bent pacing, its social sweep and intricate interweaving of private and public responsibilities, its electric sense of conveying current events and its knowing portraits of people actually doing their jobs. Who, besides Wolfe, would have thought that banking and real estate transactions could be the stuff of gripping fiction?"

On second thought, I have to mention that cover of *Time*, after all. Honestly, I do blush easily, and I pledge you my word that I go into the following only because it is essential to understanding what other people were about to do. In any field in the United States, the news that So-and-so "made the cover of *Time*" has always had a unique ring to it; and over the preceding two decades the picture of a novelist on the cover of *Time* had become a rarity. But there I was, not only on the cover, but on the cover wearing a white double-breasted suit and vest and a white homburg and holding a pair of white kid gloves in one hand and a white walking stick in the other. The headline said in big letters: TOM WOLFE WRITES AGAIN. Beneath, in smaller letters, it said: "The novelist with the white stuff is back with *A Man in Full*. More than a million copies, before anyone has read a word!" Not only that, for the first time in its history *Time* printed its logo, the famous TIME, in white against a white background, with only a gray undershading to let you know the four letters were even there. The entire cover, graphics and all, became an overture to "the novelist with the white stuff." I didn't realize it at that moment, but this was premonition music, as they say in cinema circles, for what was about to occur.

And sales? This is the most embarrassing subject of all for me to be talking about, and I do apologize, but I have no choice; as we are about to see, *others* insisted on bringing it up. Sales of *A Man in Full* skyrocketed from the moment it reached the stores. *The Wall Street Journal* ran a feature on the book's depiction of the city of Atlanta with the headline "Tom Wolfe Burns Down Atlanta," and former Atlanta mayor Sam Massell announced he was withdrawing an invitation to me to speak before a business group, the Buckhead Coalition. So I didn't know what to expect when I reached Atlanta on my book tour the following week. They were waiting for me—in lines at the bookstores. My first night in town, at the Borders bookstore in Buckhead, I signed books for 2,300 people in four hours. Borders is a vast place, but the line spilled out onto the sidewalk on Lenox Road. The book sold so rapidly, it didn't have to climb its way up the *New York Times* bestseller list. It jumped on at number one and stayed at number one for ten weeks, throughout the Christmas season and well beyond. It sold in hardcover like a paperback bestseller, at a rate three to four times that of the usual number-one bestselling hardcover. Not only did the huge first printing sell out, but so did seven subsequent editions of 25,000 each.

It's uncomfortable being compelled to sum things up so baldly, but here, in as few words as possible, is what we have: a critically acclaimed novel selling at an astonishing clip in a blaze of publicity. The scene is now set for the extraordinary thing that happened next. I have searched, and I can come up with nothing else like it in all the annals of American literature. Three big-name American novelists, heavy with age and literary prestige—John Updike, Norman Mailer, and John Irving—rose up to denounce *A Man in Full*. Three famous old novelists rousing themselves from their niches in literary history to declare a particular new novel anathema—if anything even remotely comparable had ever occurred before, it had certainly escaped my attention.

John Updike, who was sixty-six, went on for four pages in *The New Yorker* before concluding with considerable solemnity that *A Man in Full* was not to be taken as literature but as "entertainment," not even—he continued, as if to make sure his readers understood the crucial distinction between a pleasant experience and the higher things—not even "literature in a modest aspirant form." Furthermore, its author was not a novelist but a "journalist." Henry James, said Updike, has taught us that literature must be "exquisite," and this journalist, Wolfe, had "failed to be exquisite." Norman Mailer, who was seventy-five, went on for six pages in *The New York Review of Books*—six pages in a newspaper-size journal dense with print—to reach the verdict that *A Man in Full* was not to be taken as literature but as a "Mega-bestseller." Furthermore, its author was not a novelist but a "journalist" who "no longer belongs to us (if indeed he ever did!)" but has moved away and now "lives in the King Kong Kingdom of the Mega-bestsellers."

"*Us?*" I remember saying to myself. "Did he say *us*? Who is *us*?"

Frankly, I was amazed, not that the two of them didn't approve, but that at this stage of their lives they had taken the *time*. "My God, those two old piles of bones!" I said to the reporters who began clamoring for interviews. "They're *my* age!"

I was sixty-eight. I *knew* how it must have drained them. How could they have spent those untold hours, ground out those thousands and *thousands* of words—the two old codgers had gone on for pages—*pages!*—to review a novel? How could our two senior citizens have found the energy in those exhausted carcasses of theirs? In interviews Updike was already complaining about his aging bladder. Mailer, I noticed, was appearing in newspaper photographs supporting himself with two canes, one for each rusted-out hip.

The way John Irving, who was fifty-seven, joined his fellow oldsters in this obsession with *A Man in Full* did not involve such debilitating toil, but his emotional toll may have been even greater. Irving threw a temper tantrum on television.

He was in Toronto appearing on the show *Hot Type*, plugging a book about how he had retreaded his novel *The Cider House Rules* for the movies, when *Hot Type*'s adept and provocative young host, Evan Solomon, brought up *A Man in Full*, knowing full well the rise it had gotten out of Updike and Mailer. I found the next five minutes riveting when I got a glimpse later on videotape. Irving's face turned red. His sexagenarian jowls shuddered. He began bleeping. It was all the show's technicians could do to hit the bleep button fast enough. "Wolfe's problem is, he can't bleeping *write*! He's not a *writer*! Just crack one of his bleeping books! Try to read one bleeping sentence! You'll gag before you can finish it! He doesn't even write literature—he writes . . . *yak*! He doesn't write *novels*—he writes journalistic hyperbole! You couldn't teach that bleeping bleep to bleeping freshmen in a bleeping freshman English class!"—and on and on in that mode. It was spellbinding. I don't pretend to be a lip reader, but it took no particular expertise to decode bleepos that began with such bitterly lower-lip-bitten *f*s. Evan Solomon kept covering his face with his hand and smiling at the same time, as if to say, "How can the old coot make such a spectacle of himself—but, wow, it's wonderful television!"

Evan liked it so much, in fact, he called and asked me if I would like to appear on *Hot Type* and respond. I told him if he would be so kind as to come to New York for the taping, I'd be delighted. So he did, and the tape rolled, and he asked me:

"One of the foremost novelists in the United States, John Irving, says you simply can't write. You're not a writer. Does that make you feel bad?"

"Bad?" I heard myself saying. "Why should I feel *bad*? Now I've got all three."

All three?

"Larry, Curly, and Moe. Updike, Mailer, and Irving. My three stooges."

Stooges?

Seemed like the right word to me. A stooge is literally a straight man who feeds lines to the lead actor in a play. My three stooges were so upset by *A Man in Full,* they were feeding me lines I couldn't have dreamed up if they had asked me to write the script for them.

"Are you saying they're envious of your success? Is that all it is?"

By no means. Granted, the allergens for jealousy were present. Both Updike and Mailer had books out at the same time as *A Man in Full,* and theirs had sunk without a bubble. With Irving there was the Dickens factor. "Irving is a great admirer of Dickens," I told Evan. "I think he would like to be compared to Dickens. But what writer does he see now, in the last year, constantly compared to Dickens? Not John Irving, but Tom Wolfe. It must gnaw at him terribly." And who was it who had "made the cover of *Time*"? Knowing my three stooges, that all by itself would have been enough to send them ballistic. "It must gall them a bit that everyone—even them—is talking about me, and nobody is talking about them." But no, I didn't think it was jealousy in the simple sense of displeasure at a rival's success.

Did I think there was any personal animosity at work here, any old scores that hadn't been settled?

Oh, people had suggested that, but I didn't think so. Years ago, when I was a reporter for the New York *Herald Tribune,* back before I had ever written a book, I had reviewed a novel of Mailer's, *An American Dream*, and called it a clumsy paint-by-the-numbers knockoff of Dostoevsky's *Crime and Punishment*. (Which it was, or else Jung's concept of synchronicity is truer than he ever knew.) About that same time, I had made fun of Updike in a couple of newspaper articles. (One, it so happens, is available on pages 255–87 of the book before you.) But all that was decades ago. With Irving the screen was an absolute blank. We had no old scores, settled or otherwise.

Then what was it?

Something much more obvious, I told Evan. *A Man in Full* had frightened them. They were shaken. It was as simple as that. *A Man in Full* was an example—an alarmingly visible one—of a possible, indeed, the likely new direction in late-twentieth- and early-twenty-first-century literature: the intensely realistic novel, based upon reporting, that plunges wholeheartedly into the social reality of America today, right now—a revolution in content rather than form—that was about to sweep the arts in America, a revolution that would soon make many prestigious artists, such as our three old novelists, appear effete and irrelevant.

All three had risen up as one to make not merely an accusation but a plea. The plea was that *A Man in Full* be regarded as . . . *out of bounds*. Each cry was the same. Each of our seniors had cried: "*Anathema!*"

Updike had said: Look, we're not dealing with literature here, not even "literature in a modest aspirant form," but, rather, "entertainment." Irving had said: Look, we're not even dealing with a novel here, much less literature, we're dealing with "journalistic hyperbole," with "yak," with bleep. Mailer had said: Look, we're not dealing with any sort of legitimate creature here, but with a bastard, a "Mega-bestseller" whose dissolute creator "no longer belongs to us (if indeed he ever did!)." *Us*. And who was *us*? Why, *us* was we who belong to "the literary world," in Mailer's terminology. *A Man in Full* and its author inhabited another place entirely, "the King Kong Kingdom of the Mega-bestsellers." In other words, Wolfe and his accursed book were . . . *be-*

yond the pale, a *pale* (originally synecdoche for *fence*) being an area of permissible conduct with definite boundaries. That which is beyond the pale does *not count* . . . and *us* members of the literary world do not have to be measured by it.

Shakespeare, Balzac, Dickens, Dostoevsky, Tolstoy, Gogol, Zola, Ibsen, and Shaw, not to mention Mark Twain, all of whom were enormously popular in their own day—Dickens, Dostoevsky, Tolstoy, and Zola published their novels serially in magazines—Ibsen and Shaw *gloried* in their box-office appeal—all would have been highly amused by this attempt to place literature here on this side of the fence and entertainment and popularity over there on the other. How could my three stooges ever have maneuvered themselves into such a ludicrous position? That wasn't hard to explain. You only had to think of the sort of novels they had been writing.

The novel Mailer had on the market at the time *A Man in Full* was published was an autobiography of Jesus—yes, an autobiography of Jesus—called *The Gospel According to the Son*. The book Updike had just published, *Bech at Bay*, consisted of stories about a seventy-something writer named Bech who is irritable about the sagging status of the man of letters in America. Updike's novel before that, like Mailer's autobiography of Jesus, was a fantasy, *Toward the End of Time*, about a small town north of Boston in the year 2020 following a war between the United States and China. Irving's last novel, *A Widow for One Year* (1996), had been about two neurotic writers who seemed unable to get out of a house in Bridgehampton, Long Island. As the pages wore on, I kept waiting for them to kindly make it into town, just once, even though town—I've been there—is only a two-block strip along a two-lane highway. At one point the two of them . . . leave the house! They get in a car! They're driving through a nearby hamlet called Sagaponack, a lovely little Hamptons Rural Chic retreat—I've been there, too—and I'm *begging* them to please stop—park next to the SUVs and German sedans and have a soda at the general store there on Sagg Main—take a look, just one look, at a $125,000 show-circuit hunter pony in the pasture over there at the Topping Riding School—

do something—*anything*—to show that you're connected to the here and now, that you actually exist where the author claims you exist, on Long Island, U.S.A.! But they don't listen . . . they just drift on, encapsulated in their neurasthenia . . . and disappear behind the walls of another timeless, abstract house . . .

So was I saying that John Irving was untalented, just the way he said I was untalented?

"Not at all," I told Evan. "John Irving is a talented writer. Norman Mailer is a talented writer. John Updike is a talented writer. All I'm saying is that they've wasted their careers by not engaging the life around them," by turning their backs on the rich material of an amazing country at a fabulous moment in history. Instead of going out into the world, instead of plunging into the (to me) irresistibly lurid carnival of American life today in the here and now, instead of striding out with a Dionysian yea-saying, as Nietzsche would have put it, into the raw, raucous, lust-soaked rout that throbs with amped-up octophonic tympanum all around them, our old lions had withdrawn, retreated, shielding their eyes against the light, and turned inward to such subject matter as their own little crevice, i.e., "the literary world," or such wholly ghostly stuff as the presumed thoughts of Jesus.

But how could I say that about Mailer? asked Evan. What about *The Executioner's Song*, Mailer's 1979 novel based on the Gary Gilmore case (in which a convicted murderer insisted, to the distress of anti-death-penalty activists, on becoming the first American executed by the state in more than ten years)?

I *wouldn't* say that about *The Executioner's Song*, I told him. "That book should have taught Norman a lesson, but obviously it didn't."

Mailer's career had been floundering for the better part of a decade when one day a remarkable Santa Claus named Lawrence Schiller turned up. With him he had bales of transcripts of interviews he had done with Gary Gilmore, his family, and other people involved in Gilmore's life and internationally publicized death. He had visited Gilmore in jail many times and had witnessed his execution. Schiller was a photographer who had developed into a reporter with an unusual specialty. He amassed material for books on hot topics and then looked for writers to write them in co-ventures. Mailer took Schiller's reportorial gold mine and wrote what turned out to be the only good novel he would ever write after his first, *The Naked and the Dead*, back in 1948. Schiller said later that he interviewed "close to a hundred people over a year-and-a-half period and prepared all that material . . . He [Mailer] never interviewed any of the people or was at any of the events." Why Mailer hadn't drawn the obvious conclusion and headed out into the country himself as a reporter before doing his next novel, or at least signed up with Schiller again, instead of writing the ghostly novels that were to follow, I can't imagine.

For that matter, what on earth prompted John Irving to spend more than four years writing a 633-page novel set in India, *A Son of the Circus*, and publish it (in 1994) with a preface that said: "This isn't a novel about India. I don't know India. I was only there once, for less than a month. When I was there, I was struck by the country's foreignness; it remains obdurately foreign to me"? *I don't know India.* It was true—which only makes it odder. *A Son of the Circus*, all 633 pages of it, is not a novel about India or any other place in this world. It sank without a trace.

Since my interview with Evan Solomon, John Updike has published a new novel, *Gertrude and Claudius*, yet another otherworldly story, this one about what transpired in Hamlet's family prior to the events depicted in Shakespeare's play. It was received congenially, respectfully, collegially by . . . *us* . . . in *the literary world* . . . and then, dismayingly, it dropped off the radar. *Us* was one thing; *they*, the book-reading public, were quite another. *They* lost interest so completely, so rapidly, that *The New York Times* ran a story about it, also mentioning other highly "literary" writers whose current novels, likewise duly praised by *us*, had suffered the same fate. Since the others (Saul Bellow was one) were about the same age as Updike, the *Times* raised the question of whether or not it might be a generational matter, a case of older writers no longer resonating with a younger audience.

But Updike had his own unique analysis: it was the readers' fault.

Their "tastes have coarsened," he said in an interview. "People read less, they're less comfortable with the written word. They're less comfortable with novels. They don't have a backward frame of reference that would enable them to appreciate things like irony and allusions. It's sad." The airport bookstores didn't stock anything one could characterize as literature, he said, and when one got on the airplane, people were reading not literature but the trash sold at the airport bookstores. With a Twilight of the Gods resignation, he told of how it used to be, back before readers became what they are today, i.e., coarse, dumb, and dumber. "When I was a boy, the bestselling books were often the books that were on your piano teacher's shelf . . . Someone like Steinbeck was a bestseller as well as a Nobel Prize–winning author of high intent. You don't feel that now. I don't feel that we have the merger of serious and pop—it's gone, dissolving . . . The kind of readers that would make it worthwhile to print a literary writer are dwindling."

Were my eyes deceiving me? Was this man actually saying that the lack of interest in the "literary" novel in the year 2000 was the *readers*' fault? He, John Updike, was a victim of a new cultural disease, Reader Failure? And he was invoking the name of John Steinbeck, who wrote in a happier time, back when Updike's piano teacher read great writers? How could he risk even *mentioning* Steinbeck—unless he actually does consciously and willfully regard himself as my stooge, a straight man whose role is to feed me such lines?

The crowning triumph of Steinbeck's career was *The Grapes of Wrath*, his novel of the Great Depression of the 1930s, published in 1939. He had already written a bestseller, *Tortilla Flat* (1935), and sold it to the movies, plus the highly praised and reasonably well-selling *In Dubious Battle* (1936), and was completing *Of Mice and Men*, which became an even bigger bestseller in 1937 and subsequently a play and a hit movie, when he accepted an assignment from the *San Francisco News* to write a series of newspaper articles on the Okies, who were pouring into California from the drought-stricken Southwest, seeking work on California's sprawling agribusiness farms. Steinbeck was not interested in the money or the journalism but in amassing material for what he envisioned as a "big book," a novel on a grander scale than the comparatively spare books he had written so far. He bought an old pie truck, as he called it, stocked it with food and blankets, and prepared to do his fieldwork, his documenting: studying the Okies, who were living in squatters' camps and working for wages as low as 12½ cents a day. At the time, the existence of the camps was not public knowledge, much less the appalling conditions in which the Okies lived.

Steinbeck was fascinated by the "organismal" theory of a biologist friend, William Emerson Ritter, who believed that the individual human inevitably lived, without knowing it, as part of a larger social organism, after the manner of the multiunit "superorganisms" known to marine biology, and that the whole was inevitably greater than the sum of its parts. For the same reason, no single organism could be understood without observing and comprehending the entire colony. (Which is to say, Ritter was a half century ahead in what is currently one of the hottest fields in science, "sociobiology.")

So Steinbeck headed out into the farm country in his pie truck and toured the camps day after day, documenting the entire "organismal" complex and looking for the individual "organisms" that would bring the whole alive in story form. It was at a squatters' camp in the San Joaquin Valley that he came across a man, his wife, and their three children living in a lean-to made of willow reeds and flattened tin cans and sleeping under a piece of carpet. The wife had just given birth to a dead child, her second stillbirth in a year. Their degradation gave him the idea for the tragedy of the Joad family. He conceived of the Joads as types, as specimens, as a cluster of people representing the whole experience of the Okies, and yet Ma Joad and her rebellious son Tom come to life in the pages of *The Grapes of Wrath* as two of the most compelling individuals in American fiction. Without departing from the Zolaesque naturalism of his approach, Steinbeck manages by book's end to make Tom the embodiment of the Okies' will not only to live but to fight back. Ma Joad and Tom became the soul, in Ritter's terminology, of the whole that is greater than the sum of its parts. *The Grapes of Wrath* is a textbook American demonstration of Zola's method of writing the novel: leaving the study, going out into the world, documenting society, linking individual psychology to its social context, giving yourself fuel enough for the maximum exercise of your power as a writer—thereby absorbing the reader totally.

And *Steinbeck* is the name Updike invokes to explain the failure of two novels of fantasy and a third set in that crack between the toes of contemporary life, "the literary world"?

I doubt that many people even down in that crack would dispute the proposition that the stature of the American novel has declined steadily since its palmy days, which were before the Second World War. The great period ran from the publication of Theodore Dreiser's *Sister Carrie* in 1900 to Steinbeck's *The Grapes of Wrath* in 1939. This was the age of John Dos Passos, Edith Wharton, Sinclair Lewis, Ellen Glasgow, Sherwood Anderson, Willa Cather, Ernest Hemingway, Scott Fitzgerald, Zora Neale Hurston, Thomas Wolfe, James T. Farrell, Richard Wright, James M. Cain, John O'Hara, and William Faulkner. It was the period in which American fiction not only began to be taken seriously in Europe for the first time but also began to influence European writers. Sartre was so impressed by Dos Passos that he wrote his World War II trilogy, *The Age of Reason*, *The Reprieve*, and *Iron in the Soul*, in unabashed emulation of Dos Passos's great trilogy, *U.S.A.*

What is the vein that runs from Dreiser to Steinbeck? It was Alfred Kazin, writing in 1942 in his critical literary history of the period, *On Native Grounds*, who first isolated "the greatest single fact about our modern American literature—our writers' absorption in every last detail of their American world together with their deep and subtle alienation from it."

Their "absorption in every last detail of their American world" never varied, no matter what their mood. Steinbeck may have felt angry when he wrote *The Grapes of Wrath*, Dreiser may have felt disillusioned when he wrote *Sister Carrie*, Sinclair Lewis seemed to have a Menckenesque sense of the absurdity of the spectacle all around him when he wrote *Main Street*, *Babbitt*, *Elmer Gantry*, and *Arrowsmith*, for which he became the first American to win the Nobel Prize in Literature. But all immersed themselves wholeheartedly in that spectacle, relished "every last detail" of it, and recognized the importance of going beyond the confines of their own personal experience to get novelistic material . . . Dreiser based the plot of *Sister Carrie* on the sexual liaisons of one of his sisters, but his work as a newspaper reporter in Chicago, St. Louis, Pittsburgh, and New York provided the book's rich fabric. Lewis went forth Zola-style (and Steinbeck-style) as a reporter (using 5 x 8 cards) to gather material not only for *Babbitt* and *Elmer Gantry* but also for *Main Street*, which was about the town, Sauk Centre, Minnesota, where he grew up. Like Balzac, Dickens, Zola, and Mark Twain, they mocked, attacked, laid bare the society around them, but always as members of it. They unmasked and shocked the bourgeoisie, but never from the point of view of "artists" coming from a different world. As Kazin put it, "They were participants in a common experience" who "gave the American novel over to the widest possible democracy of subject and theme" and had a "compelling interest in people, Americans, of all varieties."

In his Nobel acceptance speech in Stockholm in 1930, Sinclair Lewis exhorted his fellow American novelists to "give America a literature worthy of her vastness." Can anyone imagine my three stooges expressing any such sentiment? Can anyone imagine them even wondering if America is due anything at all from writers? And what's all this about "vastness" anyway—literature as geography?

Unless they have been keeping it to themselves, my three stooges haven't a clue as to why their "literary world" is in such a decline—or why they themselves have become so insular, effete, and irrelevant. And here we come upon the supreme irony of American literary history so far. In the twentieth century the United States outstripped Europe in every respect save one. In matters "intellectual," as I mentioned on pages 113–30 herein, we remained sweaty little colonials forever trying to keep up with Europe and, above all, with France. In the 1830s Balzac, Stendhal, and Dickens had introduced the novel of intense everyday realism—of *petits faits vrais*, in Stendhal's phrase; of "naturalism," in Zola's—to bring alive in story form the new condition of Europe in the wake of the French and Industrial Revolutions. This became the "modern" approach to art, so much so that in 1863 even Baudelaire, whose influence would eventually be something quite different, went into raptures (in his essay "The Painter of Modern Life") about a painter named Constantine Guys who delighted in leaving the studio, observing the promiscuous hurly-burly of the Paris streets, the sporting fields, the wartime battlefronts, recording with meticulous care the clothing, the uniforms, the coaches, the carriages, horses, weapons, hairdos, expressions, and gestures of the moment. No longer was the timeless, classical, high-minded approach to art sufficient unto itself, said Baudelaire. To capture the beauty of modern life the artist had to know how to combine the sublime with the intensely real, with Stendhal's *petits faits vrais* of the here and now.

This approach elevated literature to a plateau from which it is impossible to back down without sacrificing the medium's full power—and losing much of its audience. But intellectual fashion was another matter. As Europe's reigning intellectual fashion, naturalism lasted barely fifty years. The intellectual historian Arnold Hauser recounts how in 1891 a French journalist, Jules Huret, asked sixty-four prominent French writers whether or not they thought naturalism remained a vital literary tradition and, if not, what would take its place. Overwhelmingly they characterized naturalism as dead, finished, and expressed enthusiasm for the new Symbolist poetry, the work of Mallarmé, Rimbaud, Verlaine, and, above all, Symbolism's progenitor, Constantine Guys's old fan, Baudelaire. It is at this point that poetry, if it is to be considered serious, becomes difficult. The serious poet begins to make his work hard to understand in order to show that he is elevating himself above the rabble, which is now known of course as the bourgeoisie. He is writing for what the French critic Catulle Mendès referred to as "a charming aristocracy," "an elite in this age of democracy." There was something vulgar and common about harping on "meaning." Poetry existed to produce wafts of sensibility, Mallarmé-style. Exquisite wafts; "exquisite" became a very important word. That fashion has never weakened; it has only grown stronger and spread throughout the West. Today all "serious" poets are hard for the reader—any reader—to understand, although some are more "accessible" than others. I love this word "accessible." It is as if serious poets live in caves. Some you can reach in your 4 x 4 off-road SUV. Some you can get only within several hundred yards of by vehicle; the rest of the way it's hand over hand up a hanging vine. Some you can't reach at all; you can only admire them from a great distance. Today Edgar Allan Poe, far from being accepted for publication in any self-respecting university literary quarterly, would be working for Thompson Creative, the company that specializes in radio jingles. It is at this point also that the "literary world" is created, to be inhabited exclusively by *us*, by "literary" writers, as distinct from the writers read by ordinary readers, who, as we already know, are coarse and deaf to the exquisite music of allusion and irony.

What we are looking at here in the France of Mallarmé's time is a *fashion* among self-consciously literary people, which, like a clothing fashion, exists solely to confer some special status upon the wearer. Readers were something else again. When Huret published his survey results in 1891, readers' tastes had not changed in the slightest. Zola remained the most popular writer in France (and probably in the world), and Maupassant was second. In America in the 1890s, writers like Dreiser and Frank Norris were influenced by French naturalism, not because it was French and fashionable, but because it had such power over readers. The only sort of American novelist who was immediately influenced by French aestheticism was an émigré like Henry James. James, like Proust, Joyce, and George Meredith, turned away from this vulgar business of Dickensian characters and melodramatic plots to the point where, as Hauser puts it, his characters "seem to move in a vacuum compared with the world of Stendhal, Balzac, Flaubert, Tolstoy, and Dostoevsky." James didn't even care to vie for the attentions of the coarse herd, which is to say, plain readers. He became the first great sensibility wafter in American literature.

It was not until just after the First World War that there came into being that sweaty colonial, the American "intellectual," who would value a James above a Dreiser, a Dos Passos, or a Sinclair Lewis. It was our colonial intellectuals who finally managed to transplant the "charming" and "aristocratic" French distaste for naturalism into American literary circles in the early 1950s, leading to the supreme and supremely cockeyed piece of irony I mentioned at the outset.

What happened reminds me of Malcolm Muggeridge's marvelous conceit, in another context, of an army that wins a great victory and then, at the very moment of triumph, inexplicably runs up a white flag and surrenders to the enemy. No sooner does the American version of the naturalistic novel emerge triumphant on the world stage than American intellectuals begin pronouncing it dead, finished, exhausted, impossible any longer. A Columbia University English professor, Lionel Trilling, wrote a highly influential essay in 1948 in which he said that the realistic novel was no longer a plausible approach and that the day of the novel of ideas had dawned. It so happened that he had one in his desk drawer, which was duly published and praised, whereupon it sank like a stone to the bottom of a pond and vanished. Nevertheless, the idea caught hold in the universities with a vengeance. Dreiser, Hemingway, Steinbeck, and Faulkner probably didn't have four years of college between them, but from 1950 on, the great majority of novelists came out of university writing programs. Novelists who got going before 1960 still tended toward realism, although even among them the writer who, like Lewis or Steinbeck, headed off as a reporter or documenter into unknown territory had become rare. For the postwar realist the only valid experience was his own.

After 1960 came the era of young writers in the universities educated in literary *isms*, all of which were variants of French aestheticism, products of the notion that the only pure art is art not about life but about art itself. Absurdism, fabulism, minimalism, magic realism—all shared a common attitude. One way or another the novelist winked at the reader, as if to say, "You know and I know that this isn't real. This is something more sublime: the game of art." Occasionally a writer would break off in the middle of a story to identify himself to the reader as an artist sitting alone in a room doing nothing other than demonstrating what an artist he is.

By 1980 the slump in the novel as a form had become noticeable. It was not that strong realistic fiction had completely vanished. Looking back over the past quarter century, I can think of any number of wonderful books: James Webb's *Fields of Fire,* in my opinion the finest of the Vietnam novels; Richard Price's *Clockers*, product of a reporting foray into the underbelly of the drug trade in Union City, New Jersey; Carl Hiaasen's *Strip Tease*, a newspaper reporter's romp through end-of-the-century South Florida; Pat Conroy's *The Great Santini*; Louis Auchincloss's *The Golden Calves*; Terry McMillan's *Waiting to Exhale*; Jimmy Breslin's *Table Money*; William Price Fox's *Ruby Red*; Joseph Wambaugh's *The Choirboys*; Po Bronson's *Bombardiers*. But the young talent that half a century earlier would have been interested in the naturalistic novel was being steered in other directions. New fabulists, minimalists, magic realists, and the like emerged and were duly praised, but they never excited readers the way the naturalists did. The novel itself lost the hold it once had on the imagination of college students and young people generally.

I think it's safe to say that many of them have turned to the movies and pushed the novel off into the margins so far as their interest in art is concerned. The critic Terry Teachout created quite a stir in 1999 when he wrote an article for *The Wall Street Journal* headlined "How We Get That Story" with the subhead: "Quick: Read a novel or watch a movie? The battle is over. Movies have won." He spoke of "far-reaching changes in the once-privileged place of the novel in American culture." "For Americans under the age of 30," he wrote, "film has largely replaced the novel as the dominant mode of artistic expression" when it comes to "serious storytelling." "It might even be that movies have superseded novels not because Americans have grown dumber but because the novel is an obsolete artistic technology." The Nobel-winning novelist Saul Bellow was sufficiently aroused to write an article for *The*

New York Times going over Teachout's piece point by point. He adopted what has become the familiar fallback position of novelists today when they gather at writers' conferences and bring up the subject, as they inevitably do, of how irrelevant the popularity of movies and television makes them feel as storytellers. Well, the argument goes, great novels have always had small, special (read: "charmingly aristocratic") audiences. Bellow cited Hawthorne's *The Scarlet Letter*, Melville's *Moby-Dick*, and, striking his own Twilight of the Gods note, the novels of Proust and Joyce, which "were written in a cultural twilight and were not intended to be read under the blaze and dazzle of popularity." What impressed "the great public" even in the nineteenth century, he argued, was a minor novel like *Uncle Tom's Cabin*. But if *Uncle Tom's Cabin* was a minor accomplishment in a literary sense (an eminently disputable proposition to anyone—Tolstoy, for example, or Edmund Wilson—who has actually read it), our *Götterdämmerungisch* novelists must still face up to the fact that the same "great public" also adored Tolstoy, Balzac, Dickens, Dostoevsky, and Zola.

I felt flattered, up to a point, anyway, when Teachout singled out *The Bonfire of the Vanities* and *A Man in Full* and said that not even novels like these could stem the movies' victorious tide. As I mentioned at the outset, it is *others*—not me—who insist on bringing up my sales figures, and Terry Teachout is one of them. In order to make his point, he felt compelled (by the best of intentions, I am sure) to jigger the figures and imply that *A Man in Full* did not do as well as *The Bonfire of the Vanities* in the marketplace, when in fact it sold almost 50 percent more, placing it rather high up, I haven't been able to avoid noticing (and once more I blush), on the list of bestselling American novels of the twentieth century, along with *The Bonfire of the Vanities*. And yet I don't dispute for a moment his central thesis: "For Americans under the age of 30, film has largely replaced the novel as the dominant mode of artistic expression." Over the past ten months I have made a tour of American universities doing the reporting for a novel I am now writing, and I can tell you that college students, at least, are excited not by new novelists but by new movie directors. But I don't think Teachout understands why.

Today it is the movie directors and producers, not the novelists, who are themselves excited by the lurid carnival of American life at this moment, in the here and now, in all its varieties. It is the movie directors and producers, not the novelists, who can't wait to head out into that raucous rout, like the Dreisers, Lewises, and Steinbecks of the first half of the twentieth century, and see it for themselves. It is the movie directors and producers, not the novelists, who today have the instincts of reporters, the curiosity, the vitality, the *joie de vivre*, the drive, the energy to tackle any subject, head out onto any terrain, no matter how far it may be removed from their own experience—often *because* it is so far removed from their own experience and they can't wait to see it for themselves. As a result, the movie, not the novel, became the great naturalistic storytelling medium of the late twentieth century. Movies can be other things, but they are inherently naturalistic—and I suggest that this is precisely what their audiences adore most about them: their intense realism.

Movies are team enterprises, the work of entire troupes of story creators, scene and wardrobe designers, technicians, and actors, most of them, even the actors, imbued with a reportorial zeal, an urge to get things right, and none of them daunted by their ignorance—this is entirely to their credit—of what they might be getting into. A producer at United Artists who knew nothing about the Nashville country music scene importuned a director, Robert Altman, to make a movie about it. He knew nothing about it, either, and wasn't interested at first, but undertook the project anyway, assembled a team, and got interested. The team apparently started with written sources such as William Price Fox's *Ruby Red*, headed for Nashville, took a look for themselves, talked to one and all, and produced *Nashville*. The director Oliver Stone's movie, *Platoon*, about the war in Vietnam, was based on his own experience, but thereafter, without the slightest hesitation, he plunged into subject after subject about which he knew nothing, including, lately, the world of professional football, resulting in the extraordinary *Any Given Sunday*. The director Francis Ford Coppola knew nothing about war, let alone about the war in Vietnam, but was nonetheless determined to make what became *Apocalypse Now*. So he signed on a writer who *did* know about war, John Milius, assembled a team that spent a year doing the research and reporting to get it right, and the result was a masterpiece. The director Spike Lee, famous for his movies about black life in America, turned to Jimmy Breslin and other sources to document a largely white world to make *Summer of Sam*, a brilliant naturalistic movie capturing New York City's sweltering Zeitgeist of fear and pornoviolent excitement during the summer of 1977, when a publicity-crazed serial killer known as "Son of Sam" was on a rampage.

Terry Teachout argued that movies had won the battle for a story-hungry young public "because the novel is an obsolete artistic technology." Bellow chided Teachout for "this emphasis on technics that attract the scientific-minded young," since to treat the experience of reading a great novel in technological terms was to miss the point. But I personally find it highly instructive to treat the naturalistic novel as a piece of technology. After all, it was an invention—and a rather recent one, at that. Four specific devices give the naturalistic novel its "gripping," "absorbing" quality: (1) scene-by-scene construction, i.e., telling the story by moving from scene to scene rather than by resorting to sheer historical narrative; (2) the liberal use of realistic dialogue, which reveals character in the most immediate way and resonates more profoundly with the reader than any form of description; (3) interior point of view, i.e., putting the reader inside the head of a character and having him view the scene through his eyes; and (4) the notation of status details, the cues that tell people how they rank in the human pecking order, how they are doing in the struggle to maintain or improve their position in life or in an immediate situation, everything from clothing and furniture to accents, modes of treating superiors or inferiors, subtle gestures that show respect or disrespect—"dissing," to use a marvelous new piece of late-twentieth-century slang—the entire complex of signals that tell the human beast whether it is succeeding or failing and has or hasn't warded off that enemy of happiness that is more powerful than death: humiliation.

In using the first two of these devices, scene-by-scene construction and dialogue, movies have an obvious advantage; we actually see the scenes and hear the words. But when it comes to putting the viewer inside the head of a character or making him aware of life's complex array of status details, the movies have been stymied. In attempting to create the interior point of view, they have tried everything, from the use of a voice-over that speaks the character's thoughts, to subtitles that write them out, to the aside, in which the actor turns toward the camera in the midst of a scene and simply says what he's thinking. They have tried putting the camera on the shoulder of the actor (Ray Milland in *The Lost Weekend*), so that the audience sees him only when he looks in the mirror, *and* having him speak his thoughts in voice-over. But nothing works; nothing in all the motion-picture arts can put you inside the head, the skin, the central nervous system of another human being the way a realistic novel can. The movies are not much better with status details. When it comes time to deal with social gradations, they are immediately reduced to gross effects likely to lapse into caricature at any moment: the house that is *too* grand or *too* dreadful, the accent that is *too* snobbish or *too* crude.

Which brings us to another major shortcoming of the movies as a technology: they have a hard time explaining . . . anything. They are a time-driven medium compelled by their very nature to produce a constant flow of images. Three movies have been made from things I've written, and in each case I was struck by how helpless perfectly talented people were when it came time to explain . . . anything . . . in the midst of that vital flow, whether it be the mechanics and aerodynamics of a rocket-assisted airplane or the ins and outs of racial politics in the Bronx. When a moviegoer comes away saying, "It wasn't nearly as good as the novel," it is almost always because the movie failed in those three areas: failed to make him feel that he was inside the minds of the characters, failed to make him comprehend and *feel* the status pressures the novel had dealt with, failed to *explain* that and other complex matters the book had been able to illuminate without a moment's sacrifice of action or suspense. Why is it that movie versions of *Anna Karenina* are invariably disappointing? After all, Tolstoy put enough action, suspense, and melodrama into *Anna Karenina*—think of Vronsky's disastrous, melodramatically symbolic steeplechase ride on the mare Frou-Frou—for ten movies. What is inevitably missing is the play of thoughts and feelings inside the central nervous systems of the novel's six main characters—and Tolstoy's incomparable symphony of status concerns, status competition, and class guilt within Russia's upper orders. Without those things, which even a writer far less gifted than Tolstoy can easily introduce, using the technology of print in a naturalistic novel, *Anna Karenina* becomes nothing more than soap opera.

The fact is that young people, very much including college students, were inveterate moviegoers during the first half of the twentieth century, too, during the very heyday of the American novel. I know, because I was one of them. We probably spent *more* time at movies than college students today, because we didn't have television and the Internet as other choices. And new movie directors? *We* followed them, too, ardently. I can remember the excitement at my university, Washington and Lee, in Lexington, Virginia, when a movie called *Fear and Desire*, directed by a young man named Stanley Kubrick (and produced by a man who still went by the name of S. P. Eagle instead of Sam Spiegel), arrived at the State Theater. But the Steinbecks, Hemingways, Farrells, and Faulkners were even more exciting. They had it *all*.

The American novel is dying, not of obsolescence, but of anorexia. It needs . . . *food*. It needs novelists with huge appetites and mighty, unslaked thirsts for . . . *America* . . . as she is right now. It needs novelists with the energy and the verve to approach America the way her moviemakers do, which is to say, with a ravenous curiosity and an urge to go out among her 270 million souls and talk to them and look them in the eye. If the ranks of such novelists swell, the world—even that effete corner which calls itself the literary world—will be amazed by how quickly the American novel comes to life. Food! Food! *Feed me!* is the cry of the twenty-first century in literature and all the so-called serious arts in America. The second half of the twentieth century was the period when, in a pathetic revolution, European formalism took over America's arts, or at least the non-electronic arts. The revolution of the twenty-first century, if the arts are to survive, will have a name to which no *ism* can be easily attached. It will be called "content." It will be called life, reality, the pulse of the human beast.

AMBUSH AT FORT BRAGG:
A NOVELLA

Ambush at Fort Bragg

PART ONE

I, IRV

Way past midnight, up in the network's New York control room, a man and a woman sat in a glass cubicle watching a pair of television monitors. The man was only in his early forties, but already he was bald on top except for a narrow little furze of reddish hair that arched up over his freckled dome like an earphone clamp. He had jowls, eyeglasses for nearsightedness, a shell back, rounded shoulders, and a ponderous gut, which his old gray sweater only made look worse. He also had a slovenly way of slouching in his seat so that his weight rested on the base of his spine. In short, a slob; which he realized; and the hell with it.

The woman was almost exactly the same age he was, but she had a terrific head of blond hair and correct posture to burn. She had big bones and nice broad shoulders, and she wore a pair of creamy white flannel pants, a heavenly heathery tweed hacking jacket, and an ivory silk blouse. Any single item of her ensemble, even her flat-heeled shoes, cost more than all the clothes he was likely to wear in a week.

She made him look insignificant by comparison. He also realized that, and the hell with that, too.

Every now and then he glanced at her, a big blond mama sitting there as primly erect as a thirteen-year-old girl on a horse at a horse show, and he just slumped down a little farther. He was giving up on posture, poise, graceful bearing, first impressions, and all the other superficialities at which Her Blondness excelled. What did it matter, all this poise and grace, if you were up in a cubicle in the middle of the night monitoring a remote feed, f'r chrissake? Through the cubicle's glass walls he could see an entire bank of monitors glowing and flaring in the control room outside. Or he saw them and he didn't see them. The only things on his mind right now were the two screens in front of his face and getting Madame Bombshell to pay attention to them. To him, what was going on on those screens was the most important event in the world.

Both monitors were being fed the same action, via a hellishly expensive private fiber-optic hookup, from different camera angles. On both sets he could see the same three young white men in T-shirts, twenty-one or twenty-two years old, certainly not much more than that, boys really, drinking beer in a beat-up booth with leatherette seats, a speckled Formica tabletop, and a little café lamp. All three had smooth, tender jawlines and roses in their cheeks. Their hair was cut so close, their ears stuck out. Happy and high, they radiated the rude animal health of youth, even in the gloom of a topless bar as transmitted to this cubicle over the remote fiber-optic feed.

By now, after midnight, they had reached the garrulous stage. Their conversation chundered out against the irritating thud of a Country Metal band, which was beyond camera range. And yet such were the wonders of modern electronic surveillance—in this case, the microphone planted in the café lamp—he could hear every word they said, assuming you could call them words.

The biggest of the three boys was speaking, the one with all the muscles. His voice had a babyish quality: "Man . . . was some adder wit chew?"

"Dear God in heaven, Irv," said the Blond Pomposity, "what's he *say*ing?"

"He's saying, 'Man, what's the matter with you?' " said Irv. He spoke in a low voice and never took his eyes off the monitors and slouched down even farther into his seat, as if withdrawing into a shell, to indicate that questions and comments were not welcome.

On the screen, the boy continued: "You in see no snakes. I mean, hale, you caint tale me you seen no snakes outcheer in no broad *day*light."

"Deed I did, too, Jimmy," said the rawboned boy right across the table from him. "You know, lack it gets sunny late'na moaning, toad noon? They lack to come outcheer on the *con*crete strip overt the *de*pot?—whirr it's warm?—and just stretch out fer a spale? Saw one yistitty, big ol' rattler. Sucker mussa been big araound's a *gas*'leen hose."

The big blonde let out a ferocious sigh. "What—are—these—people—*say*ing?! We're gonna have to use subtitles, Irv. And see if somebody can't do something about the light."

"I don't wanna use subtitles," said Irv in a whisper meant to admonish her to keep quiet. "I don't wanna create the impression that gay-bashers are some kind of strange alien creatures. Because they're not. I wanna show they're the boy next door. They're as American as 7-Eleven or Taco Bell, and they're bigots, and they're murderers."

"Well, that's fine," said Her Erect Highness, "but these three kids—suppose one of 'em blurts out the whole thing while we're sitting here. Suppose one of 'em says, 'Right, I'm the one who killed him,' and it comes out, 'Rat, ah'm the one whut kaled the quair.' How's the viewer supposed to know? I mean, these kids are speaking rural Romanian. I say we use subtitles."

"It's not *that* hard to understand," whispered Irv, getting testy. "I thought you were *from* the South."

"I am, but—" She broke off. Her eyes were pinned on the monitors. "Besides, the light's too dim."

Irv's voice rose. "Too *dim*?" He gestured toward the screens. "Whattaya think that is, *The Wonder Years*? That's a dive, a saloon, a gin mill, a topless bar in Fayetteville, North Carolina, Mary Cary! I mean, Jesus Christ, that's real life you're looking at, in real time, and that's . . . *the light that's there*!"

"Fine, but considering we've already gone to the trouble of wiring the place—who's the field producer on this piece?"

"Ferretti."

"Well, get him on the line. I wanna talk to him."

"I'm not calling him in the middle of a *live feed*—when he's monitoring *an undercover operation*!"

"I don't see what difference—"

"*Shhhhhh!*" said Irv, slouching down still farther and concentrating on the monitors as if the three boys were about to say something pertinent. But it was just more redneck saloon jabber about snakes and God knew what else.

The truth was, Mary Cary was right. They probably *would* have to use subtitles. But he didn't feel like giving her the satisfaction of saying so. He couldn't stand the way she was already saying *we*, as if she had actually done some work on this piece. Up until tonight, when she finally agreed to spend a couple of hours monitoring the feed with him, she hadn't done a thing. But obviously she was ready, as usual, to march in and take credit if the piece worked out. He had a very strong instinct about this piece. It was *going to work out.* And suppose he hit the jackpot. Suppose the three soldiers hung themselves right on that videotape. Who would get the credit? All the newspaper stories, the editorials, the Op Ed pieces, all the pronouncements by the politicians, all the letters from the viewers, would talk about this big, gross, aging blonde sitting up in this chair with her regal posture as if she actually ran the show. All anybody would talk about would be Mary Cary Brokenborough.

The dumb, irritating way she said her own name on the air started running through his brain. On the air she still spoke with half a Southern accent. *Merry Kerry Brokenberruh.* That was the way it came out. She pronounced her own name as if it were a piece of rhyming trochaic duometer. It was ridiculous, but people loved it:

Merry
Kerry
Broken
Berruh

He stole a glance. The light of the monitors played across her big broad face. Up close, in person, she wasn't much; not anymore. There was something gross about her supposed good looks. She was forty-two, and her skin was getting thick, and her nose was getting thick, and her lips were getting thick, and her hair was turning gray, so that she had to go to some hair colorist on Madison Avenue, or he came to her; whichever. Eight years ago, when she had first signed on with the network, she had still been—he closed his eyes for an instant and tried to envision her as she had been then; but instead of *seeing* her, he *felt*, all over again, the humiliation . . . the insouciance, the amusement, with which she had repulsed every effort of his to . . . get close . . . "*Ummmmhhhhh.*" He actually groaned audibly at the recollection of it. Little fat bald Jewish Irv Durtscher was what she had made him feel like . . . and still made him feel like . . . Well, her Southern Girl good looks were decaying fast . . . Another five years . . . although it was true that on camera she still looked great. She got away with murder. On camera she still looked like a blond bombshell; a cartoon rendition of a blond bombshell, but a blond bombshell all the same; and 50 million people tuned into *Day & Night* every week to see her.

And who the hell knew the name Irv Durtscher?

Well, that was nothing more than the nature of the business, and he had always known that. Nobody even knew what a television producer was, much less who Irv Durtscher was. Nobody knew that the producers were the artists of television, the creators, the *soul*, insofar as the business had any . . . Mary Cary knew that much. She wasn't stupid, but she suffered from *denial*, in the sense that Freud used the word. She wanted to deny that she was really nothing but an actress, a mouthpiece, a voice box reciting a script by the creator of *Day & Night*, whose name happened to be Irv Durtscher.

They'd been sitting here in front of the feed for almost three hours, and she hadn't stopped thinking about herself long enough to even acknowledge what a superb piece of investigative journalism she was looking at. Not a peep out of her about the ingenuity of what he had managed to pull off! What the hell would it cost her ego to say, "Wow, this is really fabulous, Irv," or, "Nice work," or, "How on earth did you know they'd be in that particular bar and exactly what booth they'd be sitting in?" or, "How'd you ever manage to install two hidden cameras and wire the place, for goodness' sake?" . . . or just any goddamned thing . . .

No, she sits there and complains about the *light*. The *light*!—and up until now the Army and the locals in Fayetteville have managed to stonewall this whole atrocity, utterly, and insist there's no evidence that anybody from Fort Bragg was involved. These three kids, these three rednecks he and Mary Cary were looking at right now—in real time, on these monitors—had beat up another soldier, a kid named Randy Valentine, killed him, murdered him, in the men's room of a dive just like the one they were in at this moment, for no other reason than that he was gay. Everybody on the base knew who had done it, and there were soldiers who went around giving high fives to the big muscular kid there, the one who started it, Jimmy Lowe—and yet General Huddlestone himself denied all, and *Day & Night* had Huddlestone's square, creased, lithoid, American Gothic WASP face on tape denying all—and I, Irv Durtscher, will gladly bury the general along with his three young Neanderthal enforcers . . . I, Irv Durtscher . . . I, Irv Durtscher, am the true artist of the modern age, the producer, the director, who can at one and the same time draw in television's stupendous audiences and satisfy the network's gluttony for profits—and advance the cause of social justice . . . The big thing in newsmagazine shows now was sting operations with elaborate setups, hidden cameras and microphones, incriminating statements on camera, and this case was perfect. It was *I, Irv Durtscher*, who convinced Cale Bigger, the network's News Division chief, to authorize the huge expense of the spook operation to install the equipment and a live fiber-optic field feed from a dump, a topless bar called the DMZ, in Fayetteville, North Carolina. And why did Bigger say yes? Because he cares for one second about the cause of gay rights? *Eeeeyah*, don't make me laugh. It's solely because I, Irv Durtscher, am the artist who can draw in the millions, the tens of millions, no matter what—and yet nobody knows my name . . .

He cut a quick glance at Mary Cary. She was looking straight ahead at the monitors. Why couldn't he come on at the very beginning of the program, the way Rod Serling used to in *The Twilight Zone* or Alfred Hitchcock used to in *Alfred Hitchcock Presents*? Yeah, Hitchcock . . . Hitchcock was just as short, round, and bald as he was. More so. He could see it now . . . The titles come on . . . The theme music . . . and then . . . *I, Irv Durtscher* . . . but then he lost heart. They'd never go for it. On top of everything else, he looked too . . . *ethnic*. You could *be* Jewish and still be a star in television news, an anchorman or whatever, so long as you didn't *seem* Jewish. And a name like Irv Durtscher didn't help. No fat little baldheaded Irv Durtscher was going to be the star, the personality, of a big network news production like *Day & Night*.

So he had his mouthpiece, this big, blond, white Anglo-Saxon Protestant from Petersburg, Virginia, Mary Cary Brokenborough . . . *Merry Kerry Brokenberruh* . . . What did *she* care about the cause of gay rights? Who the hell knew? Did *she* even know, herself? Well, at least she was smart enough to know that she should act enlightened about such things. She'd be savvy enough to take directions . . .

A small cloud formed in Irv Durtscher's brain. Why was he himself so passionate about gay rights? He wasn't gay himself; he'd never even had a homosexual experience; and the truth was, every now and then he worried lest his two young sons, who seemed so passive, timorous, overly sensitive . . . (effeminate?) . . . lest they turn out gay . . . Christ, that would be a real goddamned horror show, wouldn't it? Of course, he would never express anything like that to them. Their orientation would have to be . . . their orientation . . . Nevertheless, he felt so goddamned guilty . . . Ever since divorcing Laurie, he really hadn't seen that much of the boys. So if they turned out gay, it might be considered *his* fault . . . *Still*—that had nothing to do with whether he was truly committed to gay rights or not, did it? Social justice was social justice, and he was truly committed to social justice; always had been; learned it at his mother's knee, saw the importance of it in his father's anguished face—

"... gay rats ..."

He lurched forward in his chair and concentrated on the monitors and held up his forefinger so Mary Cary would do the same. The tall, rangy one, the one right across the table from Jimmy Lowe, the one with the strange last name, Ziggefoos, had just uttered the expression "gay rats," which in their patois, he knew by now, would mean *gay rights*.

"... they nebber tale you what the hale they deeud fo' they got that way. You jes see some may'shated sommitch with a fo'-day growth a beard and his cheeks lack this here"—he hollowed his cheeks and rolled his eyes up into his head—"lucking lack Jesus Christ and talking abaout AIDS'n gay rats."

"Fuckin' A," said Jimmy Lowe.

"I mean, sheeut," said Ziggefoos, "they act lack they jes flat out got sick fum ever'buddy calling 'em quairs or sump'm. Wasn't nothing they *deeud*, natcherly."

"Fuckin' A wale told," said Jimmy Lowe.

The third one spoke up, the small, wiry, dark-haired one, the runt of the trio, the one named Flory. "Member 'at little Franch feller come overt *ob*stickle course last munt with that fust bunch a UN trainees? Olivy-yay? I ever tale you what h'it was he called 'em? Be talking about some gladiola, and he'd say, 'He ain't fum our parish.' "

"Ain't fum our parish?" said Jimmy Lowe. "What's 'at spose mean?"

"It means—ovairn France everbuddy's *Cath*'lic? And ever'buddy's in one p'tickler *parish* er'nudder? Y'unnerstan'? So him'n'me, one time we seen Holcombe lane the ballin' sun out back at the Far Department with his shirt unbuttoned taking a goddayum *sun*bath, and Olivy-yay, he don't even know the sucker, but he's spishus rat away, and he says to me, he says, 'He ain't fum our parish.' "

Holcombe! Irv's central nervous system went on red alert. He leaned forward even farther and held up both hands toward the monitors as if he were Atlas ready to catch the world. Holcombe had been one of Randy Valentine's closest friends at Fort Bragg. Even Mary Cary seemed to sense the three boys were now entering a minefield. She had leaned forward from out of her perfect sitting posture.

Up on the two screens, the tall one, Ziggefoos, didn't intend to get sidetracked by Flory and his "not from our parish." He took a swallow of beer and said, "An' all 'em shows on teevee, an' all 'is sheeut abaout 'the gay lifestyle'? The wust thang they gon' show you is, they gon' show you a couple lesbians dancing or sump'm lack 'at'eh. Jevver see two faggots dancing on teevee or kissing each other on'a lips? Hale, no. Ain' gonna show you any a *that* sheeut."

"Fuckin' A wale told, Ziggy."

"Oncet my old man rented us a *ho*tel room somers up near the pier at Myrtle Beach," Ziggefoos said, "an' rat next doe's this *bow*adin haouse or sump'm lack 'at'eh, and abaout five o'clock in the moaning?—when it's jes starting to geeut lat?—me 'n' my brother, we kin hear somebuddy grunting and squealing on the roof of the *bow*adin' haouse, and we tuck a luck out the winder, and there's two guys upair on the slope a the roof, unnerneath one a them great big ol' teevee earls they used to have?—nekkid as a pair a jaybuds, and one *uv*'em's jes buggering the living sheeut out th'other'n. Me'n'my brother, we didn't even know what they was doing. So we woke up the ol' man, and he tuck a luck out the winder, and he says, 'Jesus H. Christ godalmighty dog, boys, them's faggots.' Next thang you know, the fust two *uv*'em's finished, and they go daown this little hatchway they got upair in the roof, and rat away two more *uv*'em pop up, buck nekkid just lack the fust two, and they's lane on the roof, and one *uv*'m's rubbing some kinda all on th'other'n's butt. And the ol' man, he's smoking, I mean he's flat out on far by now, he's so mad, and he yales out, 'Hey, you faggots! I'm gonna caount to ten, and if you ain't off'n'at roof, you best be growing some wangs, 'cause they's gonna be a load a 12-gauge *bud*shot haidin' up yo' ayus!' Well, I mean I wisht I'd a had a cam'ra and some fi'm, the way them faggots set to scrambling up the roof and diving down that hatchway. Come to find out that haouse was packed fulla them fucking guys. They got 'em hanging on hooks in'eh, they's so many *uv*'em, and they prolly been coming up on that roof all night long takin' tons unnerneath that big ol' teevee earl. And 'at's what I'm talking abaout. That's what they ain't abaout to tale you when they's talking about gay rats and legal madge between homoseckshuls and all 'at sheeut."

Jimmy Lowe was nodding his approval of all this. Then he leaned over the table toward Ziggefoos and looked this way and that, to make sure nobody was eavesdropping, and he said, "You just put yer fainger on it, old buddy."

Irv held his breath. It was beautiful. The kid had leaned over the table so he could lower his voice and not be overheard, but that had brought his mouth no more than six inches from the microphone hidden in the little lamp. At that range it would pick up a whisper.

"Anybuddy saw what I saw in—" He cut it off, as if a cautious impulse made him not want to say where. "Anybuddy woulda done what I deeud, er leastways they'd a wanted to. Soon's I walked inair and I looked unner that tallit doe and I seen that guy's knees on the flow, and I hud these two guys going, '*Unnnnnh, unnnnnh, unnnnnh.*' "

Even in the middle of it, in the middle of these words for which he had been lying in wait for two and a half weeks, Irv was aware of the sleazy throb of the Country Metal music in the background and the secretive sibilance of the kid's near-whisper—and—*perfection!*—it was the perfect audio background! No one with all the money and time and imagination in the world could have dreamed up anything better!

"—I mean, I knew 'zackly what h'it was. And when I walked overt the tallit and stood up on tippytoe and looked daown over the doe and seen it was a feller fum my own goddayum cump'ny daown on his fucking knees gobblin' at whangus sticking thew'at hole in the *par*tition—I mean, I saw some kind a *rayud*, and 'at was when I kicked inny doe. Broke 'at little metal tab rat off'n it."

Ziggefoos, also leaning in, right into the mike, put on just the beginning of a smile. "Summitch mussa wunner what the hale hit him."

"Whole goddayum doe hit him, I reckon. That summitch, he was lane upside the wall when I grabbed him."

And now little Flory had leaned in over the table, too. "And you nebber deeud see the other guy?" he asked.

"Nebber seen him t'all," said Jimmy Lowe. "Speck he hauled ayus real fayust, 'cause whan y'all come in'eh, y'all nebber seen nobuddy coming out."

"That's rat," said Flory.

Then the three boys, still huddled over the table, looked at one another reflectively and solemnly, as if to say, "Maybe we'd better not talk about it anymore."

An impulse like an alarm surged through Irv's central nervous system and up his brain stem, and the significance of what he'd just heard swept over him even before he could sort it out logically.

They had just hanged themselves.

He looked at Mary Cary, and she was already staring at him. The same dawn was breaking over her. Her over-made-up eyes were open wide, her too-big lips were parted slightly, and a wondering, half-questioning smile was beginning to form on her big, broad face.

That's it, isn't it? They've just hanged themselves?

Oh, that they had! They'd just confessed the actual motive: homophobia. They'd just established the fact that the killing began with an unprovoked, blind-sided assault. And they'd revealed the fact that there existed an as-yet-unidentified witness to the beginning of the attack.

Irv's mind raced on ahead. A victory for justice—oh yes! But it would be a lot more than that.

Long after the three young rednecks had departed the DMZ and the live field feed was finished, Irv remained there in the cubicle and insisted that Mary Cary review the tape with him, over and over. He was soaring. He called Ferretti, down in Fayetteville, and he went over it with him, the same things, like a hero exulting after a battle.

The nice thing was that Mary Cary seemed almost as euphoric as he was. Perhaps she could already see how terrific this was going to make her look on *Day & Night.* Perhaps she could see herself depicted as the heroine who broke the Fort Bragg gay-bashing case, which was not inconceivable. But for the moment he didn't even care. At this moment hers was the only face he could look into and see the reflection of his triumph.

"One of the beautiful parts," she was saying, "is when the sort of rangy-looking one—Ziggy, is it?—when he wakes up, and he's just a boy, I guess, and he sees the two gays on the roof, and he wakes up his father, and his father says, 'Boys, them's faggots,' and he threatens to shoot them with budshot. Speaking of which, whatta you suppose budshot *is*?"

"Birdshot," said Irv. "After you listen to these characters for two or three nights, something very bad happens to your brain and you actually begin understanding what they're saying." He was feeling so good, he didn't even mean it as a rebuke for her reluctance, up until now, to take part in the two and a half weeks of surveillance. "A bud is a bird, a bub is a bulb, a bum is a bomb, a far is a fire, a tar is a tire, an earl is an aerial—I mean, I've been sitting here for two and a half weeks. I could write you a lexicological introduction to Florida Panhandle illiteracy."

"Well, thank God *you* know what they're saying!" said Mary Cary. Irv liked that. "But anyway," she continued, "I think that whole business of the father saying they're *faggots* and he's gonna *shoot the faggots*—I think that's a very important part of what we've got here, because it shows how homophobia is implanted, father to son, one generation to another. I mean, it's a straight line from that scene in a hotel room ten or fifteen years ago to the scene in the men's room where Valentine is killed. An absolutely straight line, Q.E.D. There it is."

Irv reflected for a moment. "You're right, you're right. It definitely makes the point. But I'm not sure how much of that stuff about the roof we can use, if any."

"Why not?"

"Well, I mean it's . . . it's so *gross*. I'm not sure how much of it we can get on the air in a prime-time network show. But there's something else. It puts anal intercourse in such a vulgar light. I mean, all this about one man *lubricating*—the thing is, you could make ordinary heterosexual intercourse sound disgusting, too, depending on who you let describe it. Hell, you could turn *Romeo and Juliet* into a couple of dogs in the park, if you really wanted to get graphic about it. And frankly, we've got a similar problem with the scene in the men's room."

"Whattaya mean?"

"I mean I don't wanna be the one who broadcasts to 50 million people this homophobic maniac's claim that Randy Valentine was committing fellatio in a men's room. And all that stuff about a hole in a partition—*eeeeyah*, it's not even relevant."

"Not relevant?"

"What's it got to do with whether or not one man is justified in killing another for no good reason?"

"Maybe it doesn't have anything to do with it," said Mary Cary, "but I don't see how we can touch that tape. It's probably *evidence*. It could end up evidence in a trial, in court."

"It can still be evidence. But for *Day & Night* we edit it."

"How, Irv? That's the most crucial part of the whole tape!"

"That's the beauty of having two cameras going," said Irv.

He didn't have to explain it to her. If you had just one camera, and it was on someone who was talking, and you tried to edit something out, you would get a blip, no matter how carefully you did it, because the person would have moved, if only ever so slightly, from the moment you cut the tape to the moment you spliced it again. With two cameras you could just switch from one angle to the other at the cut, and the viewer would never know anything had been left out. On newsmagazine shows like *Day & Night*, this was standard practice whenever you wanted to eliminate something that was awkward or inconvenient.

"Well, I suppose we can *do* it, *tech*nically," said Mary Cary, "but I think we'd be asking for a whole lot of trouble."

Irv merely smiled. The truth was, he wasn't even worrying about the problem any longer. Something else she had said, a phrase she had used a moment ago—"evidence in a trial, in court"—had just begun to register. The very idea gave him a warm, rosy rush. If the tape became the centerpiece of a successful criminal prosecution, then *everything* would come out . . . the whole story of how he, Irv Durtscher, had broken the case . . . of how he, Irv Durtscher, and not the celebrated face on the screen, actually created *Day & Night* and ran it and was its mind and soul . . . of how he, Irv Durtscher, was the Sergei Eisenstein, the Federico Fellini of this new art form, this new moral weapon, television journalism . . . of how he, Irv Durtscher—

He, Irv Durtscher, let his eyes pan over the studio around him, over the now-glassy gray screens of the two monitors right in front of him and the screens of all the monitors on the wall of the control room just beyond the cubicle. These were his palettes in the new art, the monitor screens of the control rooms where the producers practiced their magic. And perhaps it would come to pass . . . *Day & Night* would become *Irv Durtscher Presents* . . . The titles, the theme music, and then the world-renowned face and roundish form of—

A sudden small stab of guilt . . . I, Irv Durtscher. He was letting himself get carried away by personal ambition . . . Mustn't let that happen . . . But then he worked it out. He was not doing all this for Irv Durtscher, or at least not *just* for Irv Durtscher. He was doing it for a dream passed on to him by his father and mother, two little but fiercely idealistic people who had eked by with a glass-and-mirror shop in Brooklyn, who had sacrificed everything to send him off to Cornell, who had never had the means, the opportunity, to bring their dream of social justice alive. This piece on the martyrdom of Randy Valentine, a poor, harmless gay soldier at Fort Bragg, North Carolina, was part of the final battle, the battle to end America's secret feudal order and her subtle but pernicious forms of serfdom. The hour was at hand. The day of the Cale Biggers, the General Huddlestones, and those who did their dirty work, the Jimmy Lowes and Ziggy Ziggefooses and Florys, the day of the WASPs and their wanna-be's with their constricted version of "families" and "the natural order"—that day was in its dusk and fading fast, and a new dawn was coming, a dawn in which no authentic genius of the future would ever need hide behind a mask of whiteness or heterosexuality or WASPy names and good looks . . . or Merry Kerry Brokenberruh.

He looked her right in the face. She stared back at him with a certain . . . *something* in her eyes, something he'd never seen there before. It was as if it was suddenly dawning on her what this all meant and she was seeing him, Irv Durtscher, in an entirely new light. Their eyes engaged in what seemed like a blissful eternity. He somehow knew that now if he just—well, why didn't he go ahead and try it? She was . . . she had just gotten married for the third time, but it was ludicrous . . . The guy, Hugh Siebert, some eye surgeon, was solemn, pompous, pretentious, a stiff neck *and* a nonentity . . . Couldn't last . . . Why didn't he just reach forward and take her hand in his, and whatever happened . . . would *just happen* . . . Irv and Mary Cary . . . There was no one around to see them . . . He upped the voltage, stared into her eyes with the eyes of a victorious warrior. A confident, manly, and yet warm and inviting, even seductive, smile stole across his face.

And then he went ahead and did it.

He reached out and took her hand in his and let the current flow from him into her, let it surge up from his very loins, all the while pouring his victorious gaze into her eyes.

For a moment Mary Cary didn't stir, except to bring her eyebrows together quizzically. Then she lowered her head and stared at his hand, which still held hers. She stared at it as if it were a Carolina anole, a tiny tree lizard, that had somehow made its way up twenty-odd stories in New York City and wrapped its little lizard self around her hand. She didn't even deign to take her hand away. She just lifted her head, cocked it to one side, and gave him a look that said, "What the hell's gotten into *you*?"

Pop. The bubble burst. The magic moment deflated. Sheepishly, oh so sheepishly, he took his hand away. He felt as repulsed and humiliated as he had ever felt in the eight years he had known this infuriating woman.

That did it. She had to go. From now on—if she actually thought her celebrated presence was the heart and soul of *Day & Night*—

Then his spirits sank all over again. The plain truth was, he needed her more than ever right now. This story, the Randy Valentine story, was far from over. In keeping with the newsmagazine format, somebody was going to have to execute the ambush. That was the term they used, the *ambush*. Somebody was going to have to confront the three violent redneck murderers on camera. Somebody was going to have to find them, surprise them on the base, on the street, wherever, and shove the incriminating evidence right in their faces, and stand there and take whatever they had to say—or do—while the cameras rolled. In his sinking heart, he, Irv Durtscher, knew he could never pull off an ambush like that, even if the network was *dying* to see him on camera. And yet it wouldn't faze Mary Cary for a second. It wouldn't worry her before, during, or after. She'd do an ambush, of anybody, anywhere, any time, in an instant, *just like that*, with gusto and without a moment's fear or regret.

He looked away, out through the glass of the cubicle at the great bank of control-room monitors, which glowed and flared from feeds all over the world. The new palettes . . . the new art form . . . the new dawn . . . The very notions began to curdle in his mind.

He looked back at her. She was still staring at him, only now with a look of boredom. Or was she merely tired?

"Well, I guess that's all we can do tonight," he said. He sounded as if he had lost his last friend. Moreover, he knew he sounded that way.

I, Irv Durtscher . . . damn that woman! . . . Why was it that everything, even the grandest designs, boiled down at last, when all was said and done, to sex?

PART TWO

THE IMPORTANCE OF LOLA THONG

Ferretti, the field producer for the Fort Bragg gay-bashing piece, had been down in Fayetteville for weeks, and it seemed as though every time he called Irv in New York he had some new war story about Bragg Boulevard. Not only that, back in New York, Irv had spent untold hours monitoring the live field feed from the DMZ itself, which was a typical Bragg Boulevard topless joint. So what could be so surprising about Bragg Boulevard? He had had a picture of this garish, hellish nightmare alley in his mind long before he got here yesterday.

But actually being on Bragg Boulevard, as he was tonight—this had unnerved Irv Durtscher. Seriously. It had rattled him so, he wanted to talk to someone about it. Immediately. But how could he? The stakeout had already begun, and soon, all too soon, any minute perhaps, the ambush would be underway. And he, Irv Durtscher, the Costa-Gavras of television journalism, the Goya of the electronic palette, was supposed to be the maximum leader of this operation.

Once more he ran his eyes over everybody who was here inside the RV with him—the RV, the recreational vehicle, a term he, having lived all his life in New York City, had never heard of before yesterday, when Ferretti showed him this monster. They were all crammed into the RV's rear compartment . . . Ferretti . . . Mary Cary . . . Mary Cary's fat makeup woman . . . the two hulking technicians, Gordon and Roy . . . and Miss Lola Thong, the Thai-American topless dancer Ferretti had recruited . . . too many bodies in too tight a space . . . too much equipment . . . lit entirely by the Radiology Blue glow of a bank of monitor screens . . . so that Mary Cary's famous shock of blond hair now looked a sickly aquamarine . . . Irv scanned his entire army, looking for emotional support and wondering if they could tell the maximum leader had the hoo-hahs.

From the outside, to anybody passing by on Bragg Boulevard or anybody turning in here to the DMZ's parking lot, the RV was just an ordinary beige High Mojave touring van, a big boxy house-on-wheels. Nobody would even look twice (Ferretti had assured him), because Fort Bragg was a huge base with more than 136,700 soldiers, support personnel, and family members, a highly transient population that practically lived in RVs, trailers, and U-Haul-its. But if anybody had been able to look inside the van, that would have been a different story. Ferretti had had a partition installed two-thirds of the way back, with a concealed door; and the technicians, Gordon and Roy, had turned the hidden rear section, where they were now, into a spaghetti of wires, cables, monitor screens, headsets, and recording equipment that reminded Irv, morbidly, of *Bone Zone*, the notorious counterterrorist movie.

They were parked right behind the DMZ, which from the rear was a crude, one-story, cinder-block-and-concrete structure with a flat roof weighed down by air-conditioning compressors and rusting ducts. The three rednecks, Jimmy Lowe, Flory, and Ziggefoos, were inside the topless joint at this moment, drinking, as usual, and jabbering away in rural Romanian, as Mary Cary called it. Mary Cary was watching them on the two monitors that took the feeds from the cameras hidden inside the DMZ and listening to them over a headset that had the unfortunate effect of compressing her Blond Bombshell hair. Every now and then she took the headset off, and the fat girl, her makeup woman, fluffed up her hair and put some more powder on her forehead. Irv wondered if all the powder meant she was sweating. Other than that, Mary Cary didn't show any sign of nervousness at all. She didn't seem to have a nerve in her body. Look at what she was wearing!—one of her creamy white silk blouses, a short creamy white skirt, a Tiffany-blue cashmere jacket, and bone-white pumps with medium-high heels. For an ambush! The blouse was unbuttoned practically down to her breastbone. It was almost as provocative as the cocktail dress the topless dancer Lola Thong was wearing, which showed so much cleavage it was ridiculous. Irv, on the other hand, was wearing regular ambush gear: jeans, running shoes, and a Burberry trench coat. (The Daumier of the Digitized

Era was unaware that if he, a short, bald, fat, fortyish little man with a freckled dome, a double chin, and bad posture, walked anywhere near Fort Bragg in the Burberry trench coat, he would be taken for a child molester; at best.)

Irv didn't even want to look at the monitors anymore. The sight of the three young rednecks in that booth, probably no more than twenty yards from where he was right now, only jangled his nerves more . . . but his eyes kept straying to the monitors all the same. All three were wearing T-shirts, and even on these two small screens you could see the muscularity of their arms and the firmness of their necks and jaws and, above all, the way their ears stuck out. Their ears stuck out because the sides of their heads were shaved, and the way their heads were shaved—

Mary Cary took off her headset again, and Irv moved over beside her and said in a low voice, "So what are our three—our three skinheads talking about now?" Breezy and laid-back, and not nervous, he wanted to sound.

"Our three what?"

"Our three skinheads," said Irv. "This whole place—I've figured out what it is." He gestured, as if to take in all of Bragg Boulevard, Fayetteville, Fort Bragg, Cumberland County, and Hoke County, the state of North Carolina, the entire South. "You wanna know what this place is? Skinhead country."

"Oh, for goodness' sake, Irv," said Mary Cary. "Relax."

"What he say about skinheads?" *Whadee say 'bout skeenheads?* It was the stripper, Lola Thong, talking to Mary Cary. "They're skinheads?" *Dey're skeenheads?*

Mary Cary shot Irv a reproachful look, as if to say, "You and your nerves and your big mouth."

Lola, offspring of an American father and a Thai mother, was a tall, slender creature with black hair and pale skin that appeared milky blue in the glow of the monitors. She had an exotic Asian look through the eyes and cheekbones, and a trace of a Thai accent, which turned the short *i* in *skinhead* to a long *e*. *Skeenhead*. But her diction and grammar, like her jumbo breast implants, were strictly Low Rent American. At the moment she was agitated, twisting about on her high heels, so that her prodigious head of teased black hair bobbed about.

"He don't say nothing to me about skinheads," she said, nodding toward Ferretti, who stood a couple of steps away, looking at the monitors.

Mary Cary said, "They're not skinheads, Lola. I promise you. They're in the U.S. Army. That's the way they make them cut their hair. You know that."

"Then why he say skinheads?" To Lola, Irv was not the maximum leader. He was merely *he*.

Mary Cary sighed and shot Irv another look. "He was only making a joke. Because they cut their hair so short."

"That's true," said Irv, whispering, afraid that Lola would start making too much noise. "It was just a figure—I was just talking about their hair. They're just kids. They're GIs. I was just trying to be funny."

Lola did not look terribly reassured.

And funny Irv Durtscher had not tried to be since he had first laid eyes on Bragg Boulevard after arriving from New York thirty hours ago. The boulevard, which was six lanes wide in some places, ran right through the eastern end of Fort Bragg. Right through it; you could see the barracks. You weren't separated from them by a wall or a fence or anything else. The soldiers could keep cars at the barracks. And did they ever! They spent everything they had on cars. You could see them barreling along Bragg Boulevard, three, four, five to a vehicle. You knew they were soldiers because you could see their shaved heads, with just little mesas of hair on top, and their ears, which stuck out. Many were black, but more were white, and it was the white ones Irv feared. Skinheads were white.

Between the base and Fayetteville, Bragg Boulevard turned into the sleaziest commercial strip Irv ever hoped to see. Not a tree, not a blade of grass, not an inch of sidewalk, not a redeeming architectural feature from one end to the other—just a hellish corridor of one-story cinderblock sheds and wooden huts and blasted asphalt and stomped-sod parking lots and garish signs and fluttering Day-Glo pennants proclaiming pawnshops, mobile homes, trailer parks, massage parlors, pornographic-video stores, check-cashing establishments (KWIK KASH), dry cleaners (SPECIAL FOR FATIGUES), car washes, multiplex cinemas, takeout stands (SUBS, CAROLINA BAR-B-Q), automobile dealerships, motorcycle dealerships, auto suppliers, auto upholsterers, gasoline stations, fast-food franchises, Korean, Vietnamese, and Thai restaurants, discount liquor stores, discount cigarette kiosks, Wal-Mart, Sam's Club, Black & Decker tools, concrete garden birdbaths and figurines, gun stores, attack dogs (K-9 C-Q-REE-T) and topless bars, topless bars, topless bars, one after the other, such as this one, the DMZ.

Last night, before Irv's very eyes, as soon as the sun had gone down, this appalling fever-line of late-twentieth-century instant gratification had lit up. Ten thousand backlit plastic signs and banks of floodlights came on in every hot toxic radioactive microwave pastel shade perceivable by the eye of man, until a look down Bragg Boulevard led your gaze right into the gaudy gullet of hell itself. Irv knew it was hell because of what he had seen late in the afternoon. Late in the afternoon, Ferretti had taken him—just him, not Mary Cary, because her face was too well known—over to a shopping center off Bragg Boulevard called the Cross Creek Mall. The place was mobbed, and with a clientele such as Irv could not have imagined. By the hundreds, the thousands, they swarmed over the Cross Creek Mall: young males with the sides of their heads shaved, young males whose ears stuck out, young males and their young females, young females and their young children and their children-to-be. To Irv all of them appeared to be . . . bursting . . . The males were all young, tough, sunburned, pumped up with muscles and bursting out of their jeans. So many bulging crotches! Made him think of codpieces in those old prints, they bulged so much. Fort Bragg was the training ground for the Army's elite divisions, the Special Operations Forces: Green Berets, Rangers, unorthodox-warfare and psychological-operations (PSYOP) units, commandos of every sort. Testosterone on the hoof! So many soldiers from Fort Bragg had fought in Vietnam, they used to call Fayetteville Fayettenam. Even now many of the wives of these young soldiers, as anyone at the Cross Creek Mall could tell, were Asians. And so many of the wives, Asian as well as American, were bursting, too. They were swaybacked from being so grandly, gloriously pregnant with the next generation of swaggering . . . skinheads . . . Skinheads they were! To Irv it had come as a revelation, a flash of insight right there in the Cross Creek Mall. Skinheads! Sex and aggression! Hell on earth! These young males, bursting with testosterone, were but the officially sanctioned, government-approved versions of the skinheads of Germany!—or the survival cults of Montana! And at night they poured out onto this nightmare alley, Bragg Boulevard, unbound, free of Army discipline, through the very gates of Hell, where he now waited inside a High Mojave RV for his rendezvous with—with—with—

What was he, a nice Jewish boy from New York, doing here, about to try to ambush—*ambush!*—three of this virulent, hormone-crazed species who had already murdered one man and would be primed with alcohol to . . . to do God knew what?

Irv Durtscher, the Zola of the Ratings Sweeps, was terrified.

Lola moved over beside Ferretti, who threw his arm around her shoulders. Even in this feeble light and these cramped quarters she rippled with sexuality beneath the little black cocktail dress. She touched Ferretti on the shoulder and whispered something to him. Then both of them looked around at Irv, who shrugged and arched his eyebrows in the look that says, "What can I tell you?"

Ferretti hugged Lola to him in a jolly fashion and turned her back toward Irv and Mary Cary. Irv envied Ferretti. He was a jovial Alley Oop of a man with a grizzled beard he allowed to grow down beneath his chin and his jawline, covering his jowls. He wore a polo shirt that barely made it over his beefy midsection, a Charlotte Hornets Starter jacket, and a John Deere Backhoe cap. He lit up when he smiled. He had the common touch. He was perfect for field assignments because he could deal with anybody, high or low. He leaned over until his head touched Lola's. He was purring to her.

"For Christ's sake, Irv," he said with a big grin, "what's this 'skinheads'? These guys are yo-yos." He hugged Lola again and said, "Yo-yos, baby, yo-yos!" He gave her such a squeeze and such a grin, it forced a reluctant smile out of her. "Besides, you don't have to deal with 'em. Mary Cary deals with 'em, Irv deals with 'em, these guys deal with 'em." He nodded toward Gordon and Roy, a Hawaiian and an Albanian, two great sides of beef in field jackets, the biggest technicians on *Day & Night*'s staff. (Irv had seen to that.) "You're just the official greeter," said Ferretti. "You issue the invitation. And Miss Lola, honey, when you issue an invitation, people are gonna come to the party. You know what I'm saying? The whole country's gonna come to the party."

Ferretti was shamelessly reigniting Lola's craving for stardom. Lola was currently performing as a topless dancer at a Bragg Boulevard joint called Klub Kaboom. Just how she and Ferretti had become such buddies Irv didn't know; on this subject, Ferretti's only comment was a smile. The deal was that for her part in the ambush, Lola would receive $2,500, and more important, 50 million panting Americans would get a look at the ravishing but hitherto unknown entertainer Lola Thong. Ferretti had provided Lola with an entire catalogue of girls who had made their fortunes through tangential involvement in sensational cases. But as the moment approached, Lola was getting cold feet.

She started to say something, but Ferretti gave her another big hug and, keeping his arm around her, said to Irv, "Lola's ready. How much longer do we give 'em? We don't want 'em to get too bagged in there."

Irv said, "Well, lemme see . . ." He suddenly had the panicky feeling that he had lost the power to make decisions.

Mary Cary broke in: "Lowe and Flory are on their third beers. Ziggy has switched to something called a vodka twilight. Or at least I guess that's what *twilat* means."

"That kid," said Ferretti, "he's so fulla shit. Well, I say we don't wait much longer. After three beers these fucking kids, they don't know it, but they're drunk. And after a few vodka twilats . . ." He grinned.

Oh, Ferretti, the big Alley Oop, had the heart for this stuff. He relished it, and Irv envied him even more. Irv himself was torn. On the one hand, his visceral self, the instinctive part of him that knew this hide he had on was the only one he would ever possess, wanted to push the moment of ambush off, eternally perhaps. On the other hand, his rational self, the one who managed the career of Irv Durtscher the Bertolt Brecht of Broadcasting, knew he should start the ambush now. An ambush of three slavering drunks would not make for very convincing television journalism—*and* might be more dangerous. A fine balance was what they were looking for. The idea was to let the three soldiers have a few drinks first, not enough to get drunk, just enough to loosen up and lose their inhibitions, which didn't seem to have a very high threshold to begin with.

Irv spoke as resolutely as he could: "Okay, you're right. Is everybody ready?"

He looked at Ferretti, who nodded; then at Gordon and Roy, who nodded; then at Mary Cary, who not only nodded but also added a little exasperated twist of the lips, as if to say, "Oh, for goodness' sake, Irv, get on with it."

So Irv smiled at Lola as convincingly as he could and said, "You're on."

Ferretti gave her another hug. "Nothing to it, babe," he told her. "You know what to say. Just be Lola. This is a cabaret act, and you're the star."

Ferretti opened the door in the false wall and led Lola into the RV's forward section, and Irv followed. The RV's big front windshield, which was high up off the ground like a bus's, framed a rectangle of North Carolina sky turned a hideous hot mauve by Bragg Boulevard's inferno of lights. Through the windshield Irv could see the backsides of electric signs all along the strip. They blazed. They blinked to electronic beats. Hyperkinetic patterns raced through fields of lightbulbs. Signs pivoted and oscillated against the sky's feverish dome. The entire strip seemed to be rutting and wallowing and doing a jack-legged Crazy Dance. Lurid streaks and blooms of light and shadow bathed the RV's darkened interior, making it hard to see at first that it was actually a living room, or an American Recreational Vehicle version of a living room, in any event. There was a built-in couch, covered in an indestructible Alumicron tweed, along one wall, with a television set, complete with built-in

VCR, opposite it, plus a compact stainless-steel kitchenette and a pair of plush passenger seats that could be folded down into beds. Up in the very front were the RV's driver's seat and a separate passenger seat, now swiveled toward the rear, both with thronelike backs that would make it hard for anyone passing by outside to peer inside. Curtains were drawn over the side windows.

Ferretti opened the RV's big right-hand door to usher Lola out, and the caterwaul of Bragg Boulevard came pouring in. Above the drone of the traffic rose the rutting wails and pounding thuds of the Country Metal music these . . . skinheads . . . loved, chundering out of their car stereos as they drove past the DMZ. From inside the DMZ itself you could hear the beat of an electric bass.

Now Ferretti and Lola were standing on the ground, outside the door, and he had his arm around her and his head close to hers, talking to her. Beams of light ran up and down them as cars drove in and out of the DMZ's parking lot, and Irv could hear young male voices talking in . . . rural Romanian . . . His heart began accelerating . . . But it was just more of the usual, more young, bursting soldiers heading on foot into the DMZ. Apparently they didn't even stop and stare. A grizzly, paunchy fellow in a Charlotte Hornets Starter jacket and a John Deere Backhoe cap hugging and nuzzling an Amerasian cocktail waitress, or whatever she might be, out by a High Mojave touring van in the parking lot of the DMZ didn't even rate a second look. After all, this was Hell; this was Fayettenam.

Ferretti gave Lola one last hug, and she began teetering on her high heels along the stomped-dirt driveway toward the bar's front entrance. Then he came back inside the RV and closed the door, shutting out the hellish noise, and he and Irv rejoined Mary Cary, who was standing in the doorway to the rear compartment.

"Well," said Irv, "she's on her way. I just hope to hell she doesn't blow it."

"Oh, don't worry about Lola," said Ferretti. "She's nervous, but once she walks up to those three meatballs and their eyes start falling out of their heads over her"—with both hands he pantomimed a big curve in front of his chest—"she'll be in Seventh Heaven. Lola's a born prick teaser. Excuse me, Mary Cary. A successfully teased—well, you know what I mean—it brings out the ham in Lola. In front of the aroused male animal she has true star quality."

"She'd better," said Mary Cary. "I'd just as soon not have to go in there and get them myself."

But Irv knew—and he marveled over it—he knew Mary Cary wouldn't hesitate to do exactly that, if she had to.

"Well, we can watch the show," said Ferretti. They went back into the rear compartment and shut the door and stood in front of the monitors receiving the live feed from inside the DMZ and put on headsets. Now Irv could see Jimmy Lowe, Ziggefoos, and Flory in their booth and hear the DMZ's Country Metal band banging and sloshing away in the background in a slow number that seemed even sleazier than the usual bawling headbangers. Jimmy Lowe was leaning back on his side of the booth. He had one hand on a bottle of beer on the table. His head was thrown back slightly, which made his neck look massive. He was trying to sing along with the chorus:

"*She won't abaout*
To give me no haaaaaaaaid,
So all's I got was
A piece uvver mind . . ."

Ziggefoos laughed and said, " 'Give me no haid'? Christalmighty, Jimmy, 'at's what 'at ol' gal *Lu*cille told me she lacks about you. You're so *sent*'mental. 'Give me no haid . . .' Hearing 'em sweet words, 'at's every gal's deepest *de*sar."

"Yeah, and you kin deep 'is here," said Jimmy Lowe, extending the middle finger of his right hand, "and leave *Lu*cille out *uv* it." He managed to twist his lips into half a smile, but his voice had a testy edge to it. Ziggy and Flory both started laughing.

Lucille, whoever she was, had come up a lot in the three soldiers' conversations over the past week, chiefly as a way for Ziggy and Flory to rib Jimmy Lowe. Apparently she worked in the Wal-Mart on Bragg Boulevard and wanted nothing more to do with Jimmy.

All three boys' heads swung in the same direction, toward some point in the middle distance. At first Irv thought they must have spotted Lola. But it soon became apparent that they were looking at one of the dancers up on the bar.

"Th'ow it, Sugar," said Jimmy Lowe with no particular enthusiasm. "Beats me how the hale they do thayut."

"Luck at the lamb chops on 'at ol' gal," said Flory. "Mussa hadda brought her up in a double-wide." After several weeks of monitoring the three rednecks, Irv had deduced that a double-wide was some sort of jumbo trailer home.

"What's 'at on her laig?" said Ziggefoos. "Lucks to me lack a open lesion."

"A open what?" said Jimmy Lowe.

"A open lesion," said Ziggefoos, "lack she's got a vernerl disease."

"What the hale's a lesion?"

"It's lack a—I don't know, a sore, I guess, lack fum syph'lis. There's a whole cohort a vernerl diseases 'at'll fuck up yer skin, but you jes don't hear 'bout 'em no more, because the onliest thang gits talked about no more is AIDS." Irv tensed. Maybe Ziggefoos was about to get back on the subject of homosexuality—and Randy Valentine. "Hale, when I was ovair, I knew guys 'at fucked evvy ho in Somalia—and you know how all the hose in Africa spose have the HIV virus?—these guys fucked evvy ho in a row, them and their sisters, too, and I never heard a one *uv*'em catching AIDS. But plenty *uv*'em, they got syph'lis and the whole dayum cohort a vernerl diseases, until their goddayum dicks was falling off on the graound. But don't nobuddy thank twice about thayut no more, because the onliest thang they wants to talk about is a buncha faggots with AIDS."

"Fuckin' A, wale tol'," said Jimmy Lowe.

Irv stared at Ziggefoos on the screen. Where did he pick up this stuff? Lesions? Cohort? *Cohort of venereal diseases?* Or maybe, as Ferretti had put it, he was just fulla shit. Ziggefoos was not nearly as muscular and tough-looking as Jimmy Lowe, and yet to Irv, he had his own special air of menace. He was lanky and rawboned with a thin face, a long nose, and a long jaw. His eyes were set close together in a way that reminded Irv of a mean dog. His arms were not bulky like Jimmy Lowe's but had big veins wrapped around the forearms like the service-station mechanics and other intimidating types Irv remembered from when he was growing up.

"Jeemy? Hi."

On the screen Irv could see the three rednecks look up. Irv looked over at Ferretti, who smiled and crossed his fingers. *Jeemy*. They couldn't see the woman who had said it, but it could only be Lola.

"You remeember me? From the Wal-Mart?"

On the monitor screen Irv could see Jimmy Lowe staring, slack-jawed. "I don' zackly," he said finally, "but I sure's hale *want* to."

Then he grinned and turned to Ziggefoos and Flory for approval of his powers of repartee. This they gave him, and you could see the three of them drinking in the hookery glories of Lola Thong.

"I'm Lola. You don't remeember? Lucille's friend?"

"How could I fergit, I reckon." Jimmy Lowe turned to his buddies again and laughed, and then all three of them laughed, and their eyes went up and down the vision before them.

"You *work* at the Wal-Mart?" asked Jimmy Lowe. Lola must have nodded yes, because Jimmy Lowe said, "Whirr you work at the Wal-Mart?"

Oh shit. What was Lola going to say to that?

"In the back."

"In the *bayack*?" said Jimmy Lowe, managing to turn *back* into two syllables. "If I was running the Wal-Mart, I'd sure's hale figger out someplace to put you 'sides the bayack!"

All three laughed heartily and drank Lola in some more.

"Well, I don't always work at the Wal-Mart, you know."

She said this so coquettishly and got such a rise out of the boys that Ferretti, wearing his headset, looked over at Irv and put a thumb up and mouthed the words "Star quality."

"Come on, Jimmy," said Ziggefoos, "ain'tchoo gon' ask your fran to sit daown? Who you with, Lola?"

"Nobody."

"Then you orta be with us. Move over, Jimmy."

Jimmy moved over. Now on the screens Irv and Ferretti could see Lola and her big bouffant hairdo and her long eyelashes and her flashing Asian eyes and her confidently smiling lips and her custom-made bosom sidling into the booth.

"Wale, whudjoo lack to drank, Lola?" said Jimmy Lowe. "How 'bout a beer?"

"A *beer*?" said Ziggy. "You got abaout as much class as a Port-o-San vac'um cleaner, Jimmy. Whyn't you have what I'm having, Lola?"

"What you having?"

"A vodka twilat."

"What's a vodka twilat?"

Jimmy Lowe said, "It's a drink fer fa—fer people lack Ziggy." He raised his right hand and gave it a limp wrist and lifted his little finger.

"Don't pay no nevermind to 'im, Lola. Him and refinement ain't never been innerduced."

It went on like that for a while, with Ziggefoos and Jimmy Lowe ragging each other to see who could be the wittiest and most manly. Little Flory didn't have much to say. Lola compromised by ordering a tequila sunrise, and Ziggefoos said that showed she was a lady and didn't want to sit around all night like some of the animals in here, swilling beer. Jimmy Lowe said Ziggefoos's problem was, they almost hadn't let him into the Rangers because he had . . . certain tendencies . . . and Lola changed the subject by asking Jimmy Lowe if it was true that part of Ranger training involved putting the recruit in a metal box the size of a coffin and shutting and locking the lid without telling him how long it would be before they let him out. This gave all three of them a chance to brag for a while and tell war stories about the rigors of Ranger training, whereupon Lola said she often had a dream just like that, about the metal box. She kept dreaming that she had been put in a metal box, stark naked, and she struggled and struggled. She pantomimed this part by twisting her shoulders and her chest this way and that. The three rednecks devoured every twist, every turn, every this, every that. Just when she thought she could hold out no longer, she said, someone would arrive mysteriously and pry the lid up, and she would wake up, trembling with excitement, before she ever found out who it was. The three boys were rendered practically speechless, trying to figure out what to do with this conversational opening without sounding totally crude.

Ferretti looked at Irv and mouthed the words once more: "Star quality."

Then Lola put on the most suggestive smile Irv had ever seen and said to Jimmy Lowe, "You like veedeos?" She looked at Ziggefoos and Flory the same way.

"What kinda videos?" asked Jimmy Lowe.

"Unusual veedeos," said Lola. The suggestive smile turned into a leer. She took a deep breath, and her breasts seemed to rise and fall a foot inside and outside the little black cocktail dress.

"Depends, I guess," said Jimmy Lowe, who already seemed to be breathing rapidly. He looked at his two buddies and then said to Lola, "I spose. Whirr they at?"

"Out back," said Lola with the same leering ham-actress smile.

"Out bayack whirr?"

"Een the parking lot," said Lola with such a breathy voice and such a smoldering look it was as if she had said, "Een my boudoir."

"In the parking lot?"

"Een my RV." She lowered her chin and opened her big dark eyes and gave a look that was the Mother of All Insinuation.

The three of them looked at one another, their eyes darting back and forth in a silent conference. The perfectly sleazy Country Metal music continued to bang and slosh away in the background.

Finally Jimmy Lowe said, "Wale, hale, won't hut to take a luck." His eyes flicked toward Ziggefoos and Flory for confirmation of the decision. Then the four of them, Lola and the three rednecks, slid out of the booth.

Irv's heart accelerated again. They were coming out. The feed from inside the DMZ now showed only the empty booth. The other monitor screens showed the RV's empty living room, still dark except for the lurid streaks that came beaming in from Bragg Boulevard and the parking lot. He took off his headset and started talking to Gordon and Roy—to try to calm himself down more than anything else. They already knew what to do. Gordon had a rheostat with which to adjust the lighting in the RV. He had him turn it up, to test it. The living room rose up on six monitors, in color. You could see the appalling brown-and-yellow-plaid pattern on the Alumicron tweed of the built-in couch. Then he talked to Roy, who was monitoring the sound. Roy assured him that the hidden microphones, which were no bigger than the head of a nail, would pick up everything, even the sound of the door handle turning when they reached the RV. Then he turned to Mary Cary and started to say something, but she cocked her head and narrowed her eyes and twisted her lips in a fashion that said, "Irv. Calm down."

Now Irv's heart was beating at a terrific clip. He could feel it banging away inside his rib cage. Suppose it went into tachycardia? Or fibrillation? And he passed out? Fainted? The six of them—himself, Mary Cary, Ferretti, Gordon, Roy, and the fat makeup woman, whose name he never had caught—were packed into the little compartment, with the curtains drawn . . . silent . . . waiting . . . In the tubercular blue light of the monitors, they looked ghastly. He could hear the sounds of the strip and the DMZ seeping in . . . He put his headset back on . . . and waited some more.

Presently Irv thought he could hear voices—redneck voices—voices so close he wondered for an instant if the three soldiers had come inside the RV without his knowing it. He looked at the monitors, and on five of the screens the RV's living room rose up in light and color before his very eyes. No one in there. He glanced at Gordon, who had his hand on the rheostat. Then, over the earphones, sure enough, Irv heard the handle of the RV door turning. Then the door opened, and the sounds of the strip came thrumming into the headset. On one of the monitors he could see Lola entering the RV. The camera was looking straight down her dress; he could see practically all of her prodigious breasts. Then in came Jimmy Lowe and Ziggefoos and Flory. Those little figures on the monitor screens, with their T-shirts, their muscles, their tight jeans, their . . . skinned heads . . . were barely six feet away from him now, on the other side of a flimsy fake wall, big as life.

Back in the secret compartment, Irv stole a glance at Mary Cary and the field producer, Ferretti. In the dead microwave glow, they looked ancient. They didn't show a trace of emotion. They were absorbed in their headsets and the monitors.

Barely six feet away, on the other side of the false wall, Lola was directing the soldiers to sit on the couch. Little Flory wound up in the middle, with Jimmy Lowe on one side and Ziggefoos on the other. One monitor now showed you all three of them, sitting there. Three other monitors gave you close-ups of them, head and shoulders, one by one. A fifth monitor showed you Lola, now settling into the front passenger seat, which had been turned around. Her little black dress was so short that when she sat down and crossed her legs, it made you wonder if she was wearing anything at all.

Jimmy Lowe was craning his head around, his skinned head. His neck muscles were huge. "This here's all yours, Lola?"

"Un-hunh."

"What it setcha bayack?" said Flory.

"Oh . . . I 'on know," said Lola. "Eet was part of a kind of a deal." She gave him a smile oozing with significance. They all looked at each other and laughed a little too loud and nervously.

Ferretti looked at Mary Cary and then at Irv and broke into a big grin, and once more mouthed the words "Star quality." He kept on grinning, even after he turned back to the monitor. Irv *wanted* to smile, but a smile was beyond him. He was amazed that Ferretti could feel so genuinely amused in the middle of a situation this tense. They were both television producers, but they were very different animals.

Lola offered the three soldiers some malt liquor, which they reckoned was a good idea. She got up and went to the refrigerator of the kitchenette and took out a 40-ounce bottle of Colt 45 and poured it into three paper cups. On the monitors Irv could follow their eyes—and their skinned heads and their ears, which stuck out—as they followed every locomotion, every twist, every inclination of her body. Then she removed a videocassette from a cabinet beneath the television set and slipped it into the VCR mechanism. Irv saw the one blank screen on the bank of monitors come alive with an abstract pattern of colors. It was fed directly from the television set in the RV's living room. Lola and the three rednecks settled back. Their eyes were pinned on the set: a pine forest . . . shady at ground level, green and gold way up above where the sun shines through the branches . . . music . . . an old Dionne Warwick number called "Anyone Who Had a Heart" . . . In the distance, the figure of a young woman in a white dress, a long, fancy, old-fashioned dress, down to her ankles. She's wearing white gloves and a big Garden Party hat. She's carrying a parasol and a small portfolio tied with a ribbon. She comes closer . . . It's Lola . . . Her bodice is demurely covered with lacework that goes up to her neck and forms a little collar . . . but her breasts are obviously yearning to be free . . . She stops beneath a soaring pine, tucks the parasol under one arm, unties the little portfolio, and takes out three photographs . . . Dionne Warwick wails plaintively in the background about lost and unrequited love . . .

On the monitors Irv could see the three rednecks staring at the television set, all eyes. You could tell they had a delicious inkling of what was coming.

Lola, in her big *belle époque* dress, looks longingly at the three photographs.

Longingly; oh yes. As an actress, it occurred to Irv, Lola was worse than the worst silent-film hambone. But in pornography, subtlety is not a virtue. A cloud crossed Irv's mind. This video was his brainchild. Ferretti and a camera crew had taken Lola out to a forest in the sand hills near a town called Southern Pines and shot it, but it was he, Irv, who had dreamed it up. Christ—had he gone too far this time? Well, no one but this lot would ever see the whole thing.

The camera follows Lola's longing eyes, then comes in tight on the three photographs . . . Jimmy Lowe, Ziggefoos, Flory . . . One by one their faces fill the screen . . .

"Jesus H. Christ," said Ziggefoos, "how the hale'd you do thayut?"

"Yeah, how the hale didja?" asked Flory.

Jimmy Lowe merely stared at Lola with his mouth open. Now the other two were staring at her the same way. In fact, the pictures were stills adapted from the footage shot by the cameras hidden in the DMZ two weeks before.

"Shhhhh," said Lola. "What I told you? Thees veedeo ees *unusual.*" She smiled with maximum suggestiveness.

In the dappled pine forest, Lola looks this way and that, as if to make sure she's alone. She stoops, puts the parasol, portfolio, and pictures on the ground, stands up, and looks about some more. She takes off the long white gloves and lets them drop to the ground. She brings her hands to her throat and begins unbuttoning her lacy bodice.

The three rednecks could see that their fond, lustful yearnings were about to be fulfilled. No more questions about the production process.

A haunting saxophone solo . . . Lola's busy taking it off . . . The Garden Party hat goes . . . With much writhing and wriggling she snakes her way out of the dress . . . She starts to go to work on her corset . . . Once more she looks longingly down at the three photographs on the ground before her . . . A still picture of Jimmy Lowe . . . All at once it comes alive and starts moving. Then Ziggefoos—same thing. Then Flory . . . Then the Country Metal music kicks in, and you see the three of them in the booth in the DMZ, drinking beer and talking.

Jimmy Lowe said, "Godalmighty dog, Lola. I mean, sheeut, whirr the hale'd you git *tha*yut? What the hale kinda video this spose a be anyhows?"

"Eenter*ac*tive veedeo," said Lola, in a way that as much as said, "Surely you know about interactive video."

Eenteractive veedeo . . . Ferretti turned to Irv and Mary Cary with a huge grin. *Star quality!* Mary Cary smiled back. All Irv could think about was: Suppose Jimmy Lowe got angry and broke through the false wall and came hunting for the Wizard of Oz?

Fortunately, no one, not Lola or anyone else, had to provide further explanation, because now the video was back in the pine forest . . . Once more, Lola amid the soaring pines . . . in a thrall of ecstasy . . . rotating her hips and thrusting her pelvis in time with the Country Metal music . . . She has the corset undone down the front. She opens it wide and discards it, consigns it to the forest floor, revealing her glorious breasts.

The three rednecks were mesmerized. They were deep in a sexual coma.

She lowers her eyes coquettishly and looks down on the ground. There are the three photographs once more . . . Jimmy Lowe . . . Ziggefoos . . . Flory . . . the photographs . . . come alive again . . . in the booth in the DMZ . . . Ziggefoos is talking: "You jes see some may'shated sommitch with a fo'-day growth a beard and his cheeks lack this here, lucking lack Jesus Christ and talking about AIDS'n gay rats." Jimmy Lowe says, "Fuckin' A."

On the video they talk about Holcombe, who is suspected of being homosexual, and Ziggefoos tells about the boardinghouse in Myrtle Beach where he and his brother had seen the "quairs" up on the roof "jes buggering the living sheeut out th'other'n—"

"It's great, great, great!" thought Irv, breathing fast. They were in such a sexual trance, they were no longer looking at each other in alarm. They couldn't see what was coming.

The camera is on Lola again . . . half-naked in the forest . . . The Country Metal music is banging away . . . Lola spreads her legs and puts her fingers down inside her *cache-sexe* and begins throwing back her head as if in an uncontrollable ecstasy . . . Suddenly the video is back to the booth in the DMZ. Ziggefoos is saying, "And 'at's what I'm talking abaout. That's what they ain't abaout to tale you when they's talking about gay rats and legal madge between homoseckshuls and all 'at sheeut." Then Jimmy Lowe, nodding away, leans over the table toward Ziggefoos and looks this way and that, to make sure nobody is eavesdropping, and he says, "You just put yer fainger on it, old buddy" . . . The sleazy throb of the Country Metal music . . . "Anybuddy saw what I saw in—" He hesitates, then resumes: "Anybuddy woulda done what I deeud, er leastways they'd a wanted to—"

Now, on the monitors, Irv could see the three of them cutting glances at each other. They weren't so drunk or so sex-besotted that they couldn't realize this was dangerous territory . . . the details of what Jimmy Lowe had done when he had seen Randy Valentine committing fellatio in a toilet booth in a Bragg Boulevard bar—

But then the video is back to the forest . . . Lola, leering, running her pink tongue around her ruby lips. The camera closes in on her loins, on her very groin, her corona of pubic hair, the lips of her vulva . . . *Bingo!*—Back in the booth at the DMZ . . . Jimmy Lowe is saying, "I mean, I saw some kind a *rayud*, and 'at was when I kicked inny doe. Broke 'at little metal tab rat off'n it." Ziggefoos says, "Summitch mussa wunner what the hale hit him." Jimmy Lowe says, "Whole goddayum doe hit him, I reckon. That summitch, he was lane upside the wall when I grabbed him."

On the monitor Irv could see Jimmy Lowe turn toward Ziggefoos. There was real alarm on his face now. "What the hale *is* 'is sheeut?" Then he looked at Lola. He was angry. "What the sheeut's going on here?"

Lola kept smiling, although Irv could detect the fear in her eyes. She rose up out of her seat, then gestured toward the television set.

Neither Jimmy Lowe nor Ziggefoos nor Flory could resist it. Their eyes swung toward the set—

—and there's Lola in the forest, her fingers pressed into her crotch, her hips rolling, her garter straps swinging like tassels, her breasts pitching and yawing—and the three rednecks were transported. They couldn't take their eyes off it.

Irv turned to Mary Cary, who was right beside him, her headset on, her eyes pinned on the monitors. He nudged her with his elbow, then held his forefinger in front of his face and revolved it clockwise, to indicate that the tape was near the end—and she would soon be on. He could barely see her, it was so dark on this side of the partition. Dark, crowded, and hot; he felt as if he could hardly draw a breath. But Mary Cary merely nodded and looked to make sure her makeup woman was still standing by, then turned back to the monitors. Irv nudged Ferretti. He couldn't believe it. Ferretti had a smile on his face.

Lola's back is arched. Both hands are on her genitals. Her pelvis is thrusting. She gasps, she sighs, she moans some more. And then she goes, "*Hanh hanh hanh HANHHHHHHhhhhhhhhhhhhhhhh*"—a dying shriek.

The camera pulls back . . . The saxophone solo refrain of "Anyone Who Had a Heart" resumes . . .

For a moment Jimmy Lowe remained agog, even though the tape had come to an end. Then Ziggefoos smacked him on the side of his leg with the back of his hand. "I 'on know, Jimmy, I 'on lack 'is sheeut."

Jimmy Lowe turned to Lola, who was now standing right beside the RV's door. She was trying to hang on to her smile and beginning to lose the battle.

"Look here, goddayum it, Lola," said Jimmy Lowe, "I wanna know what the sheeut's going on, and I wanna know rat now."

"Eenteractive teevee," said Lola, "eenteractive teevee. Eenteractive teevee." She was holding on to this term "interactive TV" for dear life.

"You kin innerack with my sweet ayus, Lola," said Jimmy Lowe. "I ax you a simple question."

"You don' believe me?" said Lola plaintively. "Eenteractive teevee. Eenteractive teevee, Jeemy!"

PART THREE

GUILTY! GUILTY! GUILTY!

Jimmy Lowe was now leaning toward Lola, beginning to snarl. Behind the partition, Irv's heart was beating wildly. He still had his headset on, although he wanted to take it off. His central nervous system was going into the fight-or-flight mode, and he was definitely partial to flight, and the headset would be an impediment. He looked at Mary Cary and mouthed a single word: "Ready?" But she had anticipated him. She already had her headset off and was standing still, facing the partition, while the makeup woman fluffed up her great blond hair and touched up her forehead and nose with powder. The two technicians, Gordon and Roy, were already up off their stools, headsets removed, standing right behind her. What a pair of great wide hulks they were! (Thank God!) They must have been in their thirties, but in the pallid glow of the monitors, their faces looked like a pair of ancient underwater rocks. Right next to them stood Ferretti. He had taken his headset off, too. He gave Irv a wink!—a wink! As if he didn't have a worry in the world! Once more Irv marveled.

"I'm gon' show you, Jeemy, right now!" It was Lola's voice, sounding in Irv's ears over the headset. She was losing her composure. He looked at the monitor screen. She was trying to recapture her concupiscent leer. She also had her hand on the door handle. Miss Lola Thong was ready to bail out. "There!" She pointed toward the partition. "You have a special vees'tor!"

Irv turned back toward Mary Cary and with a frantic look in his eyes mouthed the word "Now!" But she was already heading through the concealed door in the partition. Didn't have to be prodded! Marching straight out to confront these . . . skinheads! . . . murderers! Irv Durtscher, the Maxim Gorky of the Mass Media, involuntarily crouched. He needn't have. Gordon, Roy, and Ferretti followed right behind her. Their hulking forms filled up the opening.

Irv spun back toward the monitors. None of the hidden cameras had yet picked up Mary Cary, but he could see all three of the soldiers, sitting on the couch, staring toward her. On another monitor—there went Lola, slipping out of the RV and closing the door behind her. The soldiers didn't even notice. They were dumbstruck. Standing before them was a big blond bombshell in a creamy white silk blouse open down to the sternum, a sky-blue cashmere jacket, and a short white skirt showing off her terrific legs . . . and, moreover, perhaps the best-known blond bombshell in America.

"Hello, Jimmy," said Mary Cary, "I'm Mary Cary Brokenborough."

I'm Merry

Kerry

Broken

Berruh.

It was precisely the way she said it every week on the show! No different! Not a tremor in her voice! Irv was astounded, even though he had seen her do it before. His admiration, his envy, cut through his fear as he crouched behind the partition, staring at the monitors and listening over the headset.

"Aw, come on naow," said Jimmy Lowe, his mouth open, his head cocked to one side. "I don' believe theeus." He tried a smile, as if somehow she might respond with a smile and reveal that this was all some kind of harmless prank.

"No, you can believe it, Jimmy," said Mary Cary. "I'm Merry Kerry Brokenberruh, and I've got good news and bad news. The good news is, we're not the police. The bad news is, we're from *Day & Night*."

By now, as Irv could see on the monitors, Mary Cary had moved out in front of the couch and was being picked up by the hidden cameras. What was not picked up by the cameras, and what would not be seen by *Day & Night*'s 50 million viewers, was the line-up of heavies who now stood there as Mary Cary's glum-faced centurions: Gordon, Roy, and Ferretti.

Jimmy Lowe didn't say anything. He looked at Ziggefoos and then at Flory, and then all three looked at one another. This was the pivotal moment. The three of them were no brain surgeons, but they were bright enough to know that—*Gotcha!*—they were now in trouble. This was the moment in which they had to make a decision. An older trio, wiser or not, might very well refuse to say another word and depart or, conceivably, attack. But these three were children of the third television generation. To them, television was not a communications medium, it was an atmosphere you breathed. TV came into your life as naturally as oxygen, and you would no more think of trying to keep it out than you would the air in your lungs. A *Merry Kerry Brokenberruh* came into your home every week as inevitably as the barometric pressure—and now she had been beamed down into these boys' very presence. They were shocked, awed, mesmerized—and in that moment they lost the battle with logic. They neither fought nor fled. They stood their ground, transfixed by the aura of the broadcast goddess, who might be feared, might be disliked, but who could not be denied. She was in their lives, just like their bloodstreams, and *she had her questions.*

On the monitors Irv could see the boys' skinned heads and stuck-out ears turning. Mary Cary had moved to the seat Lola had vacated and was sitting down. She gestured toward the television set. "You recognize what you just saw, don't you?"

"Sonamabitch," said Ziggefoos. He had a small, incredulous smile on his face. "This really is *you*?"

"I think you recognize me, and I think you recognize what you just saw," said Mary Cary, motioning toward the set again. She spoke calmly and firmly as if she played a game of *Gotcha!* like this every day.

"God*day*um!" said Ziggefoos with such a crazy sort of exaggeration it startled Irv. "Merry Kerry . . . Merry Kerry . . . you're jes shittin' us, rat?"

"Didn't it look real to you?" said Mary Cary. "You, Jimmy, Flory—talking about what happened to Randy Valentine . . . in your own words?"

"Merry Kerry . . . Merry Kerry . . ." Ziggefoos had a dreamy tone and a dreamy look and a silly little smile. "Watchoo talking abaout, Merry Kerry?"

"It's what *you* were talking about, Ziggy, you and Jimmy and Flory, on that videotape. Why don't you tell me—"

"All's I saw was some hooker shakin' her fanny aout'na pineywoods, Merry Kerry," said Ziggefoos.

Mary Cary simply ignored the comment. "Why don't you tell

me"—she looked straight at Jimmy Lowe—"why don't you tell me exactly what you did when you surprised Randy Valentine in that men's room that night?"

"Merry Kerry," said Ziggefoos. He paused. "Jevver have a vodka twilat?"

"No, and if I were you—"

"Let's go git us a coupla vodka twilats, Merry Kerry. Rat'air inna DMZ." He broke into a grin.

Goddamn this kid! thought Irv. "Merry Kerry." Irv had seen this irritating familiarity before, especially among young people. The face and the voice of Mary Cary Brokenborough were so familiar, people felt as if they knew her. She already dwelt somewhere inside them. And this kid was just smart enough or just drunk enough to use this deluded sense of intimacy to try to transform the ambush into some kind of bullshit flirtation.

Jimmy Lowe's panicked expression began to dissolve as the beauty of this strategy dawned on him, and he, too, grinned and said, " 'At's a goddayum good idy! Gitcher tail up, gal, and let's go git it on!"

"Fuckin' A!" said Flory.

Ziggefoos grinned at both of them, egging them on.

"Thank you very much," said Mary Cary curtly, "but I'm not here to go honky-tonking. I'm here to get to the—"

"*Awwwwww*, come on, Merry Kerry," said Ziggefoos, "don't be lack 'at. You got on yer party clothes, gal! If you don' want a vodka twilat, I'll git us a Coors lat, long neck. If I got me a beer, you got half."

Jimmy Lowe and Flory cracked up over that. *You got half!* That was rich.

Thus encouraged, Ziggefoos said, "And a pack a Salem One Hunnerts, too. We don't git many vis'tors fum New York daown here 'ta DMZ. 'At's whirr you fum, ain't it? New York City?"

Jimmy Lowe and Flory were doubled over with laughter. Irv began to despair. Mary Cary had confronted them, but they were turning it into a farce.

"You're not going to have much to laugh about if you're faced with a charge of *murder*," said Mary Cary. She said it with such stentorian firmness, Jimmy Lowe stopped laughing. She had his attention. "On that tape, which you just saw, you describe how you made an unprovoked attack on Randy Valentine in the men's room of a bar not far from here. You—"

"Awwwwww, latin up, Merry Kerry," said Ziggefoos. "This ain't *Day & Nat*. This here's nat time on Bragg Boulevard. Jes letcher hair daown and git it on."

But Mary Cary kept boring in on Jimmy Lowe. "You just described how you kicked down a door, flattened Randy Valentine against a wall, and began beating him."

She wouldn't let up. She was staring him down. He was close enough to reach out and grab her by the throat.

"You need a drank," said Ziggefoos. "You need to latin up."

Ziggefoos continued to grin, but Jimmy Lowe and Flory no longer had it in them to be amused. They looked at each other and at Ziggefoos with alarm.

"You also described your motivation," said Mary Cary. "You made it very clear what it was. It was homophobia. You assaulted Randy Valentine because he was different, because he didn't have your sexual orientation, because he was gay. Isn't that what you just told us?"

"Didn' tale you any such thang," said Jimmy Lowe. He had a helpless expression, as if he couldn't comprehend how this national apparition, which had somehow materialized out back of the DMZ on Bragg Boulevard, was now hurling such accusations in his face.

"But we just heard you," said Mary Cary. "We just saw you. You just said it in so many words."

"All's I said was—"

"Shut up, Jimmy," said Ziggefoos.

"And we just heard from you, too," said Mary Cary. "And from your friend here, Flory. You just admitted your own involvement, and you just described your own motivation. Randy Valentine wasn't 'from our parish.' Isn't that what you said, Flory? The gay lifestyle is disgusting. Isn't that what we heard you say, Ziggy?"

Irv marveled. Mary Cary was staring them down. There wasn't even the tiniest break in her voice. The sentences were rolling out perfectly. She had them on the ropes. If they didn't stop talking now, they'd hang themselves for sure.

Ziggefoos hesitated. Then he said, "Whatchoo know abaout it?"

"I know what I've just heard you say—you and Jimmy and Flory—in your own words." She looked at Jimmy Lowe again. "If it wasn't for the reason you said, why *did* you attack Randy Valentine?"

Jimmy Lowe said, "All's I did—"

"Jes shut up, Jimmy!" said Ziggefoos. "You don' have to tale 'er a dayum thang." Then he looked at Mary Cary. To Irv, watching on the monitor behind the false wall, Ziggefoos's narrow eyes and long, lean face looked more menacing than ever. "I'm not talking abaout thayut, Merry Kerry. Didn't none a us have nothing to do with Randy Valentine. Don't none a us know what the hale happened to him. But I kin tale you one thang."

"What's that?"

"I kin tale you one thang abaout yer 'gay lafstyle.' "

"All right—go ahead."

"It won't never made fer the U.S. Army."

"Oh? And why is that?"

"You ever knowed anybuddy in the U.S. Army?"

"As a matter of fact, I have. My father was in the Army. He fought in Korea."

"You ever ask him what he thought a having homoseckshuls 'longside him?"

"No, I never did, but I'm sure he wouldn't have been in favor of kicking down doors and beating them senseless."

"You know what a soldier's spose a do? You know what he's spose a be there fer?"

"Tell me," said Mary Cary. There was irritation in her voice. She didn't like what this redneck kid was doing, taking over the role of interrogator.

"A soldier's ther to fat," said Ziggefoos. "He's ther to risk his laf." By now Irv knew the boys' redneck elocution well enough to figure out that *fat* meant *fight* and *laf* meant *life*. But Christ—did Mary Cary?

" 'At's what h'it balls daown to. Ever nawn'n'en, a country, any country, h'it needs men to fat and risk their laf. And do you think ther's any man 'at jes natch'ly wants to risk his laf?" He waited for her to answer.

Mary Cary, irritably: "Go on."

Damn! thought Irv. This kid was fulla shit, but he had a knack for taking over the script and turning things around. If only she could have gotten Jimmy Lowe talking! But Ziggefoos had cut him off. Jimmy Lowe and Flory were just sitting there with their mouths open and their eyes blinking, looking from Mary Cary to Ziggefoos and from Ziggefoos to Mary Cary. Well, maybe he could—

"Hale, no," said Ziggefoos, "ain't nobody jes natch'ly wants to risk his laf. You know what I'm trying to tale you?"

"Go on."

"You got to take 'ose ol' boys and ton'em into a unit. A unit. You know what I'm saying? The *unit*'s the onliest thang that don't know no fear. When you're in the field and you're pinned daown by spear far?"—once more it took Irv a couple of beats to translate: *spear far* meant *superior fire*—they'd have to use subtitles—"the unit's the onliest thang 'at don't run away. The *ind*'vigil? He'll run on you, Merry Kerry. I 'on keer who he is. He'll run on you. But when he's in a *unit*—ain't jes his own mind and his own heart working no more. He's got evvy mind and evvy heart in the *pla*toon inside *uv*'im, whether he wants'em'air'not, and even if he don't want to hear it, they're saying to him, 'A man don't run, a man holts his graound, a man risks his laf if he has to.' Being in a far fat's—"

Mary Cary broke in: "Well, the only man whose life was risked in this case—"

"Being in a far fat's—"

"—was a man who wasn't trying to—"

"Lemme finish, Merry Kerry. Being in a far fat's—"

"All right," said Mary Cary, "if you're so hipped on your *firefights*, let's *talk* about your firefights." *Good girl,* thought Irv, *you figured out "far" and "fat."* "When were you ever *in* a firefight? Not a training excercise—a *real* one? Or—"

"I was—"

"Or is this some grand military theory of yours?"

"I been *in* a far fat."

"*Really?* How interesting. When exactly? In Korea? In *Vietnam?*—which happened to have ended before you were born probably? You've never actually *been* in a firefight, *have* you?"

"Deed, I *have*, too."

"Oh?—exactly *when*? Exactly *where*?"

"In Somalia."

"*Somalia,*" said Mary Cary, pouring on the derision. "A UN mission to provide food to starving people. And you were in a firefight?"

"Jevver hear a Bloody Sunday?"

On the monitor in the rear compartment, Irv saw the consternation on Mary Cary's face immediately. A sixth sense told her not to say no, because "Bloody Sunday" rang some kind of bell, but she didn't know what the bell was tolling. Her expression went blank. The wheels spun—and she came up with nothing. Mary Cary might occasionally bone up on a subject for a *Day & Night* segment, but she was no daily devourer of current events, not via newspapers, not even via the nightly TV news; not the way he, Irv, was. Like a lot of people in television news today, Mary Cary had come into the business not from journalism school but from drama school; at the University of Virginia, in her case. The *star* in television news was not the newshound but the on-camera performer. When people like Mary Cary—and she was far from being the only one—were starting out as correspondents, they prided themselves on being able to go anywhere in the world, arrive with information zero, get briefed for ten or fifteen minutes by whatever researcher was on the scene, and then go on camera and regurgitate the stuff with an air of profound, fathomless, even smug, authority. That was . . . *performing*. Mary Cary's ascent from the lower ranks had begun one evening in 1979. Her producer, a lovable but carbuncled gnome named Murray Lewis, had sent her from New York to Teheran on the spur of the moment to cover the Iran hostage crisis. She raced from the Teheran airport, reached the American Embassy just in time for the evening news in the United States, stood in front of hordes of screaming, placard-waving, flag-burning, effigy-stomping Iranian demonstrators, looked into the camera, and, with information zero, with not so much as thirty seconds of briefing from the network's local researchers, flawlessly rephrased the Associated Press copy concerning the event as Lewis, who was in New York, read it to her over a satellite hookup and into a corded plug stuck in her ear and concealed by her luxuriant blond hair. Made it all roll out of those big lips of hers, she did, with an air of foreign-affairs profundity that would have made a Bismarck's or a Kissinger's jaw drop.

But at this moment she didn't have Murray Lewis or even Irv Durtscher to whisper in her ear, and so she fell back on her standard device for those rare moments when she was stymied or nonplussed.

"Go on," she said with a tone that always insinuated that the poor devil could only dig his own grave deeper.

Irv braced. Irv knew exactly what Bloody Sunday was.

"H'it was Sunday, October the thud, nanteen-nanny-three," said Ziggefoos. Suddenly he was giving Mary Cary a stern, unblinking look of rectitude. "Our unit, we was over east a the Bakhura Market, and our CO, Major Lunsford, he says—wale, the thang was, some *in*former or sump'm, he's tipped us off that this Mohammed Aidid?—some of his top *lieu*tenants, they're having a secret meeting up'eh at the—"

Mary Cary broke in: "That's very interesting, I'm sure, but let's get back to the point, and the point is the murder of Randy Valentine."

Ziggefoos was having none of it. The look in his eyes became even sterner, more accusatory. The boy *did not blink*, not even once. He just sawed away with his story in his rasping redneck twang.

"They was having a secret meeting up'eh at the Olympic *Ho*tel, *Ai*did's people was, and so the CO, he puts forty *uv*'us into a buncha MH-60s. They's helicopters. They call'em Black Hawks. It's abaout three-thuddy inny afternoon, inny brat sunlat, and they'd already sent another unit a Rangers fum the HQ, and them and some Delta Commandos—"

"I'm not interested in—"

But Ziggefoos's new voice ripped right through her. "—and in a couple minutes, all *uv*'us, and the units fum the airport, we're rat over the Olympic *Ho*tel, and if you ever hud prakly twenty MH-60 helicopters up inny air at oncet—I mean, you talk abaout *thun*der—ever 'buddy in'at whole goddayum moth-eaten town 'at had a gun, they strapped h'it on, because they knowed sump'm *big* was coming down."

Mary Cary seemed stunned by the onslaught of his words and the damning stare. *Goddamn it*, thought Irv, *you got to cut him off*! He was aware that his heart was beating much too fast.

"Our unit," said Ziggefoos, "we come *rap*pelling down abaout fifty feet a rope to the *ho*tel roof fum the helicopters, and the units fum the airport, they'd already broke in 'at *ho*tel and they'd got holt those summitches, *Ai*did's people, and them and us, all the units, we jes waitin'eh for the Humvees to come transport the pris'ners when all hell broke loose."

"You know about all hell breaking loose, don't you?" said Mary Cary. *That's it! That's it! But she doesn't have her usual air of command.* "Hell broke loose for Randy—"

"Them dayum Somali militiamen," said Ziggefoos, "they figured later mussa been four or five hunnert *uv*'em. They didn't have no uniforms, Aidid's militiamen didn't. They wasn't quartered in no billets, either. They was all over town, looking just like ever'buddy else, living in all'em dayum shacks or jes out on the dayum street. They was a goddayum *perm*'nen'ly *in*stalled living ambush ready to come daown on any *uv*'us soon's we exposed ourself. They was up in *trees*, they was hiding behind them goddayum *hootches* they got all over Mogadishu—look lack humps a dirt, one aft'other—they was lots *uv*'em men dressed lack women with AK-47s and grenades and I don't know whatall hidden under their skirts. They got rocket-propelled grenades and 'em Glock automatics an'evvy other dayum thang, them summitches did, and the next thang we knowed, one a the MH-60s, h'it's *daown*, h'it's crashed, h'it's daown in the street, and now we got to go out fum the *ho*tel inny goddayum street in the broad daylat'n form a p'rim'ter 'round the MH-60, 'cause the pilot, he's trapped inny wreckage, and he's still alive. We can hear him yelling: 'I got a man dead! I got a man dead in here!' And all of a sudden, I'm seeing guys all around me, buddies a mine, guys I've knowed ever since I was in the Rangers, they's getting blowed away, falling daown dead inny streets a Mogadishu. I move out abaout twenty feet to get a bead on a bunch *uv*'em'at's farring at us fum a treetop and—*blam!*—I'm daown on my goddayum face inny dirt. Goddayum grenade shrapnel's hit me alla way daown my left arm, my left leg, and the left side a my bayack."

With that, he lifted his left arm until his elbow was up beside his ear, and Irv could see clear as day on the monitor a huge scar on the back of Ziggefoos's upper arm that ran all the way down inside his T-shirt sleeve.

"That's jes one *uv*'em," said Ziggefoos. "I got scars lack at'air all overt the left side a my body. We was caught in a *am*bush, Merry Kerry, a *ambush*! The ambush a all *ambushes*! By the time we come out the *ho*tel with them pris'ners, they was waiting. We didn't know it, but we was in a *ambush*! Them Somalis?—and all'at spear farpower?—they'd—wale, it was lack they'd jes growed up out a the graound and sprouted like leaves on the trees, and they was jes raining that sheeut—'scuse me, Merry Kerry—jes pouring it on us from evvy which way."

On the monitor fed by the camera fixed on Mary Cary's face, Irv could see that her lips were parted and her eyes were wide. She looked as if she'd had her breath knocked out.

"Me, I couldn't *move*," said Ziggefoos. "My cheek was lying in the blood that was gushing out my own arm. Jimmy"—he motioned toward Jimmy Lowe, and on the monitors Irv could see Jimmy Lowe and Flory blinking away at a furious rate—"Jimmy come out to git me, come out inny street to git me 'thout no cover't'all, and—*blam!*—Jimmy's daown, too. AK-47 bullet tore rat thoo his shoulder and come out his bayack, and another'n went rat thoo his thigh, and the two *uv*'us, we's both *uv*'us lane out inny middle a the street bleeding like stuck pigs, and the air's full a shrapnel and the wust shitchoo ever saw—'scuse me, Merry Kerry—and I swear fo' God in heaven I could see AK-47 bullets coming at us and going overhaid. You can see'em at a certain angle. Look lack bees coming atchoo, bees fum hell. And you wanna know how we got out a that bloody street?"

"Not particularly," said Mary Cary, "and I don't—"

But Ziggefoos, his narrow-set eyes ablaze, talked right over her: "This little piece a steel ratcheer—" He reached over and put his hand on Flory's shoulder. On the monitor fixed on Flory, Irv could see the runt's eyes blinking away. "Hunnert'n forty-five pounds soaking wet, maybe, but he's a piece a steel, Merry Kerry, and what h'it takes, he got it ratcheer." He tapped his chest, right over the heart, with his fist. "Flory, he awready seen two *uv*'us cut daown, and he come out'air inny street running and crouching and weaving, and he grabbed both *uv*'us by our boots—our *boots*—and he starts dragging us back to the p'rim'ter. Shrapnel hits him in his left fo'arm and his rat calf and his neck—his *neck*!—and a bullet goes thoo 'is ribs and breaks two *uv*'em, and this little piece a steel ratcheer"—he shook Flory's shoulder with his hand—"he don't even stop. He keeps draggin' us till he got us bay-ack inside the p'rim'ter—and you wanna know if I ever been in *far fat*. Jesus Christ, Merry Kerry!"

"No," said Mary Cary, "what I want to know is—"

But no mere words in the world were going to stop the righteous Ziggy Ziggefoos now.

"We was pinned down in'at ambush fer nigh onto *fo'teen hours*, Merry Kerry, and we didn't have no medics, no morphine, no nothing. By and by it's nattime, and it's dark, and the muzzle flashes, I mean, you can see'em flashing out of the trees, fum behind the hootches, fum evvy goddayum place you look. And the grenades—it was a ambush that wouldn't stop. Charlie Company, they send the QRF—the Quick Reaction Force?—they send the QRF out from the airport to give us some cover, and *they* git ambushed, daown at the K-4 Circle. And lack you was talking abaout the *Yew* N? What a goddayum joke! They's trying to git the Pakistanis and the Malaysians to move in with some armored vehicles, and come to find out they's so yellow, them worthless bastards, they wouldn't move out till after midnight, and the onliest reason they moved out *then* was 'at one of our officers put the muzzle of a .357 Magnum upside the haid a one a their colonels, and he says to him, he says, 'You're haidin' for the Olympic Hotel with your armored vehicles or you're one goddayum stone-daid gook motherfucker—'scuse me, Merry Kerry."

"Okay," said Mary Cary, "suppose we assume, for the sake of argument, that you *were*—"

Not a word of it reached Ziggefoos, who kept on paralyzing her and the very camera and the very monitor in the hidden compartment with his glittering eyes. "Lack I was telling you, forty *uv'*us fum our unit? And twenty-eight *uv'*us was wounded, and seven *uv'*us got blowed away, got *killed*. One a our guys got blowed away out inny street, and he didn't have no Jimmy Lowe, he didn't have no Flory, to come out'air 'n'risk their lafs to drag'im back inside any p'rim'ter, and the Somalis, they got to'im fo' we could git to'im, and them fucking animals—'scuse me, Merry Kerry—they pulled the uniform rat off his body, and they drug him through the streets of Mogadishu by ropes tied to his wrists, laughing and hooting like hyenas, flat out grinning like hyenas with their teeth dripping blood after the kill because they'd slaughtered a 'Merican.

"And you stand'eh, and you ax me if I ever been in a far fat. 'Scuse me, Merry Kerry, but you're fulla shit."

"Spoken like a true credit to the military," said Mary Cary with an icy sarcasm. The insult had roused her to anger, renewed her sharp edge. Irv's heart was hammering away as he watched it all on the monitors. "So now that you've got all that out of your system, perhaps you'll be so kind as to tell me what any of it has to do with the murder of Randy Valentine."

"Okay," said Ziggefoos, "that's 'zackly what I was fixing to tale you. Being in a military unit's abaout being a *man*, and what the unit tales you and keeps on taling you is, 'This here's the *test* of a man. A man don't cut and run. A man risks his laf . . . fer the unit. 'Yeah, I reckon he risks it fer his country and fer the flag and fer the folks back home and all'at, but you talk to anybuddy's ever been in a real far fat, a real field a far, and if he's honest, he's gon' tale you what I'm taling you rat now. You risk yer laf fer the unit, and the unit's alla time hammering away at one thang: 'Be a man.' H'it don't say, 'Be a good person, and h'it shore's hell don't say, 'Be a good woman.' I mean, you start putting women in combat, and I kin tale you sump'm jes as shore's the sun comes up in the moaning: You kin fergit abaout having real fattin' units. Because the unit's got jes one thang to say to you: 'Be a man.' Same thang with hom'seckshuls. 'Zackly same thang. You try to put hom'seckshuls in a fattin' unit? You kin jest fergit abaout thayut, too. The unit caint say, 'Be a man—more or less,' or 'Be a man—in most *re*specks,' because the kinda ol' boy you got to have jes ain't gon' set still fer that, and you kin wait a thousand yers and try to *en*latin'im, and he still ain't gon' set still. Naow, you kin call 'at prej'dice if you want, and maybe h'it is, but that don't change the facks a laf a'tall. You folks, you teevee folks, you best tale 'Merica she better look after her Jimmy Lowes and her Florys, 'cause when push comes to shove, she's gonna need 'em, and push always comes to shove sooner or later, an' you gon' need somebody—you teevee folks, too—you gon' need somebody to fat yer wars for ya, and those somebodys gon' be and always has been your Jimmy Lowes and your Florys."

Long before he could begin to analyze what he had just heard, a *red alert* had gone off in Irv's head. This kid Ziggefoos was a *Tobacco Road* throwback, an unrenovated native, a true Southern primitive, a Florida redneck—a *skinhead*—and he was spouting total fascist bullshit—but no way could this rant be allowed on *Day & Night*. To witless segments of a TV audience, to the idiot millions, he might come across as a sincere young fighting man from the bosom of rural America who had risked his life in the service of his country and been grievously wounded in a *far fat* in the godforsaken streets of Mogadishu, Somalia. He wasn't blinking with nervousness the way Jimmy Lowe and Flory were. He wasn't being hysterical or defensive or evasive. He was looking Mary Cary right in the eye. There had to be something Irv could do, something in the editing—

Apparently Mary Cary sensed the same sort of thing. "That's all very well," she said, "but do you call assaulting a gay soldier 'being a man'?"

"Nawwwwww, I wouldn't call 'at being a man," said Ziggefoos, "and neither'd anybuddy ailse I know, but we don' need you to tale us 'at. I know you're ver *en*latined. Everbuddy you see on TV is ver *en*latined abaout all 'ese thangs. But I wunner how you live yer own lafs. How many hom'seckshuls you got close to *you*? How many a you want yer *own* chilrun to be hom'seckshuls? How many a you want hom'seckshuls working 'longside you? You don't mind taling the U.S. Army, you don't mind taling a fattin' unit, whirr a man's job is to risk his laf, you don't mind taling *us* to jep'dize the *in*tegrity a the unit, when it's laf and death, but what abaout you—when it ain't nothing but yer own comfort and peace a mind?"

Why, the sonofabitch! He was turning the whole thing around! He was bending the English language out of all recognizable shape, but he was managing to turn the whole thing into an attack on the so-called media elite! It was a cliché, and it was preposterous, but he was managing to do it.

"You're forgetting one thing," snapped Mary Cary. "Nobody in the television industry, nobody *I* know of, is going around murdering colleagues just because their sexual orientation is different."

It was a good retort, made under the gun, but there was something peevish and argumentative about it. Irv's mind spun rapidly; this whole last part, the skinhead's disquisition on the media elite, would have to go, too. No way would it be part of the broadcast. Much of the disquisition on the fighting unit—the *fattin'* unit—Christ!—and Bloody Sunday—most of that would have to go, too. Ziggefoos had turned those two skinhead thugs, Jimmy Lowe and Flory, into some kind of heroes, and that *Hee Haw* accent might just put it over. Of course, he couldn't cut it all, but—ahhhh! He had an idea. He'd let the sonofabitch talk,

but he'd take the camera off him. He'd use the cameras trained only on Jimmy Lowe and Flory. You'd hear Ziggefoos's voice, but you'd see the other two with their mouths open, looking alarmed and blinking . . . *blinking* . . . Lots of blinking! On television the close-ups of people blinking furiously were devastating. The blinks looked like uncontrollable admissions of guilt. Besides, Jimmy Lowe looked like a brute. If I, Irv Durtscher, kept Jimmy Lowe's animal face on the screen, blinking guiltily, while Ziggefoos spoke, no one would really be able to pay close attention to Ziggefoos's argument. He could use Flory and his guilty blinks, too. Flory looked like the usual gang runt, willing to go along with any caper the big boys dictated. Ah!—and he had another idea. Every time Ziggefoos used gross language, every time he said *sheeut* or anything else of that sort, he'd bleep it. That would make him seem cruder than the actual words would. Oh, he could fix this brute's hash, him and his Dogpatch theories about manhood and the unit and life and death. *Laf'n'death—meeyahhhh—*

"Maybe not," said Ziggefoos. "Maybe you don' go 'raound murdern each other, but you do sump'm ailse. You go 'sem'natin' stuff abaout the gay lafstyle you don' even believe yer ownsef, and don' nobuddy ailse believe it neither, and you git everbuddy worked up, and fellers 'at jes natch'ly resent hom'seckshuls, fellers 'at know dayum wale it ain't gon' work to put 'em in a fattin' unit, they git riled to whirr they do thangs they won't lackly to do if you people'd jes tol' the plain truth."

"All right," said Mary Cary, "for the sake of argument, let's say that's true. Are you telling me *that's* why the three of you assaulted Randy Valentine?"

"I ain't said nothin' lack 'at," said Ziggefoos.

"But you did!" Mary Cary said, gesturing at the television set once more. "There you were! You said it in your own words! Jimmy just spelled it all out. He said he kicked in the door. The door knocked Randy Valentine up against the wall. And then he grabbed him."

Good girl, Mary Cary! She was steering it back to the confession made on videotape.

"Wale, you got it all wrong," said Jimmy Lowe, giving the television set a dismissive wave and getting up and turning his back on it, as if to leave.

" 'At's rat," said Flory, doing the same thing, "you got it all wrong."

"But they're your own words," said Mary Cary, "from your own mouths."

"Yeah, but y'all rigged 'is all up," said Jimmy Lowe.

It was beautiful. He didn't even look at Mary Cary when he said it. It came out as a whine, not much above a mutter. For television purposes, it was as good as an outright confession. The retreat, the pout, the refusal to look the accuser in the eye, the muffled voice—it had guilt written all over it, and by now every television viewer knew the vocabulary.

Even Ziggefoos had gotten up and turned away. All three seemed like whipped dogs. They were gravitating toward the door of the RV.

Ziggefoos looked at Mary Cary and said, "If you think we're gonna set still and talk to *Day'n'Nat* abaout all 'is bullsheeut, you got another think coming."

Irv couldn't figure out what he was talking about at first. Then it dawned on him: they didn't even know the ambush had been taped! They never dreamed that four cameras had been trained on them ever since they stepped into the RV! They thought this was some sort of preinterview! They didn't even know it was an actual *ambush*!

Oh, it was beautiful. He had dreamed that this piece would work out, and now he could see that it would.

"Nevertheless," said Mary Cary, "we'd like to give you a chance to respond."

Jimmy Lowe, who was at the door, wheeled about. "Me, I'd lack a chance to respond to 'at ho 'at brought us aout here, whirrever the hale *she* went. 'At's who I'd lack to respond to. Didn' know you people hard hose to do yer dirty work."

Hard hose? Even Irv, practiced as he was in these boys' patois, needed an extra moment to translate: *hired whores*. He'd love to use that line—even though referring to Lola as a whore was a little too close to the truth—because Jimmy Lowe sounded so ominous when he said it. *Suppose he became violent? Attacked Mary Cary? (Attacked Irv Durtscher!)* Had he gone too far in using a topless dancer to make sure the three skinheads watched their incriminating tape? Well—editing would solve everything. *Could Gordon and Roy and Ferretti stop them, if it came to that? They were big, but these three skinheads were . . . Rangers!* Irv crouched there in his secret compartment, his headset on, his eyes pinned on the monitors, his world lit only by their lifeless cathode glow, his mind furiously double-tracking from . . . Irv Durtscher the crusader against . . . fascism! . . . in America . . . to Irv Durtscher the possessor of this one and only skin, which God had never intended to go up against young Lords of Testosterone such as he saw on these screens.

To his vast relief, as he watched the monitors, he saw the three boys file through the door and depart the RV. He saw Ferretti pull the door shut behind them and lock it. Then he saw Ferretti break into a silent laugh and look at Mary Cary. Then he saw Mary Cary heave a big sigh and shake her head, as if severely disappointed. Then he heard Ferretti, grinning and chuckling, say, "If you think we're gonna set still and talk to *Day'n'Nat* abaout all 'is bullsheeut . . ." And still Irv did not take off his headset and forsake his secret compartment and join them in the RV's living room. *Suppose they came back! Suppose they stormed back into the RV!*

But then, on the monitor, he saw Mary Cary heading back toward the partition. *Mustn't let—*

Quickly he took off the headset and went through the concealed door. She was right there in front of him, breathing rapidly, her eyes flashing. She looked furious.

"Mary Cary!" said Irv. "That was great! You were fabulous!"

"Oh, I blew it, Irv," said Mary Cary. "I lost 'em. I couldn't keep 'em here. And I *had* them! They were finally where we *wanted* them! They were *defensive*! They were getting *angry*!"

He stared at her. He couldn't believe it. "I don't know what you're worried about," he said. "We got everything we needed."

"That's not true."

"Besides, the big one, Lowe, he was getting pretty hot. I was afraid—you never know with a guy like that."

"Oh, *please*," said Mary Cary. "Those kids didn't know whether to whistle 'Dixie' or go blind."

"All the same—" Irv broke off the sentence and studied Mary Cary's big Blond Bombshell face. She was genuinely angry. She meant it. She actually wanted to stay here and keep slugging it out.

"I know what you mean," he said finally. "But don't worry about it. You were great."

In fact, he didn't know what she meant. He couldn't even imagine it. His hide, the mortal vessel that contained Irv Durtscher the Rousseau of the Cathode Ray, was saying, Thank God, that's over! Or is it? Keep one ear open lest those three return. Get this vehicle packed up! Let's get out of here—out of Hell!—off Bragg Boulevard!—back to civilization!—back to enlightenment!—back to New York!

PART FOUR

THE ONE WITH THE BALLS

Well, this was New York, all right. Walter O. Snackerman, the network's chairman, CEO, and corporate predator in chief, lived in one of those three-story apartments on Fifth Avenue in the sixties you wouldn't believe could exist unless you actually set foot in it the way Irv was now doing. The building, which was twelve stories high, had been built in 1916 to compete with the ostentatious mansions that lined Fifth, so that each apartment was, in effect, a containerized ostentatious mansion with an enormous entry gallery, sweeping staircases, vast rooms, views of Central Park, walls a foot thick, and a legion of doormen, porters, and elevator men dressed like a Gilbert and Sullivan Joint Chiefs of Staff.

The library, where the great Snackerman had now assembled his guests, was twice the size of Irv's living room, or at least his present living room, now that he had to foot the bill for both his ex-wife Laurie's apartment and his own. This one room, this library, had more leather couches, leather easy chairs, more antique bergères and *fauteuils* than Irv had furniture in his whole place. The assembled hotshots had their eminent fannies nestled into all the plush upholstery, with, of course, Mary Cary—*Merry Kerry Broken Berruh*—sitting at the right hand of Snackerman the Omnipotent. A ceiling projector was beaming *Day & Night* onto the 5- by 7-foot Sony television screen that had descended with such a soft, luxurious hum from a slit in the ceiling a few minutes earlier.

Irv, clad in a shapeless blue blazer, a button-down shirt, and a so-called Pizza Grenade necktie, which looked as if a pepperoni-and-olive pizza had just exploded on his shirt front, was seated over here on the side, at the right hand of Cale Bigger. In an ordinary network setting this might have been considered a prime spot. But tonight the mighty Cale was a mere hired hand, the chief executive of the News Division and a shameless, gibbering suck-up to the ruler. Most of the seats were filled by Snackerman's fellow titans and Big Names, such as Martin Adder, the general partner of the law firm of Crotalus, Adder, Cobran & Krate; Robin Swarm, the comedian and movie actor; Rusty Mumford, the forty-one-year-old dork, wuss, nerd, and billionaire founder of 4IntegerNet; and the nitwit Senator Marsh McInnes; plus their wives. Mary Cary's husband, Hugh Siebert, the eye surgeon, was sitting over on the side next to the senator's overripe second wife. The good Dr. Siebert was a long-faced, wide-jawed nullity. Tall and handsome in a certain way, Irv supposed, with a head of steel-gray hair—it looked as if he probably spent two hours each morning brushing it back *just so;* but a nullity, a big somber zero, for all of that. At dinner—prepared and served by Snackerman's own house staff of five—Siebert had sat between the Present Mrs. Martin Adder and Robin Swarm's early-twenty-ish live-in girlfriend, Jennifer Love-Robin, or whatever her name was, and he hadn't said a word. What a nullity, what a cipher, what a fifth wheel Mary Cary had married . . . What a stiff neck . . . Why would a block of wood like that even want to live in an electric city like New York?

Actually, Irv wondered if he himself would have been invited if his name hadn't been mentioned so much in broadcasts and the newspapers, not as much as Mary Cary's, naturally, but a lot. The network's PR elves had started pumping out press-screening tapes yesterday, plus transcriptions, thirty-six hours before tonight's network showing. The U.S. attorney for the Eastern District of North Carolina and the state attorney general of North Carolina and the judge advocate of the U.S. Army and the sheriff of Cumberland County, where the DMZ was physically located, were already making a lot of noise. They were torn between the fact that *Day & Night*—Irv Durtscher, producer—had violated the laws of every conceivable jurisdiction by bugging the DMZ with cameras and microphones and the fact that they had nailed three murderers dead to rights in a sensational case.

Snackerman had put together this dinner and prime-time-television viewing on the spur of the moment. The story of the *Day & Night* coup had been on every network-news program. It was too big for the rival networks to ignore. It had been on page 1 of *The New York Times* this morning. Oh, what a surge, what a mighty cresting wave of publicity! At this very moment *Day & Night* lit up the television screens of not merely 50 million but maybe 100 million souls, including Walter O. Snackerman and his friends.

On Snackerman's huge Sony screen, there was Mary Cary, in her Tiffany-blue cashmere jacket and a cream-colored turtleneck, a jersey that covered up the age lines on her neck, sitting behind a futuristic news desk.

"For three months," she was saying, "the United States Army has insisted it could find no link whatsoever between Army personnel and the savage beating and murder of Randy Valentine, a young soldier with a distinguished service record, a member of the Army's elite Rangers—who happened to be gay. We found more than *a link*. Simply by listening in on the enlisted men's own grapevine, we located three of Randy

Valentine's fellow soldiers at Fort Bragg—and you are about to see and hear them describe in harrowing detail, before our hidden cameras, how they committed this senseless assassination—and *why*: for no other reason than that Randy Valentine's sexual orientation was . . . *different* . . . from theirs."

For an instant, on the screen, Mary Cary's face seemed to shudder with emotion. Her thick lips parted, and she executed a sharp intake of air, and she leaned closer to the camera, and her blue eyes blazed. "We try to avoid being personal, but I don't think any of us at *Day & Night*, and certainly not myself, have ever stared more directly . . . down the bloody . . . *throat* . . . of wanton slaughter."

Oh, it was dynamite. Irv glanced at Snackerman and noticed the slightly giddy expression on the tycoon's wrinkled face, beneath his odd crew-cut dome, as revealed by the room's soft lights and the glow of the television screen. He was leaning toward Mary Cary, and then he tried to look right into her face, but she kept looking straight ahead at the screen, reluctant to sacrifice even one millisecond of Merry Kerry Broken Berruh ego infusion. Her blond hair was fluffed out in full backtease. She was wearing a conservative, very expensive-looking red Chanel-style suit (Irv didn't know the names of any more-recent designers), but with a creamy silk blouse open low enough to offer a hint of the lusty Brokenborough breasts and a skirt hemmed high enough to put a lot of the Brokenborough legs, sheathed in shimmering, darkish but transparent pantyhose, in Snackerman's face as she crossed and uncrossed them.

Merry Kerry Broken Berruh was not about to tell Snackerman or anybody else that every word she had just uttered *and* the catch in her voice *and* the indignant blaze in her blue eyes had been scripted for her by Irv Durtscher.

Now there was a long shot of Fort Bragg, and then there were medium shots of buildings, drill fields, obstacle courses, barracks, and packs of soldiers off-duty in the Cross Creek Mall, as Mary Cary's voice-over explained that Fort Bragg was command central for the Army's elite troops, the Special Operations Forces, the commandos, the Army's best, in short—and that one of the *very best of the best* was a young man named Randy Valentine.

Then you see some still pictures, the kinds of photographs you find in family albums, pictures of Randy Valentine in uniform shortly after his enlistment and Randy Valentine with his parents in Massilon, Ohio, and Randy Valentine in his high-school yearbook, and then two pictures of Ranger Randy Valentine at Fort Bragg.

Suddenly the shocker: Randy Valentine's handsome young smiling face was replaced by a close-up of that same face as it appeared in the morgue photo, a face battered, cut, swollen, and caved in on one side until it no longer looked like the face of a human being. Then came the Cumberland County Sheriff's Office police photo of the young man's body sprawled in a slick of blood on the floor of a men's room in a gin mill on Bragg Boulevard, as the police had found it—Mary Cary's voice explained—on that fateful night.

And next came the flinty face of General Huddlestone blinking with nervousness as he denied any knowledge of any of his men's involvement in the case, despite an exhaustive investigation, blah, blah, blah.

Now you could see gaudy footage of Bragg Boulevard as Mary Cary explained how "we" had soon learned that the word around Fort Bragg was that a certain three soldiers had beaten Randy Valentine to a pulp in a Bragg Boulevard dive in a drunken rage over the fact that he was gay . . . the sleazy neon sign of the DMZ winking away at night . . . the interior of the joint . . . bored strippers shaking their booties and their hooters up on the DMZ's bar runway . . . a medium shot of Ferretti, Gordon, and Roy installing the bugging devices, while Mary Cary's voice says, "As we were now the duly registered lessees of the DMZ, its proprietors of record for the next four weeks, we set about installing our hidden cameras and microphones" . . . Jimmy Lowe, Ziggy, and Flory in the booth . . . then Mary Cary saying, "We spent one night, two nights, three nights, an entire week—and then a second week—monitoring the conversations of Lowe, Ziggefoos, and Flory without hearing anything out of the ordinary for three young soldiers who liked to come to a bar and drink beer and look at strippers. But then, three days into the third week, came the break we had been waiting for. Virgil Ziggefoos brought up the subject of . . . *gay rights* . . ."

Now you're looking straight at Ziggefoos in that booth, and he's finishing a sentence with those very words, "gay rats."

It occurred to Irv, as he sat here in the Snackerman containerized palace on Fifth Avenue, that the camera and the light caught Ziggefoos's thin face in a *perfect* way. He looked especially lean, mean, and menacing. The kid was a redneck Dracula.

"They nebber tale you what the hale they deeud fo' they got that way," this clay-sod skinhead was telling 150—or was it 175?—million Americans. "You jes see some may'shated *bleep*"—Irv had bleeped out *son of a bitch* to make it sound worse than the term itself sounded . . . then Jimmy Lowe, with his pumped-up muscles and his brutally strong face, saying, "*Bleepin'* A."

Now you're looking at Ziggefoos again, and he's saying, "Oncet my old man rented us a *ho*tel room somers up near the pier at Myrtle Beach, an' rat next doe's this *bow*adin haouse or sump'm lack 'at'eh, and abaout five o'clock in the moaning?—when it's jes starting to geeut lat?—me 'n' my brother . . ." At this point Ziggefoos's voice fades under the sound of the Country Metal music in the background, and Mary Cary's voice comes up. You can see Ziggefoos's lips moving and his hands gesturing, but what you hear is Mary Cary paraphrasing his description of how his father had imbued him with a hatred of gays one morning in a hotel in Myrtle Beach.

And now Ziggefoos's voice comes back up, and you hear him say, "And the ol' man, he's smoking, I mean, he's flat out on far by now, he's so mad, and he yales out, 'Hey, you faggots! I'm gonna caount to ten, and if you ain't off'n'at roof, you best be growing some wangs, 'cause they's gonna be a load a 12-gauge *bud*shot haidin' up yo' *bleep*!' "

Now, via another hidden camera, we see Jimmy Lowe and Flory grinning and nodding their approval of this call for violent action in response to public displays of gay closeness, and we hear Mary Cary say:

"Thus was the lesson passed on from one generation to another, and the lesson was: You do not *tolerate* homosexuality . . . You *exterminate* the gay life, if you can . . . You do so *violently*, if necessary . . . Lessons like that, taught in a hotel room one murky dawn in Myrtle Beach, South Carolina, and, no doubt, many other places in the years that followed, led these boys"—and now we see all three of the young Rangers grinning and drinking beer—"directly, as if impelled by Destiny, to the moment in which they . . . *slaughtered* . . . Randy Valentine because he *dared* . . . to display gay affection where they could see it."

As he watched the screen there in Snackerman's regal library, Irv's heart quickened, and his spirits soared. The crux of the entire show was about to begin. The entire nation was about to hear the incriminating words of Jimmy Lowe, Ziggefoos, and Flory. He cut a glance at Snackerman, at Cale Bigger, at Mary Cary. Their faces were lit up by the glare of the great Sony television screen. This show was going to have the highest rating of any television newsmagazine show of the decade; of all time, maybe. Naturally, Snackerman, Cale Bigger, and everybody else of any consequence at the network had already seen a tape of the show. But even for them, and certainly for Irv, there was nothing quite like watching a blockbuster such as this *as it aired*, nothing quite like *feeling the ineffable thrum* of the tens of millions of other nervous systems of people all over this country and Canada who would be resonating to it *at this very moment.* Snackerman, needless to say, cared nothing whatsoever about social justice, about gay-bashing, about *Day & Night*'s artistry, or about the entire News Division, except that it was only the existence of the News Division that enabled him to give his speech about "The People's Right to Know" at conventions, conferences, annual meetings, etc., etc., etc. After all, the network's top-rated show, a sitcom called *Smoke 'at Mother*, didn't do much to lend the great man dignity and gravitas. But not even a cynical, money-loving predator like Snackerman, this shark, this corporate eating machine, could resist the communal, tachycardiac heartbeats of the millions that vibrated in your bones when you watched a triumph like this *as it aired*. Yes, even he, Snackerman, would, on the morrow, with genuine enthusiasm, look into the faces of other American television watchers and say, "Did you see *Day & Night* last night?" and "Remember the part where . . ." Oh, you could talk all you wanted to about cable TV and the Internet and all the things that were supposedly going to supplant network television, but Irv knew, if others didn't, that *the network* had a unique magic to *it*, the magic of the Jungian *communal heartbeat* . . . teased into tachycardia by the brilliance of the great producers of the new art form, the *Irv Durtschers*. True, Snackerman was listing heavily toward Mary Cary as if he just naturally assumed that all this magical tribal consciousness had been created by *her* . . . But if the whole thing ended up in court, as Irv prayed it would, even Snackerman would realize the truth at last.

And now, on the screen, Jimmy Lowe is into the evil heart of the matter. "Soon's I walked inair and I looked unner that tallit doe and I seen that guy's knees on the flow, and I hud these two guys going, '*Unnnnnh, unnnnnh, unnnnnh*'—I mean, I knew 'zackly what h'it was. And when I walked overt the tallit and stood up on tippytoe and looked daown over the doe and seen it was a feller fum my own goddayum cump'ny—"

And now Jimmy Lowe's voice sank below the Country Metal throb of the DMZ, and Mary Cary's voice-over rose up, and once more she paraphrased, just the way Irv himself had written it:

"Now it was Jimmy Lowe who was witnessing—by eavesdropping—a display of gay affection. Randy Valentine was in that locked toilet booth, embracing another man—the two of them driven there by the public's and, more severely, the military's sanctions against amorous gestures in public by persons of the same sex."

Then Mary Cary's voice disappears, and Jimmy Lowe's rises up again, as he says:

"I mean, I saw some kinda *rayud*, and 'at was when I kicked inny doe. Broke 'at little metal tab rat off'n it."

"Summitch mussa wunner what the hale hit him," says Ziggefoos.

"Whole goddayum doe hit him, I reckon," says Jimmy Lowe. "That summitch, he was lane upside the wall when I grabbed him."

Now the Bombshell face of Mary Cary fills the screen, and she says with the sincerity that only a truly gifted video performer can summon up: "As you have just seen . . . in unmistakable terms, these three young men, these three soldiers of the United States Army, these three members of an elite corps, the Rangers, revealed the motive for the crime they had committed: homophobia, pure and simple. They revealed the fact that the killing began with an unprovoked, blindsided assault. And they revealed the fact there exists an as-yet-unidentified *witness* to this senseless murder . . . the young man who was with Randy Valentine when the assault began . . ."

Once more Mary Cary stares into the camera without uttering a sound. Another eternity seems to elapse. Those blue eyes blaze as they have never blazed before. And then she says:

"We *urge* that young man . . . to *come forward*, to make himself known. We urge anyone who may *know* his identity to come forward. This crime was too *monstrous* . . . for *anyone* to allow society's prejudice against the gay life or current military law and custom regarding the gay life to *muffle* . . . the ringing call for *justice* . . . in this case."

Now, all at once, you're back in the DMZ with Jimmy Lowe, Ziggefoos, and Flory, and they're grinning again and drinking beer again and chuckling and leering up toward what the viewer must figure is the bar and the topless dancers, as if nothing has happened, as if they don't have a worry in the world. The same old Country Metal music is banging and sloshing away. And then you hear Mary Cary's voice:

"James Lowe, Virgil Ziggefoos, and Randall Flory had made it clear, in their own words, as caught by our microphones and cameras, precisely how the murder of Randy Valentine had occurred. But here at *Day & Night* we were determined to show them what you have just seen and get their response. So we enlisted the services of a well-known Bragg Boulevard exotic dancer, Lola Thong"—now you see Lola, walking through a parking lot—"to invite the three of them back to a High Mojave recreational vehicle we had parked out back of the club. She was the one person we could find, on short notice, whose invitation . . . to view their own videotaped confession . . . the three soldiers just might accept. That night we sent Lola Thong into the DMZ . . . to make the trio a proposition. As you will see, it was not an entirely candid proposition, but it seemed to us that, under the circumstances, her less than full disclosure was justified . . ."

You see Lola at the booth inside the DMZ. "You like veedeos?"

"What kinda videos?" asks Jimmy Lowe.

"Unusual veedeos," says Lola with a full-blown, star-quality leer.

And now they're all sliding out of the booth and heading for the parking lot.

Suddenly, as Irv sat there slumped way down in an antique bergère in Snackerman's vast library, his heart began racing—even as it had raced that night when he knew the three young thugs were leaving the bar and heading for the High Mojave and the immediate proximity of his mortal hide.

Now you see a medium-long shot of the High Mojave in the parking lot. From inside the RV's living room, you see the door handle revolve, and then the door opens and in come the raucous traffic sounds and deep electric-bass strums of Bragg Boulevard, and in comes Lola, and you're staring straight down her dress at her prodigious breasts, and behind her come Jimmy Lowe and Ziggefoos and Flory . . . with their T-shirts, their muscles, their tight jeans, their skinned heads . . .

When Lola slips the videocassette into the VCR, Mary Cary's voice takes over: "Lola had promised James Lowe, Virgil Ziggefoos, and Randall Flory some 'unusual videos,' and that was what she proceeded to show them. All that she had left out was just how unusual they would turn out to be."

You see the three rednecks sitting on the couch and staring at the TV, whose own screen has that scrolling blur you get when you try to film television images. Irv had cut out all of Lola's striptease act, and now you're aware that Randy Valentine's murderers are watching the very tape on which they themselves disclose how they committed the heinous crime, and Mary Cary says: "Sitting on that couch, in that High Mojave, they watched *everything* . . . that you have just seen."

The hidden cameras focus on each of the three, and each one is blinking furiously. Jimmy Lowe's mouth is hanging open; Ziggefoos smacks him on the side of his leg and says, "I 'on know, Jimmy, I 'on lack 'is *bleep*."

And Jimmy Lowe turns on Lola and says, "Look here, *bleep* it, Lola, I wanna know what the *bleep*'s going on, and I wanna know rat now."

And Lola keeps saying, "Eenteractive teevee, eenteractive teevee."

And Jimmy Lowe says, "You kin innerack with my sweet *bleep*, Lola. I ax you a simple question."

And Lola says, "You don' believe me? Eenteractive teevee. Eenteractive teevee, Jeemy! I'm gon' show you, Jeemy, right now! There! You have a special vees'tor!"

And all at once the three young thugs are blinking, dumbstruck and agog over quite something else:

"Hello, Jimmy. I'm Mary Cary Brokenborough."

I'm Merry

Kerry

Broken

Berruh.

You see the three youths' shock and incredulity at the sudden appearance in their midst, in the living room of the RV out back of a fifth-rate topless bar on Bragg Boulevard, of the best-known female face in the United States. You see them with their mouths open and their eyes blinking and those damning blinks in the unspoken but universally known language of Newsmagazine Sting TV say: *Guilty! Guilty! Guilty! Guilty!*

Then you see the three of them, led by Ziggefoos, trying to turn the ambush into a joke. They start urging Mary Cary to "Gitcher tail up, gal" and join them inside the DMZ for some "vodka twilats." Ziggefoos is the cool, cocksure, self-possessed one throughout this exchange, and so Irv had used the cameras trained on Jimmy Lowe and Flory while Ziggefoos spoke. You hear Ziggefoos's impudent, mocking words, but you see Jimmy Lowe's and Flory's blinking eyes saying, "*Guilty! Guilty! Guilty! Guilty!*" The rest was easy—if you knew this business the way he, Irv, did. He simply eliminated Ziggefoos's Neanderthal rant, his self-pitying brute's disquisition on manhood and "the unit," and the rest of his utterly irrelevant bleat. Instead, we see Mary Cary, at the top of her form, grilling him relentlessly.

Ziggefoos says, "Whatchoo know abaout it?"

And Mary Cary says, "I know what I've just heard you say—you and Jimmy and Flory—in your own words." Then, to Jimmy Lowe: "If it wasn't for the reason you said, why *did* you attack Randy Valentine?"

Blinking furiously, looking furiously guilty, Jimmy Lowe says, "All's I did—"

Ziggefoos cuts him off. "Jes shut up, Jimmy!"

Then Irv had shifted to the camera on Jimmy Lowe's face. A damning, guilty silence, that face! With much blinking! *Guilty!* The brute looks as guilty on that screen as if he's just made a full and open confession. *Artistry!*—

He had allowed Ziggefoos to say, "Didn' none a us have nothing to do with Randy Valentine. Don't none a us know what the hale happened to him."

But then he had cut to the cameras trained on Jimmy Lowe and Flory—and not merely to capture their frightened, bugged-out, blinking faces, which said, without a word, "We do, *too*, know what happened to Randy Valentine! We kaled'at quair!"

At that point, thanks to the simple magic of multiple cameras, it was easy for Irv to jump all the way from Ziggefoos saying, "Don't none a us know what the hale happened to him," to a beaten Jimmy Lowe saying, "Wale, you got it all wrong," and giving the television set a weak, guilt-sapped, dismissive wave and getting up and turning his back.

" 'At's rat," says Flory, also getting up and retreating, "you got it all wrong."

"But they're your own words," says Mary Cary, "from your own mouths."

"Yeah, but y'all rigged 'is all up," says Jimmy Lowe, now in a full and stricken retreat to the door.

Now Ziggefoos joins Jimmy and Flory, and he looks like a whipped dog, too. It was as if the entire ambush had taken all of ninety seconds. Overwhelmed by the evidence and the sternness of the Goddess of

Television, the three thugs had mounted one brief show of loutish bravado, then buckled cravenly, the logorrheic Ziggefoos included, put their tails between their legs and slunk off like the worthless mutts they were. And so what if after the ambush, Irv had learned that in fact Jimmy Lowe and Flory had been decorated for their actions outside the Olympic Hotel in Mogadishu on Bloody Sunday? What did that have to do with their actions as homophobic goons and murderers inside a gin mill one bloody night on Bragg Boulevard in Fayetteville, North Carolina?

And now, on the screen, back in New York, is the victor, Mary Cary Brokenborough, at her futuristic desk at network command central. She begins her peroration, which she had retaped—and Irv had written—earlier this very day:

"Already, various legal jurisdictions, federal, state, local, and military, have informed *Day & Night* that in broadcasting what you have just seen, we have violated laws concerning the wire interception of private conversations." She pauses, and those fabulous blue eyes blaze. "Perhaps we have . . . Perhaps we have . . . Although we have been assured otherwise by our own legal counsel from the very beginning. Yet whatever the legal technicalities of the matter may be, we know very well—and we think that most of the citizens of our country know very well—that we have obeyed a far higher and more important law . . . and the most vital of American traditions, the tradition that values, above all else, Fairness . . . and Justice . . . regardless of what legislators and prosecutors, who come and go, might care to say . . ."

Prosecutors!

He, Irv, had written the entire thing for his Big Blond mouthpiece, but suddenly—*prosecutors!*

The implications of the word hit him, and a horrible wave of fear went rolling through his central nervous system, and his heart began drumming away at an alarming rate.

What have I *done*? Jail! They'll send me to jail—with relish! They won't touch *her*. Oh no, not her, not Merry Kerry Broken Berruh!

They'll treat me like the *accountant*, like the accountant who goes to jail when the Big Celebrity cheats on her income taxes! They'll subpoena all the videotapes! They'll see what I did! Bugged the DMZ—violated the laws of at least four jurisdictions—five years on each count—*the rest of my woulda-been working life!* The porno video I concocted with Lola Thong—that cheap little hooker thrusting the gorged red lips of her labia majora right into the camera—*entrapment!*—they'll pin it on *me*! Every insidious editing trick I played with the tapes—they'll see it all and reveal it all! We're going to make *you, Irv*, an example of everything Americans instinctively hate about the arrogance of the media and the reptilian perfidy of entrapment TV! Yes, *you, Irv Durtscher*—you coldblooded, slippery, slimy little snake, you—all fangs and *no balls*!

Now Irv's heart had gone into not only tachycardia but a terrifying series of palpitations, and he slumped way down in the bergère—*I'm having a heart attack! I'm*—

—A beeper went off. Irv looked over. It was Dr. Siebert, Mary Cary's husband, sitting over there on the far side by Senator McInnes's wife. He pulled a little cell phone out of his jacket pocket. You could hear him speaking *sotto voce*.

Then he got up and strode rapidly over to where Snackerman and Mary Cary were sitting. Mary Cary's image was still up on the screen. She was completing her stirring peroration—Irv's peroration—about residual fascism in America. Nevertheless, Hugh Siebert said to Snackerman:

"Excuse me. I'm sorry." And then he leaned right across Snackerman and said to his wife, "I'm sorry, honey. There's been an accident on the FDR Drive. An eleven-year-old girl—corneal-scleral laceration with effusion of the vitreous humor."

Then he bolted from the room. This big, square-jawed, gray-thatched, pompous piece of lumber—he literally ran out of the room and toward the elevator. Everybody, Snackerman, Rusty Mumford, Martin Adder, every last one of them, wives, Jennifer Love-Robin—all, that is, except for Mary Cary—they all craned their noggins away from the Sony TV screen and stopped listening to his, Irv's, stirring prose pouring from the mouth of Her Smugness—and stared at the galloping surgeon. A medical emergency! A brave doctor! Fearless savior!

Irritably, Snackerman turned toward Mary Cary and said, "What'd he say?"

Mary Cary never for a moment took her eyes off herself on the screen as she replied, "An eleven-year-old girl's had her eye sliced practically in two, and the insides are gushing out."

That did it. Irv sat bolt upright. His heart was still hammering away, but no longer with fear. Now—clean, old-fashioned hate, in normal sinus rhythm. That son of a bitch! Him and his Dr. Daring stage whisper! *Corneal-scleral laceration—meeeeeyah!* Probably beeped himself and then faked the call! A pathetic failure at the dinner table who couldn't even pick up, much less carry, his end of the conversation—and so now he has to try to steal the scene by playing Emergency Medical Hero during the very climax of his own wife's triumph—as orchestrated by me, Irv Durtscher! Why, that ice-sculptured *son—of—a—bitch*!

". . . what we know it to be, in our hearts: a wake-up call for America."

It was over. The last of Irv's words had passed through the lips of the blond and Tiffany-blue goddess on the huge screen.

Now they were on their feet, Snackerman and all his assembled hotshots. They had all turned toward Mary Cary, and they were grinning and applauding. Mary Cary herself stood up, a modest, almost misty little smile on her famous face, as if the whole subject was too serious for her to break into the big donkey-toothed bray of triumph she'd obviously like to cut loose with.

Snackerman grabbed her around the shoulders and grinned down at her and hugged her, and the whole mob started applauding all over again. Even Cale Bigger, who knew exactly how these shows were put together, was over there in the Mary Cary/Snackerman huddle, giving them both his best lifetime-lackey's shit-eating grin. Irv found himself standing alone. He was *damned* if he was going to walk the subservient eight feet it would take for him to join in the après-triumph pile-on.

Presently Cale walked away from the chattering, laughing, exulting hive and came over to Irv and stuck out his hand and said, "Great job, Irv! Great job!" Then he smiled and cast his eyes down and shook his big florid head and then looked up at Irv and said, "Jesus Christ. That girl's got *some balls*, hunh?"

THE NEW YORKER AFFAIR

Foreword: Murderous Gutter Journalism

May I offer you, here at the end, something on the order of those two gold foil–wrapped, silver dollar–sized, chocolate-covered peppermint coins the franchise hotels put on your pillow when they turn down your bed at night?

Just for the flavor of it, come with me back to the 1960s, to a time when the newspaper wars still raged in New York City; to 1963, when the struggling New York *Herald Tribune* completely transfused its Sunday supplement and changed its name from *Today's Living* to *New York*. In due course *New York* had a new editor, a young man named Clay Felker, who had come to the *Trib* from *Esquire* magazine. As editor of *New York*, Clay had one full-time assistant editor, Walt Stovall, and two part-time staff writers: Jimmy Breslin, whose main task was turning out a column for the *Trib* five days a week, a column based entirely on reporting (and probably the greatest column in New York newspaper history), and me. Five days a week I worked at the beck and call of the city desk as a general assignment reporter. In our so-called spare time, Jimmy and I were supposed to turn out a story apiece each week for this new Sunday supplement, *New York*. I'd heard of skeleton staffs before, but this one was bones.

Nevertheless, one day Clay, Walt, Jimmy, and I were crowded into the little bullpen of a cubicle that served as *New York*'s office, when Clay said, "Look . . . we're coming out once a week, right? And *The New Yorker* comes out once a week. And we start out the week the same way they do, with blank paper and a supply of ink. Is there any reason why we can't be as good as *The New Yorker*? Or better. They're so damned dull."

At that moment, I must say it seemed like nothing but talk. Dull or not, *The New Yorker* was one of the two or three most eminent weekly magazines in the country, certainly in terms of prestige. But Clay meant business, and thanks to his *Esquire* days he managed to persuade some great outside contributors to join Jimmy and me in our brave ride on Rosinante, writers the likes of Peter Maas, Richard Condon, Robert Benton, and David Newman, along with the *Trib*'s own outstanding critics, Walter Kerr, Judith Crist, and Walter Terry. Sure enough, by mid-1964 our little Sunday supplement, *New York*, had started making the town take notice. You know the current expression, "the buzz"? Well, by late 1964 the Buzz buzzed not for *The New Yorker* but for us, so much so that *The New Yorker* began paying us the left-handed compliment of making fun of us, first in items in their Talk of the Town column and then in a full-blown parody that went after Jimmy and me specifically.

It so happened that 1965 was *The New Yorker*'s fortieth anniversary. The magazine was, in fact, so eminent that the usual, predictable tributes to its illustrious traditions and its thises and its thats began effusing in print, like gas inflating a balloon, when the simple truth was that Clay was right. *The New Yorker* had become dull, dull, dull—dull and self-important—under William Shawn, who had succeeded the magazine's founder, Harold Ross, as editor. So . . . what better time to pop the balloon?

Our idea was to take a page from *The New Yorker*'s early days, back when Ross was running the show and the sheet was alive, and do a parody in the form of a profile of Shawn. One of *The New Yorker*'s greatest coups, under Ross, had been a parody of *Time* magazine in 1936 in the form of a profile by Wolcott Gibbs of *Time*'s founder and editor, Henry Luce. The town, or the part of the town that buzzes, had dined out on that one for a year. Not only was Gibbs's parody of *Time*'s famous breathless style gorgeous stuff ("Backward ran the sentences until reeled the mind" . . . "Where it will all end, knows God!"), but the personal details got under Luce's skin . . . At Yale he had adopted the mucker pose of going around unshaven and not wearing garters but was actually a puritanical "conformist" . . . he talked jerkily, stuttered, and avoided people's eyes . . . wore baggy clothes . . . seethed secretly over all the visiting Asians who looked him up in New York because he had been born in China, where his parents had been missionaries . . . Ross sent Luce an advance copy of Gibbs's story, and Luce got so angry he confronted Ross in Ross's apartment and, the way the story was always told, threatened to throw him out the window.

So a parody profile of Shawn it would be. The very form, "the profile," the very term itself, was a *New Yorker* invention. And in this case there was a news peg that went beyond the fact that this was *The New Yorker*'s fortieth: there had never been a profile of Shawn anywhere. Despite the fact that he was one of the most prominent figures in American journalism, he never showed his face to outside journalists. "Intensely private" was apparently putting it mildly. There was *only one known photograph* of the man, the official *New Yorker* portrait, which he had commissioned, paid for, and controlled.

The first thing I did was ring up Shawn at his office to ask him for an interview. By and by he came to the telephone and, in his quiet voice, said:

"Here at *The New Yorker*, if we tell someone we want to do a profile and that person doesn't want to cooperate, we don't do the profile. We would expect you to extend us the same courtesy."

"But, Mr. Shawn," I said, "we're a newspaper, and we consider you and your magazine's fortieth anniversary news."

That argument got me exactly nowhere. Obviously I would have to get my material from present and former *New Yorker* employees and others who knew Shawn and the magazine. That very night, or soon after, I was having dinner with a group of people down in Greenwich Village, and at the table was a young woman named Renata Adler. It was she, not I—I had no idea who she was—who brought up the fact that she was a staff writer for *The New Yorker*. I will admit I encouraged her to dilate upon the subject, however. I can't remember anything particularly riveting or revealing that she divulged, but she never forgot the conversation, as it would turn out. Anyway, it must have been shortly after my telephone call to Shawn, because soon the word was out at *The New Yorker* that nobody was to talk to anybody from the *Herald Tribune*.

Nevertheless, I found my sources, and I managed to observe, from the wings, as it were, *The New Yorker*'s fortieth birthday celebration at the St. Regis Hotel. Then I started writing the parody, and I ran into something I hadn't counted on. Wolcott Gibbs's parody of *Time* back in 1936 had been hilarious precisely because it was a caricature of an original, lively, radical departure in journalistic writing, the already famous *Time*style. But a parody of a style as dull as *The New Yorker*'s could be funny for about half a page, which is to say, only until you got the joke. After that, due to parody's law of hypertrophy, it would become literally duller than dull. The *New Yorker* style was one of leisurely meandering understatement, droll when in the humorous mode, tautological and litotical when in the serious mode, constantly amplified, qualified, adumbrated upon, nuanced and renuanced, until the magazine's pale-gray pages became High Baroque triumphs of the relative clause and the appository modifier. The only solution, it seemed to me, was to turn all that upside down, shake it out, get rid of the dust, and come up with a counter-parody, a style that was everything *The New Yorker* wasn't: urgent, insistent, exclamatory, overstated—and fun.

By the time I had finished it, it was so long it would have to run in two parts. Clay showed them to the *Herald Tribune*'s editor, Jim Bellows. Bellows read them, rubbed his palms together, and smacked his lips. Jim Bellows, although young, was a newspaperman of the old school. A month that went by without a good brawl was a pretty dull month. It so happened that the Sunday supplement, *New York*, was printed each Wednesday for insertion in the Sunday *Trib* four days later. So on Wednesday, as soon as my first installment was off the presses, Bellows had two copies delivered to Shawn at *The New Yorker*, whose offices were on West Forty-third Street, about four blocks from the *Trib*'s. The piece was entitled "Tiny Mummies! The True Story of the Ruler of 43rd Street's Land of the Walking Dead." With the two copies Bellows included a card on which he had written, "With my compliments."

Shawn's reaction was too good to be true. In his own minimomaniacal way—Malcolm Muggeridge once wrote that the world was full of megalomaniacs but that William Shawn was the only minimomaniac he had ever met—in his own way Shawn outdid Henry Luce of three decades earlier when it came to overreacting to a profile. Bango! He had a letter hand-delivered those same four blocks to the *Trib*.

The letter was not addressed to Bellows, however, much less to Clay Felker or to me. It was addressed to the *Trib*'s owner and publisher, Jock Whitney, who was not only a very rich man but also a very distinguished gentleman, lately, in fact, United States Ambassador to the Court of St. James's. It was at the distinguished gentleman in Jock Whitney that Shawn's letter seemed to be aimed. He called "Tiny Mummies" libelous, to be sure, but also worse than libelous. It was "murderous." Not only that, this single reckless, heedless, needless collapse of judgment—the publication of this pointless article—would forever consign the *Herald Tribune* and its long and honorable heritage, dating back to the great Horace Greeley, to "the gutter" along with the worst yellow journalism of the 1920s. He beseeched Whitney to withhold it from publication, to keep the magazine out of the *Herald Tribune* on Sunday.

A stunned Jock Whitney brought the letter in to Bellows, whose office was right next door, and said, "What do we do, Jim?"

Bellows read the letter and chuckled and said, "I'll show you what we do, Jock."

With that, while Whitney stared, Bellows got on the telephone and called up *Time* and read them the letter. Then he called up *Newsweek* and read them the letter. "Tiny Mummies" was published, as scheduled, on Sunday. On Monday accounts of the article and Shawn's letter were all over the Press sections of *Time* and *Newsweek*, and a perfect storm broke. It reached all the way into Lyndon Johnson's White House.

Tiny Mummies! The True Story of the Ruler of 43rd Street's Land of the Walking Dead!

Omertà! Sealed lips! *Sealed lips*, ladies and gentlemen! Our Thing! We are editing *The New Yorker* magazine, Harold Ross's *New Yorker*. We are not running a panopticon. Not exactly! For weeks the editors of *The New Yorker* have been circulating a warning among their employees saying that someone is out to write an article about *The New Yorker*. This warning tells them, remember: *Omertà*. Your vow of silence—but *New Yorker* employees are not the only people in the world who have to take this vow. White House employees have to take it—none of this gratuitous libel, my G-6 lovelies, about how "I Saw What Lyndon Drinks for Dinner"—Buckingham Palace employees have to take it—those graceless alum-mouthed butlers and everything—everybody in the Mafia and at the G. & C. Merriam Co. of Springfield, Mass.—a lot of people. The G. & C. Merriam Co. puts out *Webster's Dictionary*, and they don't want a lot of flip anecdotes published about how, for example, they sit down to decide whether certain popular but . . . dusky words are going to get in the book this time around. Right?

One wouldn't even have known about the warning going around the *New Yorker* except that they put it in writing, in memos. They have a compulsion in the *New Yorker* offices, at 25 West Forty-third Street, to put everything in writing. They have *boys* over there on the nineteenth and twentieth floors, the editorial offices, practically caroming off each other—bonk old bison heads!—at the blind turns in the hallways because of the fantastic traffic in memos. They just *call* them boys. "Boy, will you take this, please . . ." Actually, a lot of them are old men with starched white collars with the points curling up a little, "big lunch" ties, button-up sweaters, and black basket-weave sack coats, and they are all over the place transporting these thousands of messages with their kindly old elder bison shuffles shoop-shooping along. They were boys when they started the job, but the thing is, *The New Yorker* is forty years old—four decades, even, of *The New Yorker*!—and they all have *seniority*, like Pennsylvania Railroad conductors.

The paper the thousands of messages are on is terrific rag-fiber paper. It comes in pads gum-bound up at the top, but it is the best possible paper. It is like the problem with dollar bills wearing out with use. If there is this fantastic traffic in memos and things all day long, one has to have paper that will *hold up*. There are different colors for different "unit tasks." Manuscripts are typed on maize-yellow bond, bud-green is for blah-blah-blah, fuchsia demure is for blah-blah-blah, Newsboy blue is for blah-blah-blah, and this great *cerise*, a kind of mild cherry red, is for urgent messages, immediate attention and everything. So here are these old elder bison messengers batting off each other in the halls, hustling cerise memos around about some story somebody is doing.

Well—all I can say is that it is a great system they have going up there—but—nevertheless—people *talked*. These . . . *people talked*! They talked about things like William Shawn and the Leopold and Loeb case, Shawn being editor of *The New Yorker*, and about auto-lobotomy, many fascinating things.

But! These people were . . . *thinking out loud*. People do that a lot at

The New Yorker and wonder what is going on. They get that way, for example, because a guy gets hired one day and some whispery guy in old worsteds shows him to a cubicle and he sits down at his desk in there and for the next two months he never *meets* anybody. Everybody is in *other* cubicles with the doors shut. Whole days go by. He just sits there, and every now and then Old Messenger comes in and hands him a communiqué, in maize-yellow, fuchsia demure, bud-green, hello-out-there beige, hello-help-help canary, kiss-me-somebody cerise, please-I-love-you-anybody cerise—until he goes stir crazy and starts prowling the halls and opens a door, and he sees these . . . women with their backs arched over desks in this . . . *unusual* place, the Transferring Room; or he hits this *weird zone* in the back corner of the nineteenth floor, the *Whisper Zone*, all this sibilance up there.

Eventually he finds that all these things, the Whisper Zone, the Transferring Room, the memos, the System, *omertà*, everything, leads back to one man—Shawn. William Shawn—editor of one of the most powerful magazines in America. The Man. Nobody Knows.

That is why they bring up things like this business of Shawn and the Leopold-Loeb case. They, themselves, want an . . . *explanation*. In this story, one of the stories told repeatedly, it is May 21, 1924, and Richard Loeb is crouching in the weeds with Nathan Leopold, and he says, "Nathan, look! How about William Shawn—" William Shawn is such a quiet, bright little kid, neat—you know?—no trouble, secretary of his class at the Harvard School for Boys, you know the class-secretary kind. His father is "Jackknife Ben." They live in a big place at 4355 Vincennes. Easy ransom!

Only they don't tell it too well. In the first place, Loeb didn't call Leopold "Nathan." He called him "Babe," or something like that. And they would have never squatted in the grass. They had these great *clothes* on, they were *social*, one understands?

What the records show, actually, in the Cook County (Chicago) Criminal Court and at the Harvard School, now the Harvard–St.

George School, is the following: Shawn—then called Chon—and Bobby Franks were classmates at the Harvard School for Boys that year. Shawn was a junior, sixteen years old, one of the brightest students in the school, and Bobby Franks was fourteen years old, a couple of years behind him. Leopold and Loeb were very methodical. They had a whole set of specifications. They wanted a small and therefore manageable teenage boy, from the Harvard School, with wealthy parents who would pay up fast on the ransom. They went over six names, the first one of which was "William." The court records do not give the last name. Shawn's father, Benjamin W. "Jackknife Ben" Chon, had made a lot of money by opening a shop, The Jack Knife Shop, at 838 Exchange Avenue in the aromatic, full-bodied Union Stock Yards on Chicago's South Side, in 1889, and selling 150 different kinds of jackknives. Great jackknife country! Wealthy parents! And judging by the Harvard School yearbook for 1924, William Chon was a small, quiet teenage boy. In fact, even in 1940, the year of the school's seventy-fifth anniversary, everybody from the Harvard School still remembered him that way. Billy Chon was senior class president, and the 1925 yearbook, *The Review*, had said, " 'Bill' is certain to succeed in life, and will always remain the pride of the Class of 1925"—but *still*, the way they remembered him in the seventy-fifth anniversary book was "Who would have ever thought that little Billy Chon would have become one of the big shots on the editorial staff of *The New Yorker* magazine?" But so what? Not just Billy Chon but every small quiet boy in the Harvard School that year—who blames them!—must have felt as if the intellectual murderers, Leopold and Loeb, had fixed their clinical eyes upon him at some point. They dropped the idea of "William" only because they had a personal grudge against him and somebody might remember that. They gave up on three or four others because they knew them too well or because their fathers were too tight with the money and might refuse to pay a good ransom. Intellectual crime! How could anybody in God's world be safe if there were people like Leopold and Loeb going around killing people just for the . . . *aesthetics* of the perfect crime.

The whole story, and others about Shawn, supposedly help explain why Shawn is so . . . *retiring*, why he won't allow interviews, why he won't let his picture be taken, why it *pains* him to ride elevators, go through tunnels, get cooped up—why he *remains anonymous*, as they say, and slips *The New Yorker* out each week from behind a barricade of . . . pure fin de siècle back-parlor horsehair stuffing.

Incredible! Shawn attended the University of Michigan, 1925–'27, married Cecille Lyon in 1928, worked on two newspapers, then in 1933 joined *The New Yorker*'s "Talk of the Town" department as a reporter. At some point he dropped Chon for Shawn. Shawn took over as editor when Harold Ross died in 1951. Thereby he became one of the most prominent and powerful editors in the country. By World War II, *The New Yorker* was already the most prestigeful "quality lit" magazine in America. And since World War II, largely under Shawn's stewardship, it has become—new honors!—the most successful suburban women's magazine in the country. Mountains of prestige. Yet from that day to this, the outside world has learned practically nothing of William Shawn. Nobody seems to know him except for a few "inties"—intimates—at *The New Yorker*, like Lillian Ross.

Elusive pimpernel! The Shawn legends! The one of how he tries to time it in the morning so he can go straight up to his office on the nineteenth floor, by himself on the elevator, and carries a hatchet in his attaché case so he can chop his way out if it gets stuck between floors—crazy stories like that!

Shawn is a very quiet man. He has a soft, somewhat high voice. He seems to whisper all the time. The whole . . . *zone* around his office, a kind of horsehair-stuffing atmosphere of old carpeting, framed *New Yorker* covers, quiet cubicles, and happy-shabby, baked-apple gentility, is a *Whisper Zone*. One gets within forty feet of it and everybody . . . is whispering, all the secretaries and everybody. The *Shawn whisper;* the whisper zone radiates out from Shawn himself. Shawn in the hallway slips along as soundlessly as humanly possible and—chooooo—he meets somebody right there in the hall. The nodding! The whispering! Shawn is fifty-seven years old but still has a boyish face. He is a small, plump man, round in the cheeks. He always seems to have on about twenty layers of clothes, about three button-up sweaters, four vests, a couple of shirts, two ties, it looks that way, a dark shapeless suit over the whole ensemble, and white cotton socks. Here he is in the hall, and he lowers his head and puts out his hand.

"Hello—Mr."—he begins nodding—"Taylor—how—are—you," with his head down, nodding down, down, down, down, "—it's—nice"—his head is down and he rolls his eyes up and looks out from under his own forehead—"to—see—you"—and then edges back with his hand out, his head nodding, eyes rolled up, back foot edging back, back, back, back—"very—good—to—see—you"—nodding, smiling—infectious! *Good* for one! One does the same, whispering, nodding, getting the old head down, nodding down, down, smiling, edging back, rolling the eyeballs up the precipice of the forehead. One becomes quiet, gentle, genteelly, magnificently, numbly, so—

All right. Let's deal by note, memo, or telephone at *The New Yorker*. But—embarrassment! Shawn calls up—and even the secretary down where Lillian Ross is—and he calls up Lillian Ross all the time—and even this secretary *does it again*:

"Hello, may I speak to Miss Ross?"

"Whom should I say is calling?"

Whum, dramatic, grammatic pause—whisper—"Mr. Shawn."

Zonk! Mr. Shawn! She has flaked it again. He slipped in under the tympanic membrane with the whisper. One of the four or five most prominent men in Communications! Unrecognized in his own office. But does Shawn himself care? Shawn doesn't care; he has a passion for anonymity. Always he has this passion. Except—well, such as the times some writer or somebody, a young novelist, goes to a party in Shawn's apartment on Fifth Avenue. It is on the first floor and looks out on Central Park. It is a very full view. One can see who is coming from all directions. Nothing but trees across the street, no peering windows, no elevators, nothing like that. Philip Hamburger is at the party. Philip Hamburger has written a feature in *The New Yorker* called "Notes for a

Gazetteer" fifty-two times. Hamburger and a lot of people from *The New Yorker* are there. It is a "very nice" party. Shawn puts on some records from his jazz collection: Jelly Roll, Bix, Bunny Berrigan, Willie the Lion, Fats, Art. We were all very hippie along the Mississippi in naughty naughty oughty-eight. And Young Novelist writes a note the next day thanking him, addressing it to "Mr. Ted Shawn." One means, well, everybody knows Shawn is editor of *The New Yorker* and everything, but he is . . . so *quiet*, so passionately anonymous, so these names get mixed up. Ted Shawn is a famous dancer. And the next day a call comes and it is *Mrs.* Shawn saying, "Thank you so much for your nice note, and by the way—

"Mr. Shawn's name is William, not . . . Ted. Mr. Shawn prefers to be anonymous but not . . . *quite* that anonymous."

All the same! He is *Shawn of The New Yorker.* Many *New Yorker* writers are devoted to him. They have dedicated at least six books to him. He is self-effacing, kind, quiet, diligent, an efficient man, courtly, refined, considerate, humble, and—Shawn uses this quiet business like a maestro. He has the quiet moxie to walk through the snow at 3 a.m. to the apartment of somebody who owes him a story—the magazine is at the absolute deadline, and this writer is revising and revising and won't turn loose of the story, so Shawn just turns up at the door with snow caked all over his boots, boots with clackety buckles, and layers of clothes, and he knocks on the door, and the poor guy's wife, who is asleep on the couch in the living room, gets up and answers the door, and Shawn says:

"Hello—Mrs.—Taylor"—he is nodding and smiling—"is—your—husband—in?"—nodding, smiling, rolling his eyeballs up and down his forehead, edging in—"uh—I'm afraid—I'm—going—to—have—to"—

"Good evening, Mr. Shawn," or something, she says. "I mean, he's in the bedroom, he's working—"

"—take—a—manuscript—from—your—husband—how—have—you—been—Mrs.—Taylor?"—edging, nodding, sliding the old booty feet, ever nodding back, nod, smile—"your—lovely—daughters?"—

edge, edge, eye-roll, right over to the bedroom, and he opens the door and walks in, nod, smile, peeking eye: "Oh—good—evening—Mr.—Taylor—yes—I'll—have—to—take—this—now—thank—you—very—much—how—is"—he pulls the story up out of the typewriter and off the desk, with Taylor falling back in his wooden chair like a burnt-out cigarette filter—"Mrs. Taylor?—you-are-very-kind—yes—thank—you—very—much"—he edges back toward the door, nods his head down, down, down, smiles, rolls his eyes up from under his forehead, edges back, the booty buckles clackle—"goodbye—Mrs.—Taylor—thank—you—how—is—"

Floonk, the door closes. Quiet! Shawn wins.

Yes! And suddenly, after forty years, it all adds up. Whispering, inconspicuous—but courtly—formal, efficient—but sympathetic—perfection!—what are those but, precisely! the perfect qualifications for a museum custodian, an undertaker, a mortuary scientist. But of course! Thirteen years ago, upon the death of Harold Ross, precisely, that difficult task befell William Shawn: to be the museum curator, the mummifier, the preserve-in-amber, the smiling embalmer . . . for Harold Ross's *New Yorker* magazine.

Harold Ross! Practically nobody, except at *The New Yorker*, remembers what a . . . *charismatic* figure Ross was as *The New Yorker*'s founder and editor. James Thurber told a story in his book *The Years with Ross* that shows it, however. About a year after Ross died, *The New Yorker* entertained the editors of *Punch*, and a couple of weeks later Thurber was talking about the party with Rowland Emmett of *Punch* and told him it was too bad he never met Ross. "Oh, but I did," said Emmett. "He was all over the place. Nobody talked about anything else." Ross was from Aspen, Colorado, got mixed up with literati in Paris after World War I, and came to New York and entered the literary world with a kind of Rocky Mountain reverse-spin mucker stance, "anti-intellectual." Ross was moody, explosive, naïve about many things, and had many blind spots when it came to literature and the arts—and all of this partially disguised the real nature of his sophistication. Ross's sophistication actually had a rather refined *English*—Anglo-Saxon—cast to it. To Ross, sophistication involved not merely understanding culture and fashion but avoidance of excesses, including literary and artistic excesses. He didn't want anything in the magazine that was too cerebral, Kantian, or too exuberant, angry, gushing, too "arty," "pretentious," or "serious." He used those three words, "arty," "pretentious," and "serious," quite a lot. He didn't want it to seem as if anybody were straining his brain and showing off or wringing his heart out and pouring soul all over you. This idea was very special, very English.

Great stuff! Ross started *The New Yorker* in 1925, and despite the depression, it was a terrific success. Sophistication in America! The thing was, in the twenties the New York intelligentsia still felt . . . very *colonial*. They were like those poor Russian timber magnates who used to sit in their Bourbon Louis salons in St. Petersburg and make their daughters speak only French on Thursdays and talk to guests about "*l'Opéra*," as though that great piece of angel's-food cake were just around the corner on the Nevsky Prospect. They were terribly hung up on French Culture. In New York the model was English Culture. Ross may have had plenty of those lithoid Colorado eccentricities, but *The New Yorker* was never anything more than a rather slavish copy of *Punch*. Nevertheless, literati in America took to it as if they were dying of thirst. The need was so great that *The New Yorker* was first praised and then practically canonized. By the 1950s, funny things were happening. Some of *The New Yorker*'s host of staff writers, such as E. B. White, were receiving very solemn honors, such as honorary degrees at Yale.

No magazine in America ever received such *literary* acclaim before. Of course, it was hard to review the work of these *New Yorker* writers—e.g., Thurber, E. B. White, Robert Benchley, Wolcott Gibbs, Dorothy Parker, A. J. Liebling—and put one's finger on any . . . major work. What had any of them done that would measure up to, say, Hemingway, Fitzgerald, Dos Passos, or Steinbeck or Nathanael West? People who don't *really understand* just see *New Yorker* writers pistling away their talents within the old Ross mold year after year, decade after decade, until finally somebody writes an affectionate obituary. But what is all this about *major work*? Never mind! Ross himself never minded it. They had achieved the perhaps small-scale but still special goal he had set for them—Anglo-Saxon sophistication—very well. *Ecce homines!* Tiny giants!

The atmosphere at *The New Yorker* itself, however, was something else. William Shawn came to New York in 1933, at the age of twenty-six, with the idea of writing a book about *The New Yorker*. Instead, he joined the staff as a reporter for the "Talk of the Town" section. The "Talk of the Town" was nothing more than *The New Yorker*'s version of *Punch*'s "Charivari" section, but—all right!—in the United States, at any rate, *The New Yorker* was in a class by itself. One went to work there, and one—how does one explain it?—began to get a kind of . . . *religious* feeling about the place. There were already a lot of . . . *traditions*. From the first, according to his old friends there, Shawn felt as if he were entering a priesthood. Hierophants! Tiny giants—all over the place—Shawn could look out of his cubicle and there they were, those men out there padding along in the hall were James Thurber, Wolcott Gibbs, and Robert Benchley *themselves*. That gangling man out there with the mustache, that is *James Thurber*—one is not *reading about* James Thurber, *that is he*, and one is now, actually, physically, a part of his universe; one can study the most minute details about the man, the weave of his yellow-ocher button-up sweater, the actual *knit* of it, the way the loops of yarn intertwist, the sweater James Thurber has on—not a photograph of it—but the sweater he *has on*, has on *his own body*. Actually! *Grace!*

Harold Ross was forever looking for a managing editor who could somehow convert his conception of *The New Yorker* into a systematic, ongoing operation, and Shawn—faithful hierophant!—was the most successful managing editor he ever appointed. He was . . . *totally committed*.

There was a lot of speculation about what would happen to *The*

New Yorker "after Ross"! One of the *New Yorker* writers, A. J. Liebling, said, "The same thing that happened to analysis after Freud." He was righter than he knew. There was never any question of Shawn's setting a new policy. The old Museum Curator just set to work with his whole heart. Tiny Mummies!

Part of Shawn's job as embalmer is actual physical preservation. For example, there is the Thurber Room, the cubicle James Thurber had up there in his last days at *The New Yorker.* Thurber's eyesight was failing, and he tried out some of his ideas for drawings with a big crayon on the wall; nutty *foot*ball players, or something, and a bunch of nuns, some weird woodland animals on the order of the Barefaced Lie and the White Lie. James Thurber! The room is right next to the men's room, because it was hard for Thurber to navigate the halls. The room is kept like the Poe Shrine in Richmond, Virginia; *pure* Poe, *pure* Thurber. The new man, the writer in the cubicle now, understands. Nobody touches those walls, no other pictures *of any sort* go up on those walls. The custodians stand around late in the day trying to decide how best to preserve these . . . well, one means, these things are not scrawls, I don't care what Thurber would have said. These things are bona fide . . . *murals* we have here. Museum! Shrine! Maybe someday, all these offices of all these giants, like Robert Benchley, James Thurber, Wolcott Gibbs, everybody, can be restored, like Colonial Williamsburg, all the original objects and curios, Benchley's little porcelain hussar figures, Gibbs's amber walrus, animals, and things, but for now—well, only the people who were working here when Ross was alive may keep offices in the old *donnish* clutter, all these things on the *walls* and so forth. The Mr. Old-Timers, like Brendan Gill, the movie critic, who has been here twenty-five years, or something like that, may keep all these *vines* growing all over his office—picturesque!—donnish clutter!—but we keep all these men on one floor, and as they retire or . . . pass on . . . the rule is, nobody else may do up rooms like that. Nobody else may put all those *curios* up on their walls, all those maps of Hartford, *before the*

Turnpike, all that strange stuff—nothing on the walls but *New Yorker* covers. That is, of course, understood? One means, well, it is not a *written* rule or anything like that, but one soon gets the idea, by example, as it were, like this business of everybody wearing white shirts at the IBM offices. Nobody comes in and beats one over the skull with a rule book or anything, but the day may come when some unplugged bastard comes in with a light, practically *thin ice* blue shirt on, and about 3 p.m. a superior calls him into an office where the fluorescent ice tray on the ceiling hums, and he says, "Let me ask you, tell me, have you ever noticed any of our executives wearing a . . . *pastel* shirt like yours?" One means, well, of course, everyone was genuinely sorry, even stricken, over the death of A. J. Liebling, "Joe," in 1963, but, well, the man *did* have the most unbelievable clutter in his cubicle, pictures right up on the walls of fifth-ranking bantamweight boxers with their hair pomaded, photographed against dark backgrounds on *glossy* paper with *white ink* inscriptions, "Best of Luck," cretinish handwriting, circles over the *i*'s. The man went really rather *beyond* the orthodox donnish clutter. That was quite bad enough, but his style, his *writing* style, yes, he *did* write under Ross, and he quite belonged here—no one will deny that for a minute—but doesn't one think that Liebling was . . . *baroque*, and hearty at times, and did he really *fit in* around here?

Tenor! Yes! Shawn's greatest task, of course, was not preserving these shrine rooms but preserving the *style*, the *tenor* of the magazine. The tenor, the atmosphere, is important. Newcomers are schooled in it immediately. To begin with, getting hired at *The New Yorker* is nothing merely *personnel-office-like* or *technical*. It is more like fraternity rushing. A person's attitude is important. Everybody wants to know if the candidate will fit in, if he has the makings of a genuine . . . hierophant; not a lot of bogus enthusiasm and so forth, but more an attitude of—well, humility, about *The New Yorker* and its history. Humility has come to be a very important thing here, and lately *The New Yorker* has settled upon small people, small physically, that is, who can preserve through quite a number of years the tweedy, thatchy, humble style of dress they had in college. After the age of forty-one is encouraged, by tacit example, to switch to hard-finished worsteds.

Earn one's worsteds!

A lot of traditions are kept up very well. One is that the cocktail lounge in the lobby of the Algonquin Hotel and the Rose Room are actually a private club *practically owned by The New Yorker.* The Algonquin Hotel is across the street and down toward Sixth Avenue a little from the Forty-fourth Street entrance of *The New Yorker* building. The other cocktail lounge in there, the Blue Room, or whatever it is, and the other dining room—not the Rose Room but the other kind of *hearty* oak-woody dining room off the lobby—are not part of *The New Yorker,* and all kinds of hearty beef-trust people turn up in there, businessmen and one thing and another. But the cocktail lounge in the lobby—well, it is not *actually,* but it is *practically* a *New Yorker* club; you know? Or at least it seems so if one works for *The New Yorker.* It even looks like a club, a fine club like the Century Club. One sits in leather chairs at lamp tables and coffee tables and things, not at ordinary Formica cocktail-lounge tables, and there is a great deal of dark wood all around, and one summons the waiter by banging a little clerk's bell on the table—just like in a club, one understands? Well, one means, it is a public place, but if one works for *The New Yorker,* he does not simply *show* up in there—the thing is, this is the place where Ross used to come, and Thurber, and everybody, and now Shawn sometimes comes there around six, but even Shawn watches himself. A lot of times he doesn't even eat lunch in the Rose Room; for example, he and Lillian Ross will drift off up to this delicatessen near Rockefeller Plaza for a very quiet, unpretentious couple of corned-beef sandwiches. So one waits until he is invited to the Algonquin by some senior member of the staff. It is like the second round of initiation, like being really accepted. Months go by, but finally the day comes when Brendan Gill or another top member says, in this most offhand casual way, as if it really didn't mean a thing, "Mr. Toddy, would you care to join me for lunch at the Algonquin?" Zoom! Grace!

Lost in the Whichy Thickets: *The New Yorker*

William Shawn, editor of *The New Yorker* magazine—well, he is a very, as they say, homey person. That is one side of him. He is a small, quiet man, and he talks in this halting whisper. He seems to wear layer upon layer of clothes, all sorts of sweaters, vests, coats. He smiles, nods, nods, nods; he makes courtly, sort of *down home* pleasantries. And if—there may be an ashtray on his desk by now—but if there was no ashtray, he would go out himself! Mr. Shawn of *The New Yorker*!—and bring back a Coca-Cola bottle for use as an ashtray. Easygoing!

"Why—hello—Mr.—Cage—um—yes—how—are—you—here—let—me—how—is—Mrs.—Cage—um—take—your—coat—oh-oh—didn't—mean—to—um—there—if—I—can—just—slip—it—off—unh—here—have—a—"

"Well, thank you very much, Mr. Shawn—"

"—a—seat—right—over—here—well—it—uh—always—does—

that—ha-ha—well—now—oh—I—see—you're—smoking—let—me—"

"Oh, I'm sorry, Mr. Shawn, I didn't—"

"No, no, no, no, no, no, please—perfectly—all—right—it's—please—keep—your—seat—I'll—be—right—back—"

Whereupon he goes out of the office, smiling, and comes back in a moment with an empty Coca-Cola bottle in his hand. He puts the Coca-Cola bottle on the desk for Cage to use as an ashtray.

So one can imagine Cage saying something like he has a great many *viable* ideas about this story, but it is funny, he can hear his own voice as he talks. The words are coming out all right—"several really very *viable* approaches, I think, Mr. Shawn"—but they sound *hollow*, as if in an echo chamber, because inside his brain all he can focus on is the cigarette and the Coca-Cola bottle. The thick glass in those bottles, and Jeezus, that little hole in the top there—it *looks* big enough, but if you try to knock the ash off a cigarette here into the Coca-Cola bottle, you see that the glass is *thick* and the hole *isn't* big enough. Cage is practically down to the end of the cigarette—"Well, I'm not absolutely sure the ethnocentric idea *works* in a case like this, Mr. Shawn, but"—and then what is he going to do? There's nothing to put the cigarette out *on*. He's going to have to just drop the cigarette down the hole in the Coca-Cola bottle, and then it is going to hit the bottom of the bottle, and then it is going to hit the bottom of the bottle and just keep *burning*, you know? And there is going to be this little smelly curl of smoke coming up out of the Coca-Cola bottle, like a spirit lamp, and this filthy cigarette lying in the bottom, right there on Shawn's desk, and obviously Shawn is not crazy about cigarettes in the first place, and old Cage hasn't even sold him on the idea of the story—

But! That is the beauty of the man! On the *outside* he is quiet and homey, easygoing. Underneath, however—William Shawn is not nodding for a moment. Like the time the people in the Checking Department started having these weekly *skits*, sort of spoofing some of the old hands—does one really wish to know about how long that kind of thing lasted? That is a . . . *rhetorical question.* Shawn is not nodding. William Shawn has not lapsed for a moment from the labor to which he dedicated himself upon the death of Harold Ross.

To preserve *The New Yorker* just as Ross left it, exactly, in . . . perpetuity.

Yes! And to do so, William Shawn has done nothing halfway. He has devised an editing system that is in some ways more completely *group journalism,* or *org-edit,* as it is called at *Novy Mir,* than anything *Time* magazine ever even contemplated.

To start with, one can believe, most assuredly, that no little . . . comedians in the Checking Department are going to schmarf around in there doing skits about the old hands—the men who worked under Ross, many of them. Those men play an important part in Shawn's system. The *physical* part of the preservation—such as preserving the Thurber Room—that was easy. Shawn's hardest task was to preserve the literary style of Ross's *New Yorker.* The thing to do, of course, was to adopt, as models, the styles of men on the magazine who had been working under Ross—the so-called Tiny Giants, viz., E. B. White, Joseph Mitchell, Wolcott Gibbs, James Thurber, A. J. Liebling, people of that sort.

Well, Shawn's first step was brilliantly simple. In effect, he has established lifetime tenure—purity!—for nearly everybody who served under Ross. Seniority! Columnists and so forth at *The New Yorker* have lifetime seniority, and if any ambitious kids there *aspire*, they wait it out, earn their first pair of hard-finished worsteds by working and waiting for them; one understands? This has led to a certain amount of awkwardness. *The New Yorker*'s movie, theater, and art sections have come to have an eccentric *irrelevance* about them. They have a kind of knit-sweater, stoke-the-coal-grate charm, but . . . somehow they are full of

Magooisms. Such as: "It was evidently intended to be a very funny account of a lower-middle-class London family jam-packed with lovable eccentrics, but when, after thirty minutes, I found that nothing funny had happened and that my accustomed high spirits were being reduced to audible low moans, I got up and made my way out of the theater, which, as far as laughter was concerned, had been, and I suspect remained, as silent as a tomb." Evidently intended; audible low moans; as silent as a tomb: huckleberry preserves! Mom's jowls are on the doily!

The "Letter from London" and "Letter from Paris" features, written by two more seniors, have the same trouble. They started off in the 1930s, when not too many Americans were traveling to London or Paris, the idea being to introduce readers to what was current in the way of Culture and *modes* in Europe. Today all sorts of people fly to London and Paris all the time, and these "Letters" from abroad have taken on the tone of random sights seen from the window of a second-best hotel.

Shawn, of course, is well aware of all this. It is just that he has a more . . . specific mission. Museum curator! He apparently wanted a permanent mold for *The New Yorker*'s essays, profiles, and so forth, and he did it with unerring taste. Lillian Ross! The last really impressive thing *The New Yorker* published under Harold Ross was Lillian Ross's profile of Ernest Hemingway in 1950. Lillian Ross is no kin to Harold Ross, by the way. This piece of hers was terrific, and the technique influenced a lot of the best journalists in the country. She gave up the usual historical format of the profile entirely and, instead, wrote a running account of a couple of days she spent following Hemingway around New York. She put in all his little asides, everything, a lot of terrific dialogue.

This story gave a wonderful picture of this big egomaniac garruling around town and batting everybody over the head with his ego as if it were a pig bladder. The piece impressed Ross, and that gave Lillian Ross the right cachet around *The New Yorker*, right off. A small, quiet, inconspicuous, sympathetic girl from Syracuse, whose father had run a filling station and kept a lot of animals, she had a great deal of womanly concern for underdogs. Also, her prose style had a nice flat-out quality about it, none of those confounded curlicues of the man at the other extreme, Liebling. Liebling verged on Ross's Anglo-Saxon sin of "excess," straining at the brain, as they say. Anyway, Lillian Ross's style became the model for the *New Yorker* essay.

That was all right, but most of the boys never really *caught on*. All they picked up were some of her throwaway mannerisms. She piles up details and dialogue, dialogue mainly, but piles it all up very carefully, building up toward a single point; such as, Ernest Hemingway is a Big Boy and a fatuous ass. All that the vergers who have followed her seem to think is that somehow if you get in enough details, enough random fact—somehow this *trenchant portrait* is going to rise up off the pages. They miss her strong points—namely, her ear for dialogue and her point of view—and just run certain *sport* devices of hers into the ground. The fact-gorged sentence is one of them. Lillian Ross wrote another essay that also had a lot of impact, about the making of a moving picture, *The Red Badge of Courage*, and the opening sentence of that story was the ruination of at least fifty "Letters" and "Profiles" by the *New Yorker* foot soldiers who followed in her path. That sentence read:

> The making of Metro-Goldwyn-Mayer movie "The Red Badge of Courage," based on the Stephen Crane novel about the Civil War, was preceded by routine disclosures about its production plans from the columnist Louella Parsons ("John Huston is writing a screen treatment of Stephen Crane's classic, 'The Red Badge of Courage,' as a possibility for an M-G-M picture"), from the columnist Hedda Hopper ("Metro has an option on 'The Red Badge of Courage' and John Huston's working up a budget for it. But there's no green light yet"), and from *Variety* ("Pre-production work on 'Red Badge of Courage' commenced at Metro with the thesp-tests for top roles in drama"), and it was

> preceded, in the spring of 1950, by a routine visit by John Huston, who is both a screen writer and a director, to New York, the headquarters of Loew's, Inc., the company that produces and distributes M-G-M pictures.

Miss Ross was just funning around with that one, but *The New Yorker's* line troops started writing *whole stories* that way. Unbelievable! All those clauses, appositions, amplifications, qualifications, asides, God knows what else, hanging inside the poor old skeleton of one sentence like some kind of Spanish moss. They are still doing it. One of the latest is an essay in the March 13 issue. It began with what has become *The New Yorker* formula lead:

> One afternoon just after the spring semester began at the University of California, I passed on my way to the Berkeley campus to make a tour of the card tables that had been set up that day by student political organizations on the Bancroft strip—a wide brick sidewalk, outside the main entrance to the campus, that had been the original battlefield of a free-speech controversy that embroiled and threatened the university for the entire fall semester.

That is just the warm-up, though. It proceeds to a *New Yorker* style specialty known as the "whichy thicket":

> But, unlike COFO workers, *who* still can't be sure their civil-rights campaign has made any significant change in Mississippi, F.S.M. workers need only walk a block or two to witness unrestricted campus political activity of the kind that was the goal of their movement, and to anyone *who* has spent some time listening to their reminiscences, the F.S.M. headquarters, *which* is a relatively recent acquisition, seems to be a make-work echo of the days *when* the F.S.M. had a series of command posts, with names like Strike Central and Press Central—a system of walkie-

talkies for communication among its scouts on the campus—and an emergency telephone number, called Nexus, to be used *when* the regular number was busy.

Wh-wh-wh-wh-wh-whoooaaaaaaugh!—piles of whichy whuh words—*which, when, where, who, whether, whuggheeee,* the living whichy thickets. All that was from a story called "Letter from Berkeley" by Calvin Trillin, but it is not a rare case or even Trillin's fault. Trillin can write very clearly, very directly, left to his own devices. But nobody is left to his own devices at *The New Yorker* today.

Shawn has . . . a System.

The system is Shawn's refinement of Harold Ross's query theory and operates something like this: Once an article is accepted, some girl retypes it on maize-yellow paper and a couple of other colors, and Shawn sends the maize copy to a chief editor. The other two copies go to the research department ("Checking") and the copy style department. The copy style department's task is seeing to it that the grammar, punctuation, spelling, and word usage in the piece correspond to *The New Yorker*'s rules on the subject. Sentences phrased in the form of a question, for example, must end in a question mark, no matter how far they have roamed from the idea of asking a question by the end of the sentence. An example, from "Talk of the Town," again of March 13, runs: "Leave it to the astonishing Italians to bring off the reverse, however, for who should fly into New York from Milan the other morning, for a five-day stay, but a hundred and thirty-six of Italy's most prominent—not to mention liveliest and most talkative—painters and sculptors, each bringing with him five or more works, to be sold here at a series of charity auctions to benefit two New York hospitals: the Italian Hospital, on West 110th Street, and the New York Polyclinic Medical School and Hospital, on West Fiftieth Street?"

The chief editor can—and is expected to—rewrite the piece in any way he thinks will improve it. It is not unusual for the writer not to be consulted about it; the editor can change it without him, something that happens only rarely at *Time*, for example. At *Time* the writer always makes the changes himself, if possible. Practically every writer for *The New Yorker*, staff or freelance, goes through this routine, with the exception of a few people, like Lillian Ross, who are edited by Shawn himself. Meanwhile, the researchers down in the checking department are making changes. The researchers' additions often take the form of filling in blanks some writer has left in the story. He may write something like: "Miss Hall appeared in Sean O'Casey's (t.k.) in 19(00) . . ." and the researcher is supposed to fill in the blanks, t.k. standing for "words to come" and (00) for "digits to come." This is precisely the way the news magazines operate. The researcher then comes up with "Miss Hall appeared in *Drums Under the Window*, a play by Paul Shyre based on Sean O'Casey's autobiographical work of that name, in 1961."

Next, the rewrite editor's changes, the copy stylist's changes, and the researchers' changes are collated and the whole thing is set on a Vari-Typer machine. The Vari-Typer machine sets the story up with even margins on each side of the page, approximating the width of an actual column in the magazine. A lot of copies of this Vari-Typer version are made, and then the paperwork really begins. Somehow, after this point, the sentences in the story, well, they begin to . . . grow *longer and longer*.

One Vari-Typer copy goes back to the chief editor, two more go back to the researchers and the copy stylists, another goes up to Shawn's office, and one goes to a "query" editor, and sometimes to two "query" editors. The query editors play an intramural game. Ross devised it. The goal is to punch a hole in every weak spot they can find in a story, really give it a going-over. According to the rules, objections are to take the form of questions—"queries." The editors compete to see how many biting, insulting, devastatingly ironic questions they can pose about one piece. *The New Yorker*'s reigning champion at "querying" is a veteran of the Ross era, Rogers Whitaker. Players may hit a story for artiness, pretentiousness, overexuberance, overassertiveness, overanything, or for plain wrong thinking, unintentional double meanings, or other naïvetés. If it isn't otherwise vulnerable, they can hit it for vagueness. There are quite a lot of queries on that score. The query takes some such form as "Are we really to assume that there are more than eighteen living persons who remember a play by Paul Shyre, based on a book by Sean O'Casey, entitled *Drums Under the Window*? Are we sure it was not *Drums Under the Milkweed* or *Weeds in the Milk Drums Under the Window*? Where did it play—at the Ciudad Trujillo World Fair of 1955?"

This query goes back to the chief editor, who rockets it to the researcher. By now galleys are flying all over *The New Yorker*, and the old boys, the magazine's senior-citizen messengers, are upping the shoop-shoop gait in the halls. The query will eventually end in a sentence that reads, "Miss Hall appeared in *Drums Under the Window*, which was a play by Paul Shyre, based on an autobiographical book by Sean O'Casey, and which ran for (00) performances at the (t.k.), an Off Broadway theater, in 1961." The writer may or may not be in on this editing and checking and shuffling. So many galleys are going around so thickly that there is only one hope for ever getting some version of the story into the magazine: the . . . Transferring Room!

In this room a small group of people is hunched over tables, pulling all these sheets together, copying everybody's scrawls and queries onto a set of master galleys. The old boys are trundling these things in, from the researchers, the copy stylists, the chief editors, the query editors, from all over, and master copies are sent back to the chief editor, to Shawn, and to the researchers. Everybody muses and puzzles over it one last time. The author then is given a glimpse of what an . . . interesting . . . mutation his story has undergone if somebody calls him in at that point to answer queries about facts and do the needed rewriting. And finally, as the culmination of this great . . . evolution, the homogenized production is disgorged to the printers—in Chicago, via electronic impulses—and the *New Yorker* Style is achieved.

One might think that sensitive young writers would get upset about this, that they would take one look at these thickets of *perhapses, probablies, I-should-says,* at the long, tendrilly *whichy* clauses that have grown up in their prose—and get, well . . . upset.

But! That is not so. A writer gets used to it very quickly, as soon as he gives himself what one disparager called the "auto-lobotomy." Paradise! The System! *We!* Ambrosial org-lit!

Out of the org-maw, however, come some unique and even important articles from time to time. John Hersey's "Hiroshima," for example. That was Shawn's inspiration. He prevailed upon Harold Ross to devote practically an entire issue of *The New Yorker* to Hersey's account of the bombing of Hiroshima. It may have been one of those memorable fat documents of our times that nobody reads, such as the issues of *The New York Times* that carry accounts of the deaths of people like Stalin and Churchill or Presidential State of the Union messages. Everybody goes out and buys these nice, fat, full news bricks and never throws them away; or reads them. One puts them in there on the shelf in the closet and preserves them, as in a time capsule, through move after move, from town to town, from urb to suburb, hanging on to these documents of our times. But that is all right. "Hiroshima" was unique. Rachel Carson's book *The Silent Spring* was first published in *The New Yorker.* So was James Baldwin's "Letter from a Region of My Mind," which was expanded into the book *The Fire Next Time.* Articles like these have had a tremendous impact nationally. Baldwin's, for example, became the favorite bogey-whip for white liberal masochists all over the country. Flay us, flay us, James, us poor guilty, whitey burghers, with elegant preacher rhetoric. Terrific!

So *The New Yorker* has the biggest literary reputation of any magazine in the country, for both nonfiction and fiction. Yet, curiously enough, it was not *The New Yorker* that launched James Baldwin in slick magazines. It was *Esquire*. James Baldwin, Sherwood Anderson, Saul Bellow, Albert Camus, Joyce Carey, John Dos Passos, William Faulkner, F. Scott Fitzgerald, Ernest Hemingway, Sinclair Lewis, Aldous Huxley, James Jones, Thomas Mann, Arthur Miller, Ezra Pound, Philip Roth, Joseph Heller, William Saroyan, Irwin Shaw, John Steinbeck, Nelson Algren, Bruce Jay Friedman, Norman Mailer, Stanley Elkin, Terry Southern, Edward Albee, Jack Gelber, J. D. Salinger—that is a roster not of *New Yorker* writers but of *Esquire* writers. Hemingway's "Snows of Kilimanjaro" and "The Short Happy Life of Francis Macomber" appeared first in *Esquire*. Fitzgerald's *Crack-Up* appeared first in *Esquire*. Hemingway, Fitzgerald, Dos Passos, Lewis, Arthur Miller, Baldwin—all made frequent contributions to *Esquire* at one time or another. Salinger was published in *Esquire* long before he was published in *The New Yorker.* Damon Runyon, Stephen Vincent Benét, James Gould Cozzens, William Faulkner, F. Scott Fitzgerald, John Marquand, Thomas Wolfe, Philip Wylie, Frank O'Connor, Robert Penn Warren, William Humphrey, James Jones, Thomas Pynchon, Saul Bellow, William Saroyan, Louis Auchincloss, Bernard Malamud, Graham Greene, Alberto Moravia, Herbert Gold, Nelson Algren, Isaac Bashevis Singer—that is a list not of *New Yorker* writers but of *Saturday Evening Post* writers. For the last fifteen years *The New Yorker* has been practically out of the literary competition altogether. Only Salinger, Mary McCarthy, John O'Hara, and John Updike kept them in the game at all. Recently, Updike's stories have become more and more tabescent, leaving *The New Yorker* with only one promising young writer, Donald Barthelme.

The New Yorker comes out once a week, it has overwhelming cultural prestige, it pays top prices to writers—and for forty years it has maintained a strikingly low level of literary achievement. *Esquire* comes out only once a month, yet it has completely outclassed *The New Yorker* in literary contribution even during its cheesecake days. Every so often somebody sits down and writes an affectionate summary of *The New Yorker*'s history, expecting the magazine's bibliography to read like some kind of honor roll of American letters. Instead, they come up with John O'Hara, John McNulty, Nancy Hale, Sally Benson, J. D. Salinger, Mary McCarthy, S. J. Perelman, James Thurber, Dorothy Parker, John

Cheever, John Collier, John Updike—good, but not exactly an Olympus for the mother tongue.

The short stories in *The New Yorker* have been the laughingstock of the New York literary community for years, but only because so few literati have really understood Shawn's purpose. *The New Yorker* has published an incredible streak of stories about women in curious rural-bourgeois settings. Usually the stories are *by* women, and they recall their childhoods or domestic animals they have owned. Often they are by men, however, and they meditate over their wives and their little children with what used to be called "inchoate longings" for something else. The scene is some vague exurb or country place or summer place, something of the sort, cast in the mental atmosphere of tea cozies, fringe shawls, Morris chairs, glowing coals, wooden porches, frost on the pump handle, Papa out back in the wood bin, leaves falling, buds opening, bird-watcher types of birds, tufted grackles and things, singing, hearts rising and falling, but not far—in short, a great lily-of-the-valley vat full of what Lenin called "bourgeois sentimentality."

Ten years ago, in the St. Patrick's Day issue, there were two short stories, one by Sally Benson and the other by Sylvia Townsend Warner. Sally Benson's was about an old couple out in the bourgeois rural countryside somewhere, out by the old highway in the "Cozy Nook" tourist home. There is a little cracker-barrel philosophizing about how the times are passing them by, there's a new expressway over there, a-yuh, a-yuh. Sylvia Townsend Warner's is entitled "My Father, My Mother, the Bentleys, the Poodle, Lord Kitchener, and a Mouse." Lord Kitchener is a cat. The story begins with a woman, the "I" of the story, describing in detail the bed she was born in. It had a starched white valance stenciled with dog paws. The story even goes back before that, to her mother's recollections of *her* childhood in India.

Ten years later, in the St. Patrick's Day issue for 1965, there are two short stories, one by Linda Grace Hoyer and the other by John Updike. Linda Grace Hoyer's has a grandmother reminiscing about her Hansel-and-Gretel, walk-in-the-gloaming childhood somewhere out in a rural bourgeois big house and grounds. John Updike's is about an unrequited flirtation, over tea, between an American novelist and a Bulgarian poetess, both of them possessed with . . . inchoate longings.

But! Shawn knows exactly what these stories are like. He knows exactly what the literati think about them, and he doesn't care what they think. Shawn has a more serious purpose. He is preserving Harold Ross's concept of "the casual." Ross always called the stories in the magazine "casuals," because that was what they were supposed to be, casual. He didn't want a lot of short stories full of literary striving, vessel-popping, hungry-breasty suffering, Freudian sex-mushed swooning—this kind of "serious" short-story writing did not fit his English concept of sophistication. Thurber's farces—they were perfect. Mild reminiscences were fine, the kind somebody might tell you at the Players Club. Clarence Day's reminiscences of *Life with Father*—they were first published in *The New Yorker* and were made into a hit play, and they were casual.

Unfortunately, since the war, very few good writers have come along who are not in some kind of "arty" tradition, as Ross would have seen it. And Shawn—ever perfect custodian!—has remained faithful to the Ross formula. He has found writers who can write casuals. Of course, there are not many Thurbers around, so he has had to make Clarence Day his working model. Many of the casual writers he has found are women, and so it comes out *Life with Mother*, but that is all right. Occasionally, and most happily, they are talented writers like John Updike who somehow have a *feeling* for the formula.

Furthermore, it may all be the wettest bathful of bourgeois sentimentality in the world, but . . . *it works*. Even Lenin would see that and appreciate it. All these stories—*Life with Mother*, sentimental grandma, inchoately longing Young Homemakers, unrequited flirtation—they, after all, add up to the perfect magazine fiction for suburban women. Not all women but suburban women. The other women's magazines, such as the *Ladies' Home Journal* and *Redbook*, and *McCall's* and *Good Housekeeping* place somewhat more . . . *elaborate* demands upon fiction writers. The stories they run tend to get the girls into *bed*, and the heroes are often considerably more revved up than they are in *The New Yorker. The New Yorker*'s stories are more like the stories the other women's magazines used to run thirty years ago. But—perfect!—since World War II America has . . . developed . . . a kind of woman for whom recent-antique women's magazine stories are just right, especially in *The New Yorker.* Suburban women!

Since the war, the suburbs of America's large cities have been filling up with educated women with large homes and solid hubbies and the taste to . . . *buy expensive things. The New Yorker* was the magazine—about the only general magazine—they heard their professors mention in a . . . good cultural way. And now here they are out in the good green world of Larchmont, Dedham, Grosse Point, Bryn Mawr, Chevy Chase, and they find that this magazine, this cultural magazine, is speaking right to them—*their language*—cultural and everything—but *communicating*—you know?—right to a suburban woman. Those wonderful stories!

Well, first of all, *The New Yorker* is a totem for these women. Just having it in the home is, well, it is a . . . *symbol*, a kind of *cachet*. But more than that, it is not like those other *cachet* magazines, like *Réalités* or *London Illustrated*—people just only barely leaf through those magazines—*The New Yorker* reaches a little corner in the suburban-bourgeois woman's heart. And in this little corner are Mother, large rural-suburban homes with no mortgage, white linen valances, and Love that comes with Henry Fonda, alone, on a pure-white horse. Perfect short stories! After all, a girl is not really sitting out here in Larchmont waiting for Stanley Kowalski to come by in his ribbed undershirt and rip the Peck & Peck cashmere off her mary poppins. That is not really what the suburbs are like. A girl—well, a girl wants Culture and everything, but she wants a magazine in the house that *communicates*, too, you know? And you don't have to scour your soul with Top Dirt afterward, either.

Not only that—glorious!—the ads. To thousands of suburban

women, *The New Yorker* is a national shopping news. Every issue of *The New Yorker* is a gorgeous picture gallery, edited not by Shawn but by the most gifted advertising directors in New York. Here are castles at Berchtesgaden, courtesy of Air France, balding biggies with their arms around golden girls at the ship's rail at sunset, courtesy of Matson Line cruise ships, chauffeurs in leather boots and jodhpurs carrying cases of liquor out to Rolls-Royces beneath the glistening glass of Park Avenue at Fifty-third Street, courtesy of Imperial Whiskey, women of expensive languor sitting up in bed against a Louis XVI headboard with diamonds as big as a pig's knuckle on their fingers and white Persian cats and small escritoires on their laps, courtesy of Crane writing paper—all of this great, beautiful stuff. *The New Yorker* grossed $20,087,952 in advertising income in 1964. *New Yorker* stock was selling at $132 to $139 in 1964. It was only $20 to $29 ten years ago. The magazine averaged 115 pages of advertising per issue last year. The entire magazine, editorial and ads, ran only 96 to 112 pages thirty years ago. *The New Yorker*'s advertising department is in a position to reject ads at will. In 1963 the magazine threw out all ads with a picture of women's underwear on the grounds that too many of the ones the agencies presented struck a "sour" note and *The New Yorker* was tired of arguing each case individually.

The New Yorker has put out a booklet for advertisers—actually, *The New Yorker*'s "Department of Market Research" put it out. Marvelous! Very much like *Good Housekeeping*. The booklet is entitled "The Primary Market for Quality Merchandise." On the face of it, the booklet is just a service to companies to show them where the "quality" buyers are concentrated in the country. The real idea apparently is to show advertisers that *The New Yorker*'s circulation is concentrated in the same places—these great beautiful postwar American metropolitan areas. Exquisite! They show that the *New Yorker* circulation runs along the same curve as the purchase of Cadillacs and Lincolns, fine jewelry and silverware in the wealthiest American suburbs. Exquisite! One may watch *The New Yorker* in the curve of beauty with Cadillacs, Lincolns, filigree bowls, Winslow table settings, on through the zoning commission Elysiums of Stamford and Newton Square.

The March 13 issue of *The New Yorker* ran 204 pages, and running between these tropical forests of ads is a single thin gray column of type, editorial matter. The pattern now, usually, is that there are full pages of editorial matter, prints, and cartoons, only for the first fourth of the magazine. After that, typically, practically to the end of the magazine, will be a full-page ad on one page and two columns of ads and one column of print on the page facing it. This thin connective tissue—the column of print—seems to grow paler and paler all the time, in actual physical appearance. And sure enough it has. Yes! Several years ago *The New Yorker* shifted its printing operation from the Condé Nast Press in New York to the Donnelly Press in Chicago. At this juncture they made the connective tissue, the print, paler. They "leaded out" the lines a fraction of an inch, put more white space between them. This made the ads—beautiful lush ads!—stand out more, especially in cases where, for technical reasons, the blacks in the ads could not be made as intense as the blacks the *New Yorker* presses were running. The palest possible print! Like a modest silver-plated setting for . . . jewels.

One of *The New Yorker*'s former editors said—he couldn't help it—he said, "Every time I see those little skinny strips of type running on and on through those big fat gorgeous ads—all I can think of is, well, I sort of want to cry—all I can think of is all those little shabby men slaving away every week over their little albino columns that nobody is going to read."

Shabby little men? What is he talking about? It is impossible for the men, these dedicated men who put out *The New Yorker*, who—who—whuh—well, it is impossible, *genetically impossible*, for them to be . . . *shabby*, or anything close to shabby. Yes! It looks like Shawn has a complete *genetic program* under way to make certain that Harold Ross's *New Yorker* is preserved . . . *in perpetuity*.

But! How can one possibly understand *The New Yorker*'s eugenics without actually seeing something like the magazine's fortieth anniversary party in the St. Regis Hotel's Roof ballroom. It is a closed affair. People who thought of inviting outsiders were gently, firmly warned not to. Our Thing! All these men and women from the editorial and the advertising departments are up there on the twentieth floor at the St. Regis, in the ballroom, amid so much . . . *effervescence*, amid a lot of cherub decorations and a lot of snug windows on the Fifty-fifth Street side, looking down upon the City Lights. A society band is on the bandstand, and they are playing a lot of this . . . *current* . . . as they say, *pop* music, twist music or *frug* music, or whatever one calls it. But—marvelous!—they have the society-band knack of reducing everything to the most wonderful woodwind toot-toot boopy sort of . . . well, *swing*, from out of the 1930s. There are tables with white tablecloths all around the edge of the dance floor, and everyone is having drinks or dancing or having some of the buffet, so much fine ham and turkey and aspic and these carapaced rolls. Some of the younger people are even *doing* some of these dances, such as the twist and the frug—but the main thing is that everyone is *together* up here—everybody—from both editorial and advertising, all these so-called *shabby little men* who turn out the so-called albino columns of print in the magazine and these dapper people who manage one of the great advertising empires in journalism, these very-well-turned-out people like Hoyt (Pete) Spelman, an advertising executive, all there in the St. Regis Roof ballroom—happy fox-trot!—for the fortieth anniversary of *The New Yorker*.

Yes! The music stops, the bandleader stops his men, then turns around with the bandstand full-moon smile, then turns to his men, and they start playing "Happy Birthday," that good reedy woodwind society-band way, the reedy toot. And up from one side comes—indeed, it is *him*, Mr. Fleischmann, *bringing in the cake*. Mr. Fleischmann, of the family with the bakery fortune, founded *The New Yorker* with Harold Ross. He sank the money into it, and Ross turned out the magazine. Mr. Fleischmann is seventy-nine, and at his side, right at the elbow, with that old cake moving along on the silent butler, is his forty-three-year-old son, Peter Francis Fleischmann. Peter is . . . straight as an arrow. He wears a lighter blue suit, good worsted, as he is now past forty, of the shade known as headmaster's blue. The woodwinds are toot-tootbooping "Happy Birthday," and everyone is standing up amid the stagy valances and white tables, and the first emotion is very sentimental. But *next* suddenly one feels . . . yes! confidence. *The New Yorker's eugenics*! There is Raoul Fleischmann's progeny, Peter, at his side, and Peter is not just along to be with Dad; he is also *treasurer* of *The New Yorker*. Of course, it used to be even more solid. Stephen Botsford used to be president of *The New Yorker* . . . "Happy Birthday." Toot-toot boopy and the band men may be aging 1930s musicians, woodwinds toot-toot-boopy, but that . . . *swing* goes out like a supersonic industrial tool bath, out upon not just the old great tiny giants of American Culture but their sons and daughters as well. Brendan Gill, Mollie Panter-Downes, Janet Flanner, Winthrop Sargeant, Robert Coates; they worked under Ross himself, and they are still here—Shawn has faith in them. And not just them, however, but—heritage!—people like Susan Lardner, niece of Ring Lardner and daughter of *The New Yorker*'s former television columnist John Lardner. And—Donald Ogden Stewart, Jr., son of Donald Ogden Stewart, an American humorist of the 1920s and 1930s; Tony Hiss, son of Alger Hiss; Michael Arlen, Jr., son of Michael Arlen, the author of *The Green Hat* and one of the most sophisticated writers of the 1920s with one of the most sophisticated styles of life—even in the brief, bad days of the Depression, Michael Arlen had style. There was still such a thing, such a *mode* for him as evening clothes time; he had style, that was the—well, the atmosphere, the kind of tone that one can preserve. Yes! The toot-toot-boopy supersonic industrial tool cleaner bathes everyone—*vibrating!*—in the eugenic heights of the St. Regis Roof, with the city lights stretched out like an open box of Loft's candy down below. But why simple similes for such a night? The genetic convolutions build up, build up, like Leonardo da Vinci's drawings of waves and wavelets washing up, washing up, washing back off the beach, meeting, convoluting, building up again, with weight, a . . . natural force. John Updike is not actually here in the room, nor is Linda Grace Hoyer. One remembers! They wrote the two short stories in that one issue last month, March 13, and—too beautiful!—Linda Grace Hoyer is John Updike's mother, Mrs. Wesley A. Updike. Her maiden name was Hoyer, and John's middle name is Hoyer. They are modest, for if they wished to, they could appear in *The New Yorker* as Linda Hoyer Updike and John Hoyer Updike. That could *mean so much* to women who say to themselves if only they *could* be close to their sons—for here are mother and son writing . . . together. *Overpowering eugenic advantage!*

And all the while it keeps rolling up, rolling up, the cake—well, the cake is shaped like *The New Yorker* magazine; it is a thick magazine, and in bas-relief on the icing is the face of Eustace Tilley, the dandy looking at a butterfly through a monocle, the *New Yorker* symbol. One candle is on it. The band builds up to a toot-toot-boopy-rat-tat climax on the woodwinds and the drums. An old band member in dinner clothes rolls the drum, looking inimitably cool. Peter Fleischmann says a few words, in the voice of the genetic combination, nothing emotional, but That Voice. And Raoul Fleischmann himself blows out the candle on the cake—and everyone is standing and applauding, the applause piles up like—*genes!*—clap clap clap clapat pat pat pat pat pat pat. One can envision William Shawn patting the arm of one of his beautifully stuffed chairs in his Fifth Avenue apartment, pat pat pat pat pat pat pat. Pat, he can keep time with one of these . . . so fine! . . . Dixieland records there on the hi-fi. He could sink into the stuffing. He could get up and go over to the piano and play along with the record, as he sometimes does—he does it very well!—but tonight he will just relax. Forty years. William Shawn does not go to these celebrations. Celebration, like good blood, should be in the . . . heart. And the true focus of celebration is that the future is certain. Bunny Berrigan is right in the middle there, in the middle of "I Can't Get Started," that wonderful light zinc plumbing sound of Berrigan blowing through a trumpet. Those other trumpet players, like Harry James, they never played the real "I Can't Get Started." No—I'm—sorry—Mr.—James—but—I—am—afraid—you—are—not—Forty-third—Street—material—how—is—Mrs.—James—Chorus, chorus, a bridge, and *The New Yorker* will never be caught out, caught short. Shawn, it is said, has picked his own successor, just as Ross would have wanted it. And—the final brick in the indestructible structure!—one can afford an exclamation point in the privacy of certitude!—his successor, it is said, is Roger Angell. Heritage! Genes! Harmony! Ross! Roger Angell is managing editor under Shawn just as Shawn was managing editor under Ross. He has just passed forty and thereby earned his worsteds, and he looks . . . comfortable, and—the *Ross cachet* that man has! Angell is the son of Katharine Angell and the stepson of E. B. White. Katharine Angell was one of the *original staff members* of *The New Yorker,* starting right there in 1925 as assistant to the literary editor. And the next year, 1926, she *hired* one of the greatest of the tiny giants, E. B. White, "Andy" White, he was called. They grew close right there in the offices of *The New Yorker.* Roger, her son by her first marriage, was very young at that time, and he grew up in the *house*hold, the *at*mosphere, of Katharine Angell and Andy White, both of whom were, you know, just like *this* with Harold Ross, right from the beginning. It all *locks,* assured, into place, the future, and pat pat pat pat pat pat pat pat patclap clap clap clap clap clap clap, Raoul Fleischmann watches a single wisp of smoke cuney-cuneying up from the candle he blew out, up from the silent butler, toot-toot-boopy-clap City Lights pat pat pat Bunny Berrigan! Berrigan hits that incredible high one, the one he died on, popping a vessel in his temporal fossa, bleeding into his squash, drowning on the bandstand, like Caruso. *That* was the music of Harold Ross's lifetime, the palmy days, the motion of life. Don't talk to one about heat, hot music, the heat of the soul; it was Harold Ross's lifetime, and here, on that phonograph, those days are *preserved*. Berrigan! Fats! Willie the Lion! Art! Satchmo! The Count! Harold Ross! pat pat pat pat pat pat pat pat, four-four, we were all very hippy along the Mississippi in naughty naughty naughty oughty oughty oughty-eight. Done and done! Preserved! Shawn, God bless you! Pat pat pat pat pat pat pat.

Afterword: High in the Saddle

The storm broke immediately after the publication of the first installment, "Tiny Mummies," and went on for months. There were many bizarre moments and odd touches, but one stands out most vividly in my mind to this day: J. D. Salinger checked in.

Salinger was *The New Yorker*'s most celebrated fiction writer during Shawn's time, famous for the anguish he could make rise up between the lines of seemingly casual, lighthearted prose. By now, he was also a famous recluse, not quite as famous as Howard Hughes, but close. He was holed up on a farm somewhere in New England, totally incommunicado as far as the press was concerned. But now, for the first time since the publication of the novel that made his name, *The Catcher in the Rye*, he communicated with the press. He sent a telegram to Jock Whitney, and he left nothing between the lines. It was the clearest, most direct prose he ever wrote for publication in his entire career:

"With the printing of that inaccurate and sub-collegiate and gleeful and unrelievedly poisonous article on William Shawn, the name of the *Herald Tribune* and certainly your own will very likely never again stand for anything either respect-worthy or honorable."

From that day to this, he has never been heard from again.

Four other *New Yorker* regulars also immediately sent letters to Whitney: E. B. White, Richard Rovere, Ved Mehta, and Muriel Spark. Muriel Spark said Wolfe's "style of personal attack is clearly derived from Senator McCarthy." I groaned; at *The New Yorker* even their epithets had liver spots on them. E. B. White compared me to "a rider on horseback . . . sitting very high in the saddle" dragging a small, helpless man along the ground "at the end of a rope." At first I was excited by my steroid-like bulking up. Just a few months earlier, in the Talk of the Town, I had been a child playing in a sandpile. Now I was Stark Wilson, the hired gunslinger in *Shane*. Then I realized it was merely preposterous. The small, helpless man on the ground was one of the most powerful figures in American magazine publishing. The heavy way up there in the saddle was a general-assignment newspaper reporter who did man-on-the-street interviews ("How do you think Governor Rockefeller's divorce will affect his political future?") and crime stories ("Mrs. Tony Bender: 'My Husband's No Mobster!' ") and wrote for a Sunday supplement in his spare time.

Others, thank God, wrote in to say *The New Yorker* had it coming and to add a note of grim biblical eye-for-an-eye humor. William Styron wrote: "I was quite amused to read in *Newsweek* that William Shawn feels that Tom Wolfe's brilliant study of himself and *The New Yorker* 'puts the *Herald Tribune* right down in the gutter . . .' I have become fairly resilient over the years in regard to criticism, but since the only real whiff of the gutter was in a review of one of my books in the pages of *The New Yorker*, I found Shawn's cry of Foul woefully lacking in pathos. '*I receive of the Lord that which also I delivered*' (Corinthians I:11, 23)." Barton Kane wrote: "There's an old folk adage that if you can't take it, you should not dish it out." He cited *The New Yorker*'s skewerings of Luce and *Time* and of *The Reader's Digest* and closed with: "Let him who is without sin cast the first stone."

That put things in perspective, the way I saw it, but over the following couple of weeks the outcries began spreading beyond *The New Yorker*'s inner circle. Murray Kempton, a newspaper columnist much admired by literary folk for his British-essayist mannerisms, tossed the *Trib* and me into the aforementioned gutter with a flourish of tropes and *figurae sententiae*. Well . . . who cared? Kempton used so many elegant British double and triple negatives, half the time you couldn't figure out what he was saying. But then Joseph Alsop, the nationally syndicated political columnist, did likewise in a letter to the *Trib*, and that was a bit of a shocker. Alsop wrote out of Washington, and his column appeared in hundreds of newspapers, but his home base—most of the columnists had home bases—was the *Trib* itself.

Then Walter Lippmann weighed in. He consented to the publication of a letter he had sent Ved Mehta on the subject of my *New Yorker* articles and said I was "an incompetent ass." Walter Lippmann! There is no columnist today the equivalent of Walter Lippmann. He was the dean—that was the word everyone used, "dean"—of American political pundits. "Pundit" was another word everybody used when Lippmann's name came up. In fact, my impression was that it was expressly for Walter Lippmann that the word "pundit" had been imported into the English language from the Sanskrit. I tried to take the long view, the larger view. At that time, 1965, the Berlin Wall was up, the Soviets had the hydrogen bomb and the missiles to deliver the payloads with, the Mideast was coming to a boil, China was a restless giant—but Walter Lippmann had time to be interviewed about a Sunday supplement and me. If so, then how bad a shape could the world really be in? To tell the truth, that line of reasoning wasn't very reassuring. The great Walter Lippmann's home base was . . . the *Trib*, too!

J. D. Salinger, E. B. White, Murray Kempton, Joseph Alsop, Walter Lippmann—although we tried to put on a brave front, for about ten days there Clay Felker and I thought the sky was falling down. But Jock Whitney, after the initial shock, held firm, and I had never seen our maximum editor, Jim Bellows, happier in my life. He loved every minute of it. He ate it for breakfast and put some in his double espressos at night. After a couple of weeks Clay and I realized the only thing that had really changed in our lives was that we were beginning to be invited to parties by rich and famous people we had never laid eyes on before. It had to do not with us personally but with the definition of "a party" in New York. In New York, a party was something to which you invited people you didn't know but figured you should.

So Clay and I had become fairly battle-hardened by the time the shadow of Lyndon Johnson's White House stole across our heads a few days later. Clay was sitting in his little bullpen office at the *Trib* when the telephone rang and a voice announced that "the White House" was calling and that Clay should hold on. After he had held on a properly deferential five minutes or so, a voice came on the line and said, "This is Richard Goodwin. I'm calling from the White House." Richard Goodwin had been a speech writer and policy wonk for John F. Kennedy and was now serving Lyndon Johnson. He proceeded to tell Clay what poisonous, gutterish, despicable stuff our *New Yorker* articles were. The bill of particulars was pretty familiar by now. The only thing that made Goodwin's different was that he couldn't let twenty-five words go by without interjecting, "Here at the White House." Golly, what were we to conclude? Johnson was already sending half a million American troops to Vietnam on the basis of a ten-cent gunboat incident in the Gulf of Tonkin. What chance did *we* have? But by now Clay's instincts and Jim Bellows's were the same.

"Excuse me, I don't mean to interrupt," said Clay, "but if you'll do me a favor and write down everything you've just said on White House stationery and send it to me, I promise you we'll print it."

We never heard another word from Richard Goodwin there at the White House. *The New Yorker* was far from finished, however. Dwight Macdonald, a self-styled "man of letters" known in 1965 mainly for a long piece in *The New Yorker* denouncing Webster's Dictionary for allowing too many new words through the portals of approved English usage and into its recent third edition, wrote a two-part attack on the *Trib*, *New York*, Clay, and me for *The New York Review of Books*, command central for America's "intellectuals." By now *The New Yorker* had decided to take a page from a master, namely, Aristotle, who had advised that if the argument was giving you problems—in this case, the argument that *The New Yorker* was a dull magazine edited by a minimomaniac—then go after the facts and try to invalidate the argument that way.

Macdonald was joined in this task by two of *The New Yorker*'s in-house salt miners, a journeyman writer named Gerald Jonas and my new acquaintance Miss Adler. In an article published in the *Columbia Journalism Review*, they drew up a vast list of "mistakes," a list notable for two things. One: half the items—such as the museum-like preservation of Thurber's wall drawings—were in due course validated by *New Yorker* writers themselves as they began to write their memoirs. Two: the other half were things Shawn himself could have validated—or denied—but the team of Adler & Jonas wrote as if there was no way they could possibly ask him. They made much of my mentioning something that was in point of fact constantly bruited about at *The New Yorker* itself, namely, that Shawn grew up thinking it might easily have been he, instead of Bobby Franks, whom Leopold and Loeb singled out for kidnapping. To try to prove me wrong, Adler & Jonas went to Chicago to see an old lawyer named Elmer Gertz, who had apparently hung on to transcripts of the Leopold and Loeb trial. Nowhere could they find any record of the two killers ever considering a boy named "William." Honest, it wasn't all that hard. I found it three blocks from the *Herald Tribune* and one block from *The New Yorker*, at the New York Public Library on West Forty-second Street. But the larger question is: Why didn't they ask Shawn? *He* knew whether or not he grew up thinking he might just as easily have been the target. What did *he* have to say about it? He wouldn't talk to me, but we know he would talk to Miss Adler. In her own *New Yorker* memoir (in 1999) she recounted how she went in to see Shawn that very year, 1965, to try to block publication of the greatest piece of writing to ever come across his desk, Truman Capote's four-part series, *In Cold Blood*, and then got poor Jonas to join her in protesting to Shawn in writing. Miss Adler found *In Cold Blood* "lurid," "sensationalistic," and "prurient."

My biggest concern in reprinting "Tiny Mummies" and "Lost in the Whichy Thickets" has been that readers in the year 2000 would wonder what all the fuss was about. What was it that would draw the likes of Joseph Alsop, Walter Lippmann, and Richard Goodwin into the fray? Alsop, I was told later, envisioned going out to pasture writing long think pieces for *The New Yorker* once he gave up the daily grind. And Goodwin? Was it anything more than the usual power-muzzy courtier showing somebody he could do him a favor? Quite possibly. Goodwin had literary aspirations. *The New Yorker* had published a solemn bit of poetry of his the year before and ran a short story, a book review, and three solemn think pieces of his over the next three years. And Dean Lippmann? Beats me. Who can read the mind of a pundit?

Of course, the biggest puzzle of all was Shawn himself. What on earth could have set him off to the point of trying to stop publication of another magazine? The other day somebody suggested to me it was because he thought my two articles revealed to the world how close he was to Lillian Ross, a matter Madame Ross, for reasons best known to herself, chose to retail in embarrassing detail recently (1998) in *her* memoir of Shawn's time at *The New Yorker* entitled *Here But Not Here*. I knew Shawn was closer to her than to anybody else at *The New Yorker* and said so. But if someone had come to me back then and shown me chapter and verse of their "affair"—I wouldn't have believed it. I'm sorry, but they weren't affair material.

By the way, Renata Adler titled her book *Gone: The Last Days of The New Yorker* and opened it with the portentous sentence, "As I write this, *The New Yorker* is dead." I tried to tell her that thirty-five years ago. I tried to save her decades of dead end in her career. What else did she think "tiny mummies" and "the land of the walking dead" were supposed to mean?